January 17. 10?—

For Art and

"A faithful [...] [...] the

medicine of life."

[signature]

IDENTITY
· AND ·
COMMUNITY

IRVING MASSEY

IDENTITY
REFLECTIONS ON ENGLISH,
· AND ·
YIDDISH, AND FRENCH
COMMUNITY
LITERATURE IN CANADA

WAYNE STATE UNIVERSITY PRESS DETROIT

LIBRARY OF CONGRESS

CATALOGING-IN-PUBLICATION DATA

Massey, Irving.
Identity and community : reflections on English, Yiddish, and
French literature in Canada / Irving Massey.
p.   cm.
Includes bibliographical references and index.
ISBN 0-8143-2518-1 (alk. paper)
1. Canadian literature—History and criticism—Theory, etc.
2. Roberts, Charles George Douglas, Sir, 1860–1943—Criticism and
interpretation.   3. Tremblay, Michel, 1942–   —Criticism and
interpretation.   4. Maza, Ida—Criticism and interpretation.
5. Canada—Literatures—History and criticism—Theory, etc.
6. National characteristics, Canadian, in literature.   7. Jews—
Québec (Province)—Montréal—Intellectual life.   8. Identity
(Psychology) in literature.   9. French Canadians in literature.
10. Community in literature.   11. Massey, Irving.   I. Title.
PR9184.3.M37   1994

809'.8971—dc20   94-20233

∎

DESIGNER

S.R. TENENBAUM

For Al Cook and Art Efron

■

AMICUS FIDELIS MEDICAMENTUM VITAE

Ecclesiasticus 6.16

Contents

CONTENTS

3

Quebec 104

■

4

La Grosse femme, Macbeth, and Des nouvelles d'Édouard 124

■

CONTENTS

Preface

∎

I should begin by saying that this book is a study of three Canadian authors in terms of identity and community rather than a survey of the identity-community problem in Canadian literature as a whole. Each of these authors requires different treatment, both because of their differences and because of the different ways in which they must be used to cast light on the central theoretical issue. I do not attempt to apply the same methodology to all three cases. In the first instance (Sir Charles G. D. Roberts) the emphasis is on the nature of isolation and the problem of influence; therefore the chapter focuses on the influence of Roberts's style on mine, and the paradox created when a philosophy of isolation becomes the source of an influence. In the second case (Ida Maza) the interest lies in the opposite situation: namely, the communal character of the Montreal Yiddish-speaking community. Here there is an attempt to provide information, both in the form of historical detail and through translations of Yiddish poetry. In the third case (Michel Tremblay) the approach is more broadly literary and philosophical, dealing with ideas of community and individuality derived from *La Grosse femme d'à côté est enceinte* and *Des nouvelles d'Édouard*, with *Macbeth* as a source of comparison for problems in politics and ethics.

Having examined these works, each in a different way, I go on to deal with broader theoretical concerns. By placing these theoretical chapters at the end of the book I hope to enable a reader, now equipped with some specific examples, to see the attitudes of these three Canadian writers against the wider problems of identity and community as they are understood in an international context, and from a philosophical point of view. (Those readers who are primarily interested in such general questions may in fact prefer to begin by looking at chapter five). In my conclusion I venture some comments on the relation between politics and the individual in Canada, using Ferdinand Tönnies's *Gesellschaft-Gemeinschaft* model as a point of departure.

Throughout the book, even in the autobiographical passages, I have tried to keep the philosophical background of the specific issues in mind. I have been especially interested in finding ways in which the Canadian works with which I have been dealing enable one to formulate new ideas about identity and community, rather than in merely applying standard, accepted concepts to my material. In other words, these works, if they are as significant as I think they are, should serve as a catalyst for fresh approaches to social theory, rather than just exemplify or reflect it. The section on Michel Tremblay's *La Grosse femme* can serve as a clear illustration of this procedure.

Some readers may be puzzled by the mixture of personal reminiscence, philosophical commentary, and literary criticism in this work. A blending of these elements is important if we are to achieve a form of criticism that is not doctrinaire or scholastic; I share Fichte's conviction that the personal and the philosophical are inseparable. Though the recent debates over the political records and the personal behavior of several major philosophers and critics may be a lamentable context in which to make the point, it does show that the connection between life and ideas can never be ignored.[1]

Besides these general purposes, I intended, in the Roberts chapter, to restore some currency to the concept of solitude, usually dismissed as a Romantic fantasy. In the chapter on Maza, as I have said above, I have tried to make a more specific contribution by fleshing out our knowledge of cultural life in the Montreal Jewish pre-war community with a number of specific details. (Interspersed among my own translations of poetry in this chapter are noteworthy examples by MacArthur Fellow Irving Feldman.) In the Tremblay section of the book I have tried to use *Macbeth* as a model for certain problems of Francophone identity in Quebec that are not taken into account in the usual analogies with *Hamlet*.

My reasons for choosing these three writers may not be immediately apparent, but the choices are not arbitrary. In each case, besides the fact that there was a personal connection for me with the author's work, milieu, or both, there was also a specific strategic motive. For a writer representing the atmosphere of Jewish communal life I picked someone from the very center of Canadian Yiddish culture during its richest period. This was also the case for Tremblay, the chief representative of French urban communitarian values; Roberts, illustrative of isolation, especially in *Red Fox*, comes, appropriately, from pre-industrial rural New Brunswick. The question whether each of these authors is truly typical of the cultural community with which he or she is identified may be decided differently by different readers: their decisions will probably depend on which they regard as the key texts of Canadian literature. Some readers will undoubtedly argue that the authors I have selected and/or the attitudes with which I identify them are not at all representative of their respective cultural groups. (See Sherry Simon versus Micheline Cambron on the question whether there is even such a thing as a coherent French-Canadian literature in the first place, whom any single author could be said to "represent.")[2] I am ready to acknowledge that all generalizations about cultures are open to dispute, and I offer my own as suggestions rather than as fixed propositions, mindful as I am of alternative views and countervailing examples.

Once more, I must emphasize that this book is not intended to be a survey of Canadian literature and the whole spectrum of its attitudes towards community and identity, but rather one that uses examples from Canadian literature and couples them with a theoretical study of the larger issues. I am not seeking to obtain a panoramic view of Canadian literature, but to achieve some depth in a study of a limited number of texts. My intention is to show the ways in which these texts illustrate, illuminate, or contribute to the concepts of identity and community as such. For this reason, there is sometimes more material for background and comparison than there is on the primary works themselves. This pattern reflects the fact that in every case the ideas form the horizon of interest. My purpose is to show how we can enrich social philosophy by examining this group of Canadian works.

Of course, to write a book about any national literature at this historical moment is to invite the question whether the entity that one is describing exists, or whether it will continue to exist long enough to warrant one's having written anything about it. (On this matter see Charles Taylor, *Reconciling the Solitudes: Essays on Canadian Federalism and Nationalism* [Montreal and Kingston; London; Buffalo: McGill-Queen's University Press, 1993].) The same question, though, might be asked about attempts to describe many other political and cultural entities besides the Canadian (so, for instance, is it still plausible to write about "Russian Literature"?). To the extent that states continue to exist one necessarily continues to describe them: whether any of them will long continue to exist, or whether they will be re-cast in new forms, is a question that haunts the periphery of this book. Still, it may be comforting to think that literature is one form of identity that does remain available to us in an increasingly fragmented world. We can continue to feel at home in a literature, whether or not it has a nation state to sustain it.

Acknowledgments

■

"Influence without Anxiety: Sir Charles G. D. Roberts—and Me," now revised, was first published in *The Kenyon Review* (New Series, Winter, 1987, vol. IX, no. 1. Copyright 1987 by Kenyon College). I should also like to thank Véhicule Press for permission to reprint "Ida Maza and the Montreal Yiddish Renaissance" from *An Everyday Miracle* (Montreal, 1990) as part of chapter two. I am deeply grateful to Kathryn Hellerstein of the University of Pennsylvania, who gave the manuscript a rigorous but sympathetic reading; she was especially helpful with the second chapter, made useful suggestions for the translations, and spared me numerous errors. A reader for Wayne State University Press with a superb knowledge of French-Canadian literature was of great assistance with my revisions of chapters three and four, providing me with many important references and prompting me to reconsider some hasty judgments. I should also like to express my gratitude to the State University of New York at Buffalo for a sabbatical semester and supplementary grant in 1991 and 1993, and the Academic Relations Department of the Canadian Embassy in Washington for a Senior Fellowship Award in 1991, as well as a later supplementary grant, which enabled me to write much of this manuscript. The staffs of Lockwood Library at SUNYAB and of the Jewish People's Library in

Montreal were of great assistance to me, as was the secretarial staff of my own department. My final thanks go to my sustaining presences, Ann and Rachel, who helped with both patience and advice.

Introduction

■

The six chapters of this book were written by one person, although they may seem to represent incompatible viewpoints. It is not an uncommon experience for people to be raised among diverse and conflicting cultures, absorbing and illustrating the values of all of them. Coexistence, which may prove impossible in the political world, is a necessity within the individual. Within oneself, the privileged position may be assumed now by one set of values, now by another, and some blend may even be achieved. This individual experience undoubtedly represents to some degree the experience of society at large, whether its factions acknowledge or deny it; but in the public sphere particular interests frequently exacerbate conflicts to the point at which the possibility of tolerance is suppressed.

In any case, the world appears to be undergoing a change that may require us to re-think the whole question of cultural autonomy. Political scientists, writing in the traditions of monarchy and imperialism, have, until recently, assumed that a centralized government of some sort attempts to impose its will upon various groups within a country. This model assumes some degree of congruence between the political unit (country) and the most influential economic interests within that geographical area (country). With the growth of the multinational corporation this model no longer appears stable. A multinational company does not need a country to work from; it negotiates with other companies and with its markets largely without reference to its own government or the government of its partners. Government becomes an interference or simply an independent structure with little relevance to the network of corporate activities. Strong central governments begin to appear obsolete. They may be desirable as instruments to inculcate the psychological values of obedience and uniformity among the lower classes, but they are not needed as agents of a resident corporate will.[1]

It may be for this reason that the twentieth century has seen an enormous proliferation of political independence movements. In this perspective, cultural centralization would be seen as doomed, not because governments have become more tolerant or more generous, but because they no longer represent the principal forms of political power.[2] Especially in their democratic form, governments may be a hindrance to corporate agency. Disintegration of countries may not matter much to companies as long as they can continue to do business.

The most striking consequence of decentralization has been the revelation of an enthusiastic mutual hatred among groups no longer confronted with the uniformity of oppression. It is as though the vividness of particularism could only be expressed in zealotry, with all its accompanying violence. Mutual definition by hatred emerges as a Saussurean principle in politics; like words, cultural groups are defined only through their opposition to other cultural groups. This is hardly a new observation in anthropology, except that the word "opposed" no longer means merely that one group wears a red feather and another wears a green one, but that the members of one group endeavor continuously to kill the members of the other group, and vice versa. This phenomenon becomes easier to understand if we consider the information presented by Joane Nagel and Susan Olzak in "Ethnic Mobilization in New and Old States: An Extension of the Competition Model."[3] Nagel and Olzak attempt to show that ethnic movements develop around nuclei of burgeoning economic interests rather than in weak or stagnant situations. The reason, then, why these movements seem to spring fully armed from the head of Zeus, so to speak, belligerent from the outset, is that competition with other groups enters into the very principle of their formation, while "claims of injustice and inequality follow from ethnic mobilization rather than cause it." (p. 136).

It may be reasonable to ask why such groupings, developed to take advantage of economic or social opportunities, should take a specifically ethnic form. There have always been opportunities to be seized, yet they have not always been pursued with this particular strategy. One can only surmise what the reasons may be. Perhaps ethnic groups are small enough to deal and be dealt with by companies without interference from central governments. If this is a consideration, it should result in a gradual shrinkage in the size of individual political units.

Whatever its source, the mutual hostility of innumerable groups raises major questions about political authority in our time. Do people, at least as they are now constituted, need an arbitrary oppressor to make them feel that they belong, at least enough so that they will cooperate sufficiently for some form of society to function? Is anarchism after all a hopeless ideal? Fortunately, I am not required by the terms of the issues I have raised to attempt to answer these questions. For the present purpose it is sufficient to point out that factional violence is not a crucial issue for the multi-national corporation, though it may well be for a central government. Since the company negotiates trans-nationally with other companies, local political entities may take any form (or lack of form) they wish, as long as they do not interfere with corporate activity.

Trans-national corporations may even encourage "cultural diversity" as a byproduct of the process I have described above, to upstage central governments and allow regional units to claim autonomy. In fact, cultural diversity may be, from the objective corporate point of view, merely the code name for a marketing strategy rather than an expression of creative autonomy. I quote Francis Lorentz, chairman of the great French conglomerate, Groupe Bull.

"What are the keys for winning in the global marketplace? . . . 1) The capacity to organize efficient multicultural organizations. We have to figure out something other than the multinational model of the seventies, of the early eighties. We need organizations that are more decentralized, respectful of local cultures, diverse behavior, and management styles."[4] Under another heading, "quality," Lorentz includes "the quality of services locally defined, locally supplied and managed."[5]

Lorentz dates this shift in corporate thinking to the middle and late 1980s, approximately when news broadcasters in North America began to pronounce foreign place names and words correctly rather than Anglicizing them contemptuously. Gradually, snatches of voices speaking a few words of French or Spanish began to be included, though with the English translation soon superimposed over the first voice. Now it is common to hear lengthy passages in unfamiliar foreign languages before the English voice enters.

Painful as it may be to think of multiculturalism as primarily the product of an economic strategy developed by the multinational corporations, there is no point in wishing that there were some more altruistic force behind it. If these are the economic forms that hyperindustrial society has elaborated, we have no choice but to accept them. Of course, there are advantages that accrue to us, whatever the background of these developments. We might, however, temper our enthusiasm for every new separatist movement and every new move towards decentralization throughout the world with the thought that they may be abetted by forces other than tolerance, ecumenicalism, or cultural fervor. In fact, the violence among minority groups that have achieved some degree of autonomy is curiously at variance with the tolerance that is presumably the cornerstone of their own demands for independence. This paradox may be easier to understand, as I have said before, if we realize that a change in governing economic structures, not some sudden improvement in human nature, has prompted the movements for autonomy.

One might also want to include a note of caution in one's words of encouragement to both the leaders and the followers of independence movements. While approving heartily of multiculturalism and supporting its development, one might wish to warn its spokesmen that they may be losing power in one domain while gaining freedom in another. There is some chance of influencing a government; there is very little chance of influencing a corporation. With the loss of centralized government the public loses the only possible target of influence that it has. Even in a dictatorship popular forces can be mobilized to produce change. There is no place where one can take hold of the hydra of the corporation. There are also some signs that corporate powers are engaging in a strategy of divide and conquer.[6]

To take these lines of reasoning one step further, it might be suggested that the various literatures, too, have become dissociated from their national bases, showing a certain homology with the multinational corporations. There is not much point any more in trying to figure out whether, for instance, Spanish literature written in the United States is specifically American, Latin-American, or Spanish,[7] or whether Italian literature written in

Canada is Canadian, Italian-Canadian, or Italian. The paradigm itself seems obsolete, and its underlying assumption that a literature is inherently identified with a nation state can no longer be maintained, and may even have been false in the first place. "National" literatures may be replaced by the categories of "ethnic" literatures, "language-based" literatures, or other paradigms, but the old categories no longer apply. It may be best to begin to think in the spirit of Deleuze's argument that all great literature is minority literature for its "own" culture. At the same time, as I present this book as a study in Canadian literature, I am mindful of the fact that the notion of national literature itself is entering a precarious phase. But, since the book consists mainly of studies of the identity-community issue in three writers, it is not crucially affected by the question of the unity or lack of unity in Canadian literature as a whole.

In any case, if there is a fragment of plausibility in the scenario I have sketched above, we should find many cultural groups achieving greater independence during the current phase of economic evolution, even though free trade areas may also expand to attract and accommodate the multinationals, and other movements to encourage uniformity may reappear. For the present, empires are being replaced by trading networks, and the anti-hierarchical "decentering" principle of postmodern philosophy looks more like a description of what had already happened in the economic sphere than a program for the future. Yet even the trading network or the international conglomerate may not be adequate to describe the future organization of world resources. Perhaps it will be necessary to think in terms of projects or initiatives that go forward on even larger scales. The smallpox eradication project would be a minor, preliminary example. The control of health problems, the development of communications and information processes, and, of course, the attempt to cope with environmental difficulties are others that do not fall within either state or corporate parameters. Nevertheless, despite such tendencies and their supranational implications, quite paradoxically, groups will presumably continue to define themselves by hostility to other groups. Countries that are already distinctly multicultural, such as Canada, will have increasingly powerful centrifugal forces to contend with or to balance. Of course, especially in Canada, conditions, attitudes, and events are in such a rapid state of flux that by the time any statement on the situation has been published it is necessarily obsolete; as when Malcolm asks, in *Macbeth*, "What's the newest grief?," and Ross answers, "That of an hour's age doth hiss the speaker" (4.3.174–175).

Incidentally, it seems only appropriate to ask why, at the very time when so many imperial structures have disintegrated or been overthrown, there is such a frantic preoccupation with imperialism, as if it were indeed the most pressing political problem. Short of speculating that this concern actually reflects a nostalgia for empire, one might wonder whether it does not conceal some other motive. Perhaps it enables us to overlook the influence of the power structures that have replaced empires with more insidious and wider controls. Professor Larry Porter of Michigan State University has suggested to me that we may have become so interested, belatedly, in imperialism/colonialism because we are now heavily dependent on third world countries and are afraid of them in unforeseen ways. In a world that is truly without boundaries, the developing world encroaches more and more urgently on the developed. The exploiters' guilty fear of the exploited is masked as an excessive concern for the latters' suffering; the desperate neo-Marxism of many Western intellectuals at a time when the importance of Marxism has declined noticeably in practical politics represents a kind of anxious backtracking.

This book can provide only a minute fragment of the raw materials with which to deal with these developments. As I have said in my Preface, it is a book that is sharply restricted in scope, both because it deals with only three of the many major cultural groups in Canadian society, and because it approaches even these three through a small number of authors. It is an attempt to define the attitudes of these groups towards community as reflected in representative literary works: how and to what degree the members of these groups identify with their distinct communities, and finally how and to what degree they relate to Canada as a whole. As I remarked earlier, I have approached the work through my own experience, confining it to what I have known at first hand.[8] This restriction undoubtedly gives the book a somewhat parochial character; a glance at a collection such as *Other Solitudes: Canadian Multicultural Fictions* gives one a sense of the wealth that is being overlooked.[9]

Still, I did not simply want to make this book into another treatise on the general problem of multiple identities in Canadian literature. I considered including material on Italian-Canadian literature, but I decided to write only about what I know intimately (rather than follow any other criterion, whether of quality or of distribution) in the hope that my work will compensate in concentration for what it lacks in breadth. At the same time, I find myself obliged to admit the force of Barbara Godard's proposition that for many Canadian writers the very idea of a literary identity is little more than a contradiction in terms.[10]

What I have done is looked at my materials through each of the three lenses my background makes available to me as an Anglophone Jewish Quebecer. (It was in that order that the qualifiers occurred to me.) I surely do not represent all three constituencies in my cultural personality fully and equally, but I do have an intimate awareness of all of them. My first language (until I was five) was Yiddish, then I began to learn English, and, about a year later, French. Now my primary language is English (still with an occasional touch of my high school teacher's Glasgow accent), but I have begun to resuscitate my Yiddish, and occasionally I speak to myself and to some members of my family in Quebec French. I mention these anecdotal matters not in order to establish my technical credentials but to emphasize the fact that all three cultures are embedded in me, different as they may seem even in my own account of them.[11]

I will not attempt to minimize these differences. Rather than round the edges and create the illusion of continuity or compatibility, I prefer to let each stand independently. This quality of separateness will be most apparent in the first section, on Sir Charles G. D. Roberts as a representative of Anglophone Canada, since that chapter is on the idea of solitude itself. It is not only a study of the condition of solitude as symptomatic or as a cultural peculiarity of the English Canadian tradition, but is also a celebration of solitude as a defensible principle or value in its own right: in other words, as a value. This defense is offered with the full awareness that solitude as a value has of late been decried as occult colonialism towards the North and at other times ridiculed as neo-romantic foolishness, mainly to avoid political realities and the challenges of social experience: a way of keeping Canadian culture second-rate. At best, it might be palmed off as a kind of watered-down neo-Existentialism. (See below, beginning of chapter 2.) For my generation of Canadians, the values associated with solitude were in fact a part of our identity, neo-romantic undoubtedly, though not quite existential, in the sense that existential values are universal whereas these values were particular, even geographical. A winter afternoon in the Laurentians in the 1930s was, objectively speaking, no different from a winter afternoon in

Maine or in North Dakota, but, perhaps because there was no man-made border north of where one stood, it was experienced somewhat differently: as defining one, in the strict sense: as having had one's dimensions in the universe sharply drawn.

My first chapter, then, is concerned not with community but with identity, and, at that, with the most private aspect of identity: the experience of isolation, and, especially, the style in which that experience is expressed. The chapter also touches on a separate question: in what sense can isolation be said to participate in a tradition?

1

Influence Without Anxiety
Sir Charles G. D. Roberts—
and Me

■

THE INFLUENCE

I'm afraid to start rereading Roberts now, lest my topic slip
through my fingers. A dozen years ago I was searching for a
birthday present for a twelve-year-old boy. I was in the basement
of the big downtown Goodwill store in Buffalo, looking at shelves
of secondhand books. My eye fell on a set of Sir Charles G. D.
Roberts, in a green and black cloth binding: obviously, exactly the
sort of thing that no one would want: who ever wants large solid
sets of books by forgotten authors? I remembered, though, with
some embarrassment, that I myself had read a great deal of Roberts when I was a boy; could my friend's son possibly enjoy him
too? I flipped open a volume, planning to read a page or two to
see whether the set might do for a noncrucial gift. To my astonishment, perplexity, and even, I must admit, to my slight horror, I
found my own style staring me in the face. This was where, for
better or for worse, I had learned to write.

All sorts of thoughts flashed through my mind. (What a trite
sentence! assuredly not one for which Sir Charles could be held
accountable.) How had it happened? I had certainly never studied Sir Charles G. D. Roberts. I hadn't been taught to admire
him or taught anything else about him, for that matter. I had
read other nature writers just as eagerly when I was around

□

Marshlands near Sir Charles G. D. Roberts' early home. Dorchester Cape, New Brunswick, 1977.

□

Photo by Thaddeus Holownia, plate no. 4 in *Dykelands* (Montreal and Kingston: McGill-Queen's University Press, 1989). Reprinted with permission of Holownia.

twelve—the entertaining but superficial Ernest Thompson Se-
ton, for instance—yet I could detect no influence of their style in
mine. I concluded that I must have experienced what is sometimes called imprinting (a concept unfortunately out of favor
among most psychologists of late).[1] At some particularly impressionable point in my development I had been exposed to a style
that served my needs at that time, and the exposure had led to
what might be described as a "take": in mechanistic terms, something that might be compared to what happens when a photo-
graphic plate is exposed to light, or an ovum to spermatozoa. It
seemed that I had been forever inseminated by the mind of Sir
Charles G. D. Roberts, without my conscious participation in the
process. The thought was, obviously, disturbing. To be sure, I
don't write anthropomorphic stories with vulpine protagonists,
and the stylistic mannerisms that I believe I have absorbed from
Sir Charles may not be discernible to others, but the affinities are
undoubtedly there. Even my choice of writing about "Sir Charles
Goddamn Roberts," as he was referred to by Marian Engel, another Canadian practitioner of the animal story (and, as is well
known, few Anglophone Canadian writers are free of the temptation of writing about animals), cannot be completely dissociated
from Roberts's choice of writing about Red Fox. Both choices—
his and mine—represent the attraction of a naive romantic primitivism, and that primitivism, coupled with the particular Canadian Latinate flavor of Roberts's prose, is evidently what drew
me to Roberts, and made me accept the imprint of his style. It
can be adapted to quite other purposes (that interposed adverb,
"quite," is Robertsian), but the perspective is similar, whether I
am writing about "simple" Yiddish poetry, or about "basic" sexuality, and the semicolons and subordinate constructions are still
there, with the *débit*, the pace. Besides, now that I think of it, as
far as subject matter is concerned, it is not merely a coincidence
that I have written a book on metamorphosis, a book largely
peopled with animals *(The Gaping Pig)*.

But what if my own experience needs to be generalized? It may
not matter very much if the imprinting was helpful, harmful, or
indifferent in its effects on me, but did what had happened to me
happen to others? The question was not negligible. For one thing,
it raised the possibility that minor authors might routinely influence major ones, since someone who was, unlike myself, des-
tined to become a great writer could have been reading Sir
Charles G. D. Roberts, or his equivalent, at an impressionable

age. (I think of Pushkin's having been influenced—consciously, though—by the trivial French poet Parny.) It also suggested the possibility that a weak style need not necessarily cripple a good one; for, although my own style has surely not improved upon its model, it has turned certain recognizable features of Roberts's style to purposes remote from his. By analogy, one could surmise that a greater imitator could freely adjust and modify the original, making it available to deeper resonances than were ever considered in the template.

Of course, some might maintain that Roberts was himself a great fiction writer. (I will not be dealing with his poetry.) Perhaps he fits into the Fiedlerian category of the popular mythic author whom we read not for the originality of his style or the subtleties of his moods, but for certain general messages that are conveyed with strength by his work as a whole. Roberts writes a great deal about fighting, but perhaps that is what life is mainly about. In any event, even if we decide to cast Roberts in the role of minor writer, that in itself need not imply that he is uninteresting.

The entire question of "minor" writing has been raised as a major issue in critical theory by Louis Renza in "A White Heron" and the Question of Minor Literature.[2] The whole problem of canon formation and the shifting significance of "the minor" is subjected to exhaustive scrutiny by Renza, who holds no brief for the accredited works presumed central to any given tradition. He goes so far as to suggest that literary criticism itself could take a leaf from the modesty of the "minor" work, and show the courage to call its own authority into question (p. 42). He also argues plausibly that the minor work deserves a consciously minor kind of criticism (p. 41): a critical approach that takes the minor work's particular qualities into consideration and identifies in them values not available through the works that are paramount in the canon. At the very least, it is important to find a way of talking about these nonstandard works that does not overwhelm them with grandiose comparisons and references to significant sources; an idiom needs to be found that does justice in appropriate terms to their special characteristics.

Nevertheless, after all these preliminaries, I am still afraid to start reading. Part of my hesitation has to do with the difficulties I am bound to have in specifying resemblances between my style and that of Roberts; and as I have said, if I begin to read, and to analyze what I am reading, I will lose the awareness of what, exactly, my style shares with Sir Charles's, though I am perfectly aware of what it is as long as I don't try to define it. The other deterrent is the necessity of using my own workaday prose as the subject of analysis. Not even the most determined narcissist could enjoy the prospect of thrusting his unedited platitudes on a reader, even if such a procedure is necessary to make a point: yet how can one help doing so, if the characteristics of the style that are being sought are embedded in those very commonplaces and the habits of thought they reflect? In order to avoid multiplying causes of tedium, I have adopted the expedient of taking examples of my style from the essay that I am now composing. Anyone who suspects me of deliberately manufacturing sentences in the style of Roberts is welcome to explore the remainder of my *oeuvre*. (Some might suggest that *The Uncreating Word* is, in fact, perceptibly Robertsian.)

Others may ask: given the difficulties involved in using oneself as an example, as well as the possibility that the phenomenon one is trying to study may be widespread, would I not have done better to take another person's writing as my first illustration? The phenomenon is hard to demonstrate even in one's own case, though, and if one lacks the kind of detailed knowledge that one has only of one's own biography one cannot be sure it is there at all. What I am trying to describe is not influence in general (something in itself often difficult to prove at the level of style), but a specific form of influence, to which only one's own awareness and one's own perceptions can provide full witness. Accordingly, in this essay I will confine myself to my experience, reserving the consideration of other cases to a later time. Anyone who thinks of pursuing the subject outside an autobiographical context might wish to consider as a model Jeffrey Mehlman's chapter, "The Suture of an Allusion: Lacan with Léon Bloy," in *Legacies of Anti-Semitism in France*.[3] Mehlman tries to show that Lacan's style, with its gnomic, oracular tone, unconsciously echoes the voice of the weirdly anti-Semitic philosopher and novelist Léon Bloy, even in the midst of Lacan's commentary on Freud (Mehlman, pp. 23–27).

But to return to matters less notable, if not entirely unrelated: I will begin my rereading of Roberts with *Red Fox*, in a copy (Harmondsworth, Middlesex: Puffin Book, 1976) purchased, not inappropriately, in Antigonish, Nova Scotia, where I now own an abandoned upland farmstead. (God knows that, as a boy in the Saint Urbain Street ghetto of Montreal, when I was reading Roberts, I never expected to find myself anywhere near the Maritimes, much less imagined that I would one day own a farm there, or anywhere else: least of all an "upland" farm, particularly since I've never been quite sure what that word means, but Roberts uses it, as does another author with New Brunswick connections: Willa Cather.) I will have to read straight through first, rather than assay the text from the opening sentence.

Now, having gone through it, I can summarize the story for those to whom it is not familiar. The book begins with the doing to death of Red Fox's father by a pair of mongrel hounds who belong to a young farmer, Jabe. Strongest and cleverest of the orphaned litter, Red Fox avoids the doom that befalls several of his siblings as they learn through trial and error the laws of the wilderness. A boy, a "friend of the forest people," rescues Red Fox from the noose of a wild grape vine. Then the seasons begin to rotate. Red Fox finds himself a vixen. As winter grows harsh, dangers multiply: from sky and snow, owl, trap, and porcupine. Eagles, migrating bees, and pestilence make a nightmare of the summer, which ends in a devastating fire. The boy finally captures the fox to prevent his being killed, but, unable to tame him, sells him to a purchaser who claims to represent a zoo. In fact, the man is a buyer for a Hunt Club "in one of the great states farther south." There, Red Fox escapes the organized pack only by hitching a ride in the back of a passing farm wagon, which takes him to the secure solitudes of a new and still wilder mountain range.

But what of the style of Roberts's simple story, and of its putative affinities with mine? There is something I can tell as I look at the opening paragraph. The sentences tend towards the periodic; they compromise successfully between Latin and English structure, with a sufficiency of subordinate phrases or clauses, but a straightforward, no-nonsense order (that sentence of my own only half-intentionally illustrates what I am trying to define). Roberts's second and third sentences read as follows:

> The musical and irregularly blended cadence, now swelling, now diminishing, seemed a fit accompaniment to the tender, thin-washed colouring of the landscape which lay spread out under the grey and lilac lights of the approaching sunrise. The level country, of mixed woodland and backwoods farm, still showed a few white patches here and there where the snow lingered in the deep hollows; but all over the long, wide southward-facing slopes of the uplands with

□

Family picnic on the Nashwaak River, New Brunswick, 1929. Charles G. D. Roberts in right foreground, with white dog; Roberts' nephew, the artist Goodridge Roberts, painting in the background. Reprinted with permission from The Pennsylvania State University Libraries.

□

Group photo taken circa 1887 when Charles G. D. Roberts was Professor of English at King's College, Windsor, Nova Scotia. Roberts is seated with his child Edith on his lap. Mrs. Roberts is standing behind him. Rev. Canon G. D. Roberts, Charles' father, is seated on his right; the Rev. Canon Isaac Brock, President of King's College, is seated on Roberts' left. From E. M. Pomeroy's *Sir Charles G. D. Roberts* (Toronto: Ryerson Press, 1943).

their rough woods broken by occasional half-cleared, hillocky pastures, the spring was more advanced. (Harmondsworth, Middlesex: Puffin Books, 1976, p. 15)

(The third sentence has allowed itself the luxury of a delayed verb at the end.)

Another sentence that seems to me typical of Roberts in similar ways is on pp. 52–53: "The whirring coveys of the partridge went volleying down the aisles of golden birch, their strong brown wings making a cheerful but sometimes startling noise; and the sombre tops of the fir groves along the edge of the lower fields were loud with crows." In addition to the rather complex phrasal structure, this sentence displays the binary form, with the dividing semicolon, that is common in Roberts's style (and in mine). There is also a consistent drag towards literary effects that are just slightly too distinct for the presumably homey, "natural" subject matter. "Volleying" is a long word to launch along the aisles of golden birch; the retraction of "cheerful" in favor of "sometimes startling" combines a qualifier ("sometimes") with two conflicting impressions ("cheerful" and "startling"), all within a single phrase, favoring compression over a more extended, prosaic construction such as "making a cheerful noise, although. . . ." (I think of this self-negating trick, with its impacted adverb ["sometimes"], as another mannerism of mine: "for, although my own style has surely not improved upon its model, it has . . ." [p. 29 of this chapter].) The transferred epithet at the end,[4] "tops . . . loud with crows," confirms the impression that the scene is being given full literary treatment, yet without the least sense of artificiality. There is a slightly formulaic rhetoric at work which seems to convey the author's respect for his subject, rather than any deficiency of feeling.

To return to page one of *Red Fox*: "The music of the dogs' voices, melodious though it was, held something sinister in its sweetness—a sort of menacing and implacable joy." It took me a long time to correct the habit of using a single dash in the place of a colon; and I can never refrain from introducing just one more parenthetical or appositional phrase. I must also confess that "menacing and implacable joy" ("implacable" comes back on p. 55) is exactly the sort of phrase of which I might be guilty, in my not infrequent gloomy and sinister moments or, at least, might have to delete. (I see that I have not been as successful as I thought I had been in getting rid of the single dash. In this case, I haven't even deleted my equivalent "gloomy and sinister" of Roberts's offending phrase; in fact, I realize that I just picked up "sinister" from that same sentence of Roberts.) Roberts's tendency towards the periodic is evident in his treatment even of a brief descriptive formula such as the one quoted above ("menacing and implacable"). The "and" between the adjacent modifiers emphasizes the status of each as an independent element in the sentence, tending to create its own context of action. (See also "the vast and austere dawn," p. 130; "another and less monotonous quest," p. 150; "vivid and spiteful sparks," p. 164.)

As I go from detail to detail, I begin to sense an affinity between Roberts's style and that of another author who wrote about foxes, though, of course, in a very different spirit: David Garnett (*Lady into Fox*). (Not as different, still, as that of Garnett's friend, Sylvia Townsend Warner, who said of a fox cub that it had paws "soft as raspberries."[5]) Could there be something other than mere subject matter that connects the two writers, the one Edwardian, the other Georgian? This is another general question that will have to be referred to another occasion: Is Roberts's writing typical, in its basic lineaments, of his period? Whatever continuities one might find, Garnett's style is certainly more clipped and bracing: for all the appearance of prissiness in the language of the later writer's surrealist masterpiece, it is no longer laced with the neoclassical stereotypes, innocent of any ironic overtones, that abound in Roberts, and that I must still labor to avoid: "rosy veil," p. 15; "rose-fringed curtain," p. 19; "eye of the morning," p. 19; "school of life," p. 29. Occasionally Roberts will allow one of his periphrases to lure him into the ridiculous: "their mating was cemented with the blood of the long-eared victim" (p. 67). Whether because of the seventeen years that separate *Red Fox* from *Lady into Fox*, or simply because Garnett had a stricter intellect, these sentimental tags have vanished.

Like myself, too, perhaps because of a certain defect in imaginative momentum, Roberts also has to make a deliberate effort to vary his vocabulary and avoid repetition: the fox, in order to "dishearten" his pursuers, conceives a stratagem that may prove "discouraging" (p. 22). The "notable marauder" (pp. 106–107) returns after one sentence as the "audacious raider." Roberts has a tendency to wash his woods repeatedly in tender hues of lilac and saffron (p. 98 and passim), and even the occasionally successful "volleying" recurs rather frequently (pp. 158, 161).

Perhaps another generalization can be attempted at this point, one that has to do with the intrinsic character of Roberts's writing, rather than merely with his relation to other authors. I wonder whether the earmark of Roberts's style is not simply that the abstract often becomes the vehicle for the concrete.

Of the foxhounds, he says, "More than half their time and energy were spent in solving the riddles which their quarry kept *propounding* to them" (p. 21, emphasis mine). The vixen's cubs "would nip and maul and worry her till patience was no longer a virtue" (p. 29). Here the phrasing goes beyond mere anthropomorphic projection into vulpine behavior; the introduction of the personified abstraction "patience," unexpectedly raised to a still higher degree of abstraction by "virtue" (that is, the vixen was tolerant not merely because she was patient, but because she was displaying the virtue of patience), overrides and displaces the trivial action of the sentence. Of Red Fox himself, Roberts remarks, "In his tenacious memory a grudge was growing which might some day, if occasion offered, exact sharp payment" (p. 54). It is the grudge, not the fox, which will exact payment. "Engrossed in the pursuit of experience and provender, Red Fox had no time for loneliness" (p. 52). This is not an ordinary jocular zeugma: the abstract noun "experience" is deliberately put on the same footing as "provender" in order to subordinate the physical to the abstract. In another case, the mother eagle is said to be not merely searching, but "questing" along the slopes of Ringwaak (p. 130). Somewhere just over Roberts's horizon there lurks the ideal of a Miltonic phrasing, to the level of which he would like to see his subject matter elevated, so that indeed a Miltonic language would not be unsuited to it. The sky looks harmless enough to a fox cub, but it may conceal awful dangers: "the vast blue spaces overhead . . . yet held such appalling shapes of doom" (p. 34).

It is this attitude of Roberts that I was trying to define by saying that his formulaic rhetoric conveys respect for his subject. He is not inflating his language to dignify a trivial or minor theme. Hard as it may be to imagine, there is no "pathetic fallacy" or failure to confront the necessities of the objective correlative in Roberts. To begin with, he grasps his material, animal, or commonplace subjects in a context of abstraction because he already experiences them as embodying abstractions.[6] The abstractions are not added afterwards as decorations or fancied improvements on essentially insignificant materials. All the significance is already in those materials.

But at this point I find myself reconsidering what it is that I'm trying to prove. Is it that Roberts's prose in general has some valuable tone or quality to which the patches of successful writing are just a local testimony? Or, on the contrary, can one claim for Roberts's stories only limited stylistic virtues which redeem in small measure a general mediocrity of purpose and of mind? Is he an author who offers one the trifling values of a good adventure story, but little else? There is probably some degree of truth in both these appraisals; but, why, if what I am primarily trying to establish is that Roberts's style had an especially strong effect on mine, should I feel the need to evaluate his work in the first place?

The reasons seem twofold, and somewhat paradoxical. On the one hand, I need to show that, if a process something like imprinting took place, the effect was disproportionate to the cause, and that Roberts's work had a major effect on my way of expressing myself simply because I read him at a certain stage in my development, rather than because his work was in itself worthwhile. On the other hand, if the entire truth be told, I also probably want to justify my source in order to justify myself: in order to show that I wasn't such a fool, after all, to take Roberts as a model, I have to show that Roberts himself wasn't entirely a fool either. There would be little point in having been influenced by an author whose highest achievement lay in sentences such as, "As for the Boy, . . . there was not a stain of cowardice in his whole make-up" (p. 90): the Boy, who therein resembles the woodchuck, of whom we learn that "there was not a drop of craven blood in his sturdy little heart" (p. 148). Roberts undeniably reminds us all too often of what was bad in Kipling.

My affinity for certain shallow elements in Roberts no doubt records the depth of my own consciousness in those areas, but I may also have been drawn to more substantial qualities in Roberts which, if more difficult to give a name to, are nonetheless there. Without exaggerating Roberts's importance, one can take satisfaction in what he did well. What is best in an author is not necessarily disqualified by the less good things that jostle it. Whatever one may think of Roberts's formal poetry, there is a natural and quite beautiful poetic cadence in many of his prose sentences: ". . . but here and there a light, belated flake still loitered down" (pp. 62–63). As the pace of the action in *Red Fox* picks up (chapter vii), the sentences seem to grow simpler and shorter, without altogether losing their neoclassical *allure*. The book moves from event to event with conviction and speed in chapters xiii (drought) and xiv (fire). At times, also, Roberts knows how to abandon his rhetoric for a moment of direct realism. The captured porcupine in chapter vii looked as if he had been "dragged through a knothole" (p. 88). But Roberts's description of the swarming bees has an almost Virgilian richness and velocity about it (compare *Georgics* iv):

> Jabe Smith looked for a very fine swarm from that populous commonwealth, and he had a nice new hive, pale pink outside and fresh rubbed with honey-water inside, to offer to the emigrants as their new home.
>
> Presently there was a louder buzzing within the yellow hive, and an electric shock went through the yellow clusters outside. Among the combs might be heard a series of tiny, angry squeaks, as the queen bee sought to sting to death her young rivals still imprisoned in their waxen cells, and was respectfully but firmly restrained by her attendants. Foiled in these amiable intentions, the long, slim, dark queen at last rushed excitedly to the door, darted out through the clusters, and sprang into the air. In a moment, like foam before a great wind, the black clusters melted away; and the air above the bean-patch and the currant-bushes was suddenly thick with whirling, wildly humming bees, the migrating queen at their centre.
>
> Attenuated to the transparency almost of a cloud, yet held together by a strange cohesion, like a nebula soon to condense into a world, the swarm, revolving about its own mystic centre, moved slowly across the garden. (pp. 139–140)

The genre of this passage is familiar from other naturalist writing in the late nineteenth century, with its breathless astonishment at the ordered mysteries of nature. (See the last chapter of my *Uncreating Word*.)[7] Compare, for instance, the flocking of the starlings at the beginning of book v in Lautréamont's *Maldoror*, plagiarized from a scientific source, not to mention Maeterlinck's bees (*The Life of the Bee* was translated in 1901, not long before *Red Fox* was written). At the same time, it is very much Roberts's own; Roberts knew about bees first hand simply because he had, as a boy, kept his own hives. In the passage before this one, Roberts speaks of the bees' society in the conventional terms of functional order, leading naturally to—what else?—the classic imperialist move. The hive "had prospered, and multiplied, and grown overfull" (pp. 138–139). "It was time for a migration. It was time that a strong colony should go forth" (p. 139). But what goes on in the swarm is far less reassuring and predictable than their "traditions of sweetness, order, and industry" (p. 139) would lead one to expect. It is not just that they turn out to be unmanageable, ending up by driving even the settled fox family out of its lair, after having abandoned their own domesticated condition. It is rather that they circle around some center which neither Jabe Smith nor, for that matter, anyone else, can envisage for them.

The bees are there to illustrate the principle of metaphor, which is that it must remain outside any particular metaphor, and cannot be captured in any or in all metaphors. The bees can be put in a hive, but they do not belong to a hive, and, if they stay in it, they stay in it only by accident, rather as the abstract idea temporarily animates a metaphor. As I have been saying, the personified abstractions that touch Roberts's whole silly enterprise with dignity do not represent rhetorical flourishes to be charitably ignored as the weaknesses of an otherwise sensible writer.[8] They represent the assumption that the force of the natural world (expressed in a body) may have something in common with the force of the mind (expressed in an abstraction), so that, for instance, the bees, as they gather to swarm, themselves convey the power of a thought in its inception. *Mutatis mutandis,* in this "wild surmise" Roberts is not far from the late teleological chapters of Kant's *Critique of Judgment* (Part II, #61 ff.); we cannot exactly prove that nature and mind are interrelated but neither can we ignore the news from their common border. The idea is a difficult one to confront directly, but it cannot be altogether avoided either. As I suggested earlier, when we fall into the galloping vortex "whose heat was already searching hungrily under the thickets far ahead" (p. 160), or when we admit ruefully, with Red Fox, that "fortune, having seen him fumble one opportunity, would not offer him another that same night" (p. 100), we are not simply relapsing into the routines of the pathetic fallacy. Rather, we are recognizing a principle that searches hungrily under the thickets of nature for a way to express itself, not committing itself to any specific formulation, but testing any that comes to hand or mouth. To repeat: like the wild bees, whether they pass through one hive or another, the principles or abstractions that inhabit the physical world cannot settle in language; they can only traverse words, occasionally leaving a metaphor as the record of their passage. A metaphor is, after all, only the tangible conclusion to an idea. Like a yo-yo for which the momentum has been provided by the mind's invisible wrist, it is at the end of a process that begins in abstraction, and it borrows its energy from the abstraction that preceded it. By the time it is articulated, it has begun to lose connection with its source. It has then become what Shelley referred to at this stage as the "fading coal" of poetry.

It would be only reasonable to object that any romantic nature writing, no matter how trivial, could be dignified by the kind of philosophy that I have been invoking in order to interpret Roberts. No doubt this is true. It can also not be denied that the exalted claims I have been making apply to Roberts only in an oblique way, and not as a description of his conscious purpose. It is only from indirect evidence that I have been able to arrive at such a formulation of what he was doing and of what he wanted to do in his work. He certainly did not articulate such intentions explicitly, though something of the sort may have been what he was groping to express in "The Poetry of Nature," especially in his comments on Keats.[9] Perhaps the clearest sign for me of validity in the point I have been trying to make is something I have mentioned earlier: the complete lack of irony, or, on the other hand, of literariness, in some of the most literary and obviously rhetorically formulaic of his rhetorical formulae. Apparently Roberts neither recognized that these were formulae (so using them as literal truth), nor that they might have been turned to ironic purpose. Without being naively medieval, his abstractions nevertheless walk around the forest floor almost as if they were so many foxes or chickens, be they called "Fortune," "Prudence," or "Memory."

So all in all—though perhaps, of course, only as a result of strenuous special pleading—maybe I don't need to feel so bad about my style's having been influenced by Sir Charles G. D. Roberts's. Certainly, as I go back over the book there are sentences about which I feel immediately, This is my variety of sentence. This is where I learned to write, for better or for worse. "It may have been mere rash folly on his part, or it may have been the extreme of confidence in his mother's ability to protect him even at long range; but he certainly showed himself lacking in wholesome apprehensiveness" (p. 147). Perhaps I was like that fox cub, overconfident in my mother's protection, apparently venturesome yet unconsciously cloning a father: in fact, the "father of Canadian Literature," if not my own long-suffering father, who would have made it easier for me to write this chapter if he had not thrown out the diary I kept when I was reading Roberts, in which he had found ungenerous references to himself. My father, by the way, was of the opinion that he himself had learned his style from Edward Gibbon, another favorite subject for analysts of prose rhythms.[10]

It is tempting for me to imagine a biographical analogy to my own experiences even in a passage such as the following. During the drought, Roberts says:

> The streams shrank, the wells in the settlement grew scant and roiled, the forest pools dried up, leaving tangles of coarse, prostrate weeds and ugly spaces of scum-encrusted mud. Under this mud, before it dried, the water insects and larvae and small crustaceans buried themselves in despairing disgust. Many of the frogs followed this wisely temporizing example; while others, more venturesome and impatient, set out on difficult migrations, questing for springs that the drought could not exhaust. (p. 150)

It would be easy enough to labor the analogy by following the frogs on their difficult migration, but in fact I have not migrated all that far. Even if one finds another pool, it can only be the same. In this case it can be recognized by its tangles of epithets, by the spaces created by its colons and semicolons; [11] by the processionals [12] of clauses, phrases, and appositives that keep one hoping or hopping: [13] "questing [once more] for springs that the drought could not exhaust."

To change the subject briefly: what kinds of social ideals can be associated with Roberts's undertaking? For the most part, he seems to represent little more than a Boy Scout mentality of terrier courage and tender sympathy. Occasionally, as I have remarked, colonial/imperialist tones are also easy to detect. Yet these are not all. *Mutatis mutandis*, Roberts reminds one in his social thinking more of Gobineau than of Kipling: his apparently simplified values derive from a doctrine of fundamental depth. When considered carefully, Gobineau turns out to be a spokesman for native virtue rather than for artificial class; what he was searching for, through his doctrine of racial superiority, was the human decency that has somehow been lost in the disorder of civilization. In a word, he was not so much a Fascist aristocrat as a Rousseauist: he demanded that mankind exhibit the seeds of nobility it was dowered with. It seems an amusing irony that Gobineau should say, of Roberts's very stamping ground, that

> Quand la nature physique n'est pas imprégnée de la nature morale, elle donne peu d'émotions à l'âme, et c'est pourquoi les scènes les plus éblouissantes du Nouveau-Monde ne sauraient jamais égaler les moindres aspects de l'ancien. [14]

> When the physical world is not impregnated with the moral, it conveys few emotions to the soul: that is why the most dazzling scenes of the New World can never equal the most insignificant aspects of the Old.

The irony is doubled by the fact that what is arguably Gobineau's best story, "La Chasse au caribou," takes place in that least Old-Worldly of the American territories, Newfoundland.

Both authors are believers in what Roberts calls "the great game" (p. 185). As surely as Gobineau, if less obviously, Roberts has not only an ethics but an ethos: the ethos of solitude. Roberts may not be sufficiently wary of clichés, but, as I have said, perhaps because he uses them so unselfconsciously they often seem to be mere truths. (On type versus stereotype, see the end of Ruth Amossy's "Stereotypes and Representation in Fiction.")[15] In the end, stereotypically or not, one must go where the pack and, even more important, the modish scarlet hunters associated with it cannot follow. Contradictorily enough, cliché must escape itself; by its very nature, never being at one with itself, it is compelled to go in search of its lost meaning; dogged by the formal dress of sadism, by the dapper enemies of meaning, the true hunter, in the guise of Red Fox, must find a way to get away from himself as the institutionalized red-vested huntsman.

Alone with God one can engender the abstract truths that slip behind the cliché, that may sometimes be trapped in it but that will escape again. One must only find a place sufficiently pure that truth will again be possible.

But is absolute solitude necessary for such an attempt? We are accustomed to dismissing pleas for aloneness as romantic silliness. It is not possible for anything of interest or of substance to happen to someone who is entirely alone. In fact, all that does happen is that the solitary becomes bored, then unhappy, then confused: pure solitude produces only sterile suffering; the very act of thinking becomes impossible. This is probably true. But, just as, for the nonreligious, within the apparent nonsense of every religion there may be some germ of psychological or philosophical interest, so within a doctrine of solitude there may be, even for normally sociable people, a kernel of value to be discovered amidst its implausibilities.

What is at stake here then, I believe, is something more than the question of whether descriptive nature writing (Roberts's genre) as such can be great, though this is in itself a major issue

42

and has been much debated since Pope and Lessing in the eighteenth century. (Douglas Bush once said to me that Keats's "Ode to Autumn" was not a poem of the first importance, since it was only about nature, whereas, of course, the proper study of mankind . . . .) What is at issue behind this question, and more decisively, is the legitimacy of solitude: of a notion such as that of, say, Captain Joshua Slocum's, of sailing alone around the world. The concern with solitude is, as is well known, an ubiquitous concomitant of Canadian culture, for all of Canada's recent urbanization. Until some three million square miles of the North have melted, the sense of isolation or loneliness, whether romantic, existential, or practical, will remain a necessary ingredient of Canadian consciousness, an ingredient perhaps best exemplified in the "Susanna Moodie" poems of Margaret Atwood. What still has to be decided is whether this fact implies that the Canadian genius labors under a fatal disability, as Edgar Friedenberg, for instance, maintains in *Deference to Authority*. An alternative possibility is that a philosophy of solitude may entail experiences that have their own importance and their own profundity.

Such questions are implicit throughout Roberts's work, for example, in the sixth chapter of *Red Fox*. After their cooperation in the defeat of a snowy owl that had attacked the vixen, the foxes creep back into their lair, dragging their fearsome prize. A wandering mink slips by, eyes the vast white shape lying in the mouth of the burrow, and darts into his runway beneath the ice of the brook. "And the bright emptiness of the cold settled down once more upon the forest" (p. 79). That bright emptiness is what remains after even the most intimate and intense collaboration. It is something that can be perceived by only one mind.[16] It cannot be known in the sharing, and it negates all mutuality, as well as the very basis for ideas concerning intersubjectivity.

We need to be with someone else in order to think and in order to create, but we probably indulge an illusion when we believe that we think or create with someone else. This conviction of mine may even help to explain my choice of topic for this essay, as well as my title. I may have learned something of my style from Roberts, but in the end there is no possible association between us, because minds stand separate: there can be no "anxiety of influence" where there is, in the end and necessarily, only radical detachment. My renewed awareness of Roberts came about simply through an accident; I had forgotten him for forty years. The presence, the assistance, or the emotional cooperation of another person may be necessary at some point to enable us to think or work in a certain way, but it may be only in the begetting and conceiving of children that we actually produce something together. Alone, and knowing that no mind can participate with another's in creation, we pretend, in play with each other, that we make something collectively. We borrow to beget, not jointly engender beauty. Feeding on the immediate past of a relationship, or strengthened by it, at the moment of creation we turn to God and ourselves for actual inspiration, even when it seems to be coming from another person.

So the eventual solitude of the fox is like the condition that we are necessarily in when we need to communicate with the sources of knowledge, and no one can do more. Emerging from the snowstorms of our confusion, our days are, again necessarily, always such as are followed by "a clear sky of steel and buff that promise[d] . . . a night of merciless cold" (p. 99).

Roberts may be a minor author; nevertheless, he provides, whether by choice or by accident, a conduit for a kind of perception that has to be taken seriously, together with the predicaments that it forces us to recognize.

■

AN EXISTENTIAL PREMISE

The history of my relationship with Sir Charles G. D. Roberts has afforded me an opportunity to review, if not to reconsider thoroughly, a number of issues that have been of concern to me at various times. These include the following possibilities, in the order in which they are mentioned in this chapter: that some features of style may be learned by imprinting; that we may need to develop a specialized approach to the field of "minor literature," if such a category is still to be distinguished; that the relation of abstraction to personification as well as to metaphor needs to be reassessed, along with the relation of stereotypes to meaning; and finally that despite the frequent popularity of existentialism during the past century, the condition of solitude still has some dimensions that have not been, and ought to be, explored.

From the point of view of aesthetics, the most important of these problems is undoubtedly the relation of abstraction to metaphor, where I suggest a change of balance in favor of abstraction, proposing that the literary metaphor is like the Shelleyan "ash" ("Ode to the West Wind") or "fading coal" ("Defence of Poetry").

From a more general point of view, the most significant of the topics considered would seem to be the importance of solitude, and, in terms of my title, the relation, if any, of that question to the problem of influence. I seem at the same time to acknowledge an extreme form of influence and to deny influence entirely. On the one hand, I speak of having had Roberts's style "printed" on me—certainly, in some sense, a social experience. On the other hand, I deny the presence of the conditions that usually accompany influence: dependence, anxiety, resentment, or a struggle either to acquire or reject a style. Not having been aware that Roberts's style had affected me, I could not very well have been anxious about its influence. That influence, having been both unconscious and completely forgotten, did not really leave me in a state of continuing relation to my model.

One might argue, though, that beyond a certain point there never is, in any case, such a relation; faced with certain necessities, one finds that one has no sources. There is no Virgil behind one, nor, for that matter, is there a Beatrice before. I have been suggesting that the condition of solitude implied in Roberts's writing is, in some respects, a more realistic basis for a philosophy of creation than the condition of sociality. In a word, the model that Roberts's writing would have provided, had I studied it with a view to imitating it, would have been the same one I arrived at by forgetting it: the model of radical isolation. It was, in a sense, the very fact of my alienation from my source, rather than any prolonged involvement with Roberts's work, which guaranteed that my thinking would be, in the end, consistent with his own.

2

Public Lives in Private:
Ida Maza and the Montreal
Yiddish Renaissance[1]

■

PREFATORY

That Sir Charles G. D. Roberts's stories (not to mention my own reaffirmation of their values) may be taken as typical of English Canadian writing, at least until recently, is asserted in numerous critical works. Some claim the ethos of solitude as a positive heritage or a necessary condition (Atwood, MacLennan); others reject it as a pretext for avoiding more mature kinds of personal and social concern (Friedenberg), or merely as a delusion (Barnes); but few (again, until recently) would deny that such an atonic loneliness is a consistent feature of this literary corpus, whether in its naive form, as in Roberts, or in its more sophisticated versions, as in Pratt, Birney, or Atwood. Of course, by this point Canadian literature has become so multifarious that many other patterns may be identified within it. But, at least in the view of the authors I have mentioned, identity in Canadian literature was something worked out between the self and an absolute environment, rather than a compromise negotiated between the self and the social world. Edgar Friedenberg's argument, as I have mentioned above, is that a preoccupation with the overwhelming power of nature is a guarantee of literary inferiority: great literature is about human relationships, not about our loneliness vis-a-vis landscapes, no matter how awe-inspiring. My first chapter claims, on the contrary, that there are qualities recoverable only from the laboratory of isolation that are essential to a valued existence.[2] Thomas G. Barnes's sarcastic dismissal of the "boreal myth" as a meretricious fantasy, merely the byproduct of imperialistic policies towards the North, simply denies the reality of experiences that I and many other Canadians have had.[3] Every real experience has some ideological component, but the experience may be none the less real for that. As I have said earlier, to look north, or to be in a northern landscape, had, and to some extent still has, a different meaning from a point south rather than north of the Canadian border. That difference has entailed, for Canada, or at least for those in Canada who have participated in an ethos of solitude, a privilege: the availability of a certain kind of perception, a free field, that is not, or perhaps was not, to be had elsewhere. Isolation provides a condition for freedom of thought.[4]

On the other hand, I cannot say that I understand fully why English Canada has not imagined itself in communitarian terms, as have the other two groups with which I will be dealing. The suggestion that, as a majority, it does not need to assert its common value is unconvincing:[5] it does assert a common value, but that value is often solitude itself. Its threatened or equivocal status should certainly have provided motivation for expressions of solidarity, but does not seem to have had that effect. The phenomenon is all the more puzzling in view of the fact that Canada is a country in which civil authority is readily tolerated: the title of Friedenberg's book on Canada, *Deference to Authority*, is reasonably appropriate. One might expect that in a well-policed yet somewhat politically unstable country the members of the majority would make their solidarity felt, especially for one another's benefit. Whatever the historical reasons, though, nothing of the sort has happened.

Although the often-cited residual status of Canada as the remnant of the American Revolution, or its politically compromised condition as a state that never coalesced after the 1759 conquest, may have left the majority in a position of permanent historical uncertainty, without a manifest destiny, that majority was still able to project an authoritarian atmosphere; but it never achieved an organic cohesiveness. No doubt this impression is, at least in part, a personal one: but I myself have not found, in most of the English Canadian literature that I have read, satisfying images of social participation or of "stickiness" among people such as are rife in the novels of, for one, Michel Tremblay. (Even in the case of conflict between the individual and community, such as occurs in a novel by another Francophone author, Langevin's *Poussière sur la ville*, the conflict itself is conducted in the name of, and in an atmosphere of, the essential communitarian value, love; and at the end, the protagonist vows to redeem the community through that same love. Nowhere do we feel the detachment of, say, an Atwood.) If we take an author who derives from a different tradition, Michael Ondaatje, one who does succeed in setting up a weirdly harmonious mini-community in a novel such as *The English Patient*, we still find the Canadian thief left hanging in mid-air at the end, while the girl Hana drifts back to what seems to be a condition of even deeper anomie, again the limbo of the lost Canadian. But the point is that one has to go to those authors who cultivate a specifically Old World or transplanted ethnic sensibility—the Ondaatjes, the Riccis—even, to some extent, the Richlers—to find such strong communitarian qualities in Anglophone Canadian literature. Before such writers emerged, the members of Anglophone Canadian culture seemed to be like the dispersed soldiers of an army, living separately in a sort of internal Diaspora, though always ready to answer duty's call. Isolation and austerity seemed the best available models for its necessities. One might go so far as to say that for its members community existed, and perhaps still exists, only in the form of that readiness to answer the call of duty: indeed, that for Canada duty takes the place of nationality.

To be sure, such generalizations about cultures are always open to debate; but, at least as I have described the situation, almost the opposite set of values seemed to govern the Montreal Yiddish culture of the 1930s; and, in approaching it, I will be using methods entirely different from those I have been applying to the study of isolation in Roberts and his context. For Yiddish Montreal, Ottawa, fragile symbol of unity for Anglophone Canadians, was unspeakably remote. A powerful centripetal communitarianism was the outstanding feature of this particular culture, with characteristics that still need to be described and defined in detail; I will attempt to provide some of this background. One major factor in its development, though, was clearly the hegemony of Yiddish as a lingua franca, which helped to reduce potential conflicts over politics, social class, and religion; the numerous Yiddish cultural and charitable institutions that sprang up in the city reinforced this solidarity. This community was to become a major phenomenon in the history of modern Jewry. What must at the time have appeared to the participants in its development as a mere offshoot of current

East European traditions can now be seen as the independent assertion of a unique force, an unprecedented amalgam of old irony and
new energy, quietism and boldness, insularity and international-
ism: it was Judaism with a new face, and a Judaism for which a
unified community was all-important.

This unique development in Jewish history may also be seen as
a contribution to Canadian culture as a whole. The chapter which
follows can be read as an attempt to describe that contribution
from within. It may also serve to fill a gap in the history, or
histories, of Canadian literature. J. M. Bumsted quotes Jars Balan,
who remarks, in the context of Ukrainian studies, that "the most
significant gap in our knowledge is Canadian literature in languages other than English or French, which has been excluded
from most discussions and assessments of Canadian letters."[6]
"Eventually," Bumsted writes, "literary studies will appear which
regard the presence of such writing as important and even integral to the Canadian experience, and which attempt to deal with it
in such terms."[7] The following chapter is intended to contribute
to this inclusive conception of Canadian literature.

■

ESPLANADE AVENUE

Côte Henri

The snouts of the suckers, coarse yet tender. I was perhaps
five. It was evening, still light. Dimentshtein (a friend of my mother's) took me down to fish from the bridge on the creek. We stood
on the bridge and looked down into the water. Instead of water,
five feet wide and two or two and a half deep, this time, for the
first and only time, it was suckers: a mass of them; they lay
banked beneath us, motionless, all facing in the same direction,
upstream I guess. Their eyes seemed to fix us as much as they
looked ahead. But they didn't move, upstream or anywhere else.
A stream in which one could sometimes see a passing minnow or
a small trout was now a motionless phalanx of suckers.

We were jelled in eye contact with them now, as if they were
human, because it was clear that they had no practical goal. They
simply avoided dangled bait. Whatever it was that they were
about, its purpose was not an immediate one. They were indiffer-

ent to food and entirely without concern for danger. In their preoccupation with something that transcended individual appetite or
safety they were like people at their best. Some were bigger than
others, but all seemed equal. Defenseless, they yet seemed without need for defense.[8]

This was at Côte Henri, not far from St. Lin with its colony of
Jewish farmers.

At the time I wrote this page I did not myself know why I felt
the need to use this particular episode from my childhood as an
introduction to a chapter entitled "Public Lives in Private." It has
since become apparent to me that this experience does have,
through several themes—the theme of individuals fulfilling collective purposes, the theme of passing beyond concern for life, the
theme of this particular person's (Dimentshtein's) biography—a
real if indirect relation to my topic.

Esplanade Avenue, 4479B, Apartment 6

The wainscoting in the long, windowless hall was muddy
olive; it was made of a nubbly oilcloth that gleamed slightly in the
gloom. It was a brown, corrosive color that stuck like gum. It
marked itself on me with every khaki nubble. Later, I think, it was
painted a powder blue, but I may be imagining that color.

This hall was the *Via Dolorosa,* but also the *Gradus ad Parnassum,*
which postulants seeking the light from the dining room had to
negotiate. The hall was so dark that one might not have noticed
that one had passed the two entrances to the double parlor, a row
of wall hooks for hanging wraps, and the door to the bedroom, all
on the right, before one reached the dining room. When those
who had come in walked to the end of the hall and emerged into
the dining room, all of them—even Mr. Summers, who lurched
with every step so that we aped his progress down the hall (and
who, I suspect, at one point may have sought an inappropriate
familiarity with my mother)—when they came out at the end of
the hall, all of them began to "babble of green fields," in Shakespeare's phrase; or if one prefers to put it in Mordecai Richler's
terms, "they wrote the most mawkish, girlish stuff about green
fields and sky."[9] Maybe that's because the hall was so long and so
dark and the color of the oilcloth wainscoting was so depressing
that they were relieved when they came out into the dining room,
which had quite a big window overlooking the Shul on St. Urbain
Street. There was always Kaddish being said there, and I used to

wonder that my mother, although she was not religious, noticed every funeral and stopped to listen to the Kaddish or to join in it. At that time I didn't hold much with funerals.

People would start phoning early in the day. "Ida" this and "Ida" that. They were not, by any means, all poets or artists. Most of them were people who just needed something. Frequently it was a job. Others wanted somebody to share their troubles, help them out of difficulties, give them advice. Sickness; family worries. Immigrants: all of them, of course, were immigrants, only some more recent than others. Who, in those days, was "Canadian-born"? I didn't realize, myself, that I was supposed to have been "Canadian-born."

The great creation of that period was people, not literature. Some of the literature may have been great, but what stands out in the minds of those who lived through that time is people. Everyone was a person; everyone counted; everyone mattered. And everyone wrote, too. But whether they wrote, or what they wrote (indeed, come to think of it, some of them, such as our friend and living-room tenant Mrs. Ratner, couldn't read or write at all) mattered little compared to what they were as human beings. Their presence, their virtues and vices, their identity, their individuality, was what counted. Perel sometimes ate knobl (garlic). Segal wore a long coat and liked chicken—leberlach (chicken livers). The people came and went in our house, constantly. Were the people the real works of art?

They must have been, in some sense, the real works of art. I can tell, because, in my attempts to follow the history of the Maza salon, and of the individuals who took part in it, I found that the imaginations of my informants—although they were all literary people—were caught, over and over, by individuals rather than by achievements. Each time I tried to set one of my respondents on the trail of a literary question—who were the authors who visited Montreal during such and such a period, what were the major cultural events in the community at such and such a time—they would invariably veer off to follow the intersecting trail of the most interesting personality, with no reference whatsoever to the question whether that person was an author or not. One such person, who seems to be a kind of point of reference for reminiscences of Jewish Montreal around 1930, I have already mentioned: Dimentshtein. I have no idea whether he ever wrote anything of a literary nature or not, but I have no hesitation in declaring that he was a work of art, in the sense in which everyone at the time could be a

51

work of art: not as something created by oneself, or by another individual, but by the imagination of the community. As an individual, one lived a role that was conferred by the community simultaneously with the role one lived for oneself: every life was double. One carried one's public life over into one's private life, and lived it, in private, alongside one's private life; or, rather, one lived one's private life as an outrigger to one's public life. As Judith Schlanger puts it, citing Schleiermacher: "l'individualité est immédiatement immersion affective dans la communauté" (individuality is immediate affective immersion in the community) (*Les Métaphores de l'organisme*, Paris: Vrin, 1971). In Schleiermacher's own words, "Here I experience the bond that unites me with everyone as a fulfillment of my own strength in every moment of life" (Hier fühle ich die Gemeinschaft die mich mit Allen verbindet, in jedem Augenblick des Lebens als Ergänzung der eigenen Kraft) (Friedrich Schleiermacher, *Monologen*, Leipzig: Felix Meiner, 1914, pp. 50–51). In these terms one can begin to understand how Ida Maza could function as a poet whose work was inseparable from the process of her life as a member of her community; not because the themes of her poetry reflected the preoccupations of that community, but because her experience was saturated with its quality and values to the point where it could be said to be indistinguishable from herself.[10]

This situation is different from the one that prevails in the processes of socialization with which we are familiar today. We are aware that society now influences us unconsciously, by means that we have no way of observing; so, for instance, one finds oneself getting divorced for apparently cogent private reasons but then discovers that everyone else is getting divorced, each one for an apparently different but equally cogent private reason. What has in fact happened is that society has somehow signaled to all of us that it is time to get divorced. The collective unconscious, or the economic unconscious, or the political unconscious works by unknown paths, mysteriously, to direct our lives. But, in the case of the Montreal Jewish community that I have been describing, almost the reverse seemed to take place: society intervened openly in the imaginative and self-constructing activity of the individual, not so much dictating actions as joining in the formulation of each person's identity and self-projection or role, demanding that each person take consciousness of himself or herself as playing a role and being the particular person that he or she was. Instead of demanding surreptitiously that everyone be the same, society demanded publicly that everyone be different. Each person's life was a novel, and you were supposed to make your life interesting at least partly so that others might also find it interesting. No one could be a nonentity. (By the way, there was a kind of antithetical correlative to the individual: the so-called "Gesellschaftlecher Mentsch," literally, social person, such as Hershman, who devoted his entire life, as an individual, to the public good and to the welfare of other individuals). To repeat: no one could be a nonentity. One's culture would take one by the scruff of the neck, so to speak, and shake one into being somebody in particular, a distinguishable individual. If necessary, it could follow one into the very act of suicide; shape one's suicide. Hence the exemplary importance of Dimentshtein's case. For, can one's culture follow one into death? Yes, and no doubt beyond it.

In such a situation, it is sort of surprising to encounter literature at all, since literature is presumably the product of a private act; as such, it was basically irrelevant. If we stumble upon it, in studying the lives of these people, characters in a collective novel, we wonder where it came from. As something meant to have either private or universal value, and that therefore, by implication, escaped the conditions of communitarian life, it was almost a betrayal: a leak, a rebuttal of the imagination of the collectivity. (Part of the purpose of this chapter will be to show how Ida Maza's life and work as an artist constitute an exception to the impropriety of art in her milieu). Although, in the recently secularized society of Jewish Montreal the issue would not have been conceived in such terms, the fact is that, from a certain point of view, it is an aberration for art to be the expression of an individual rather than of a community's needs and values. The practice of literature, in these circumstances, even while fulfilling the criterion of making one interesting, represented, if successful, an alternative to community which cast a doubt upon the supreme value of the group.[11]

Perhaps it is for these reasons that the phenomenon of the "graphoman" (graphomaniac) was so important. For better or for worse, people were deemed equal; they were all struggling to survive, and there was no sense of rank. As far as literature was concerned, there were no clear standards, and none to impose them if there had been. Besides, they were all, appropriately or otherwise, permeated by an aspiration to culture. Walter Benjamin puts it beautifully, in another context: "Poverty produced a stretching of borders that is the mirror image of the

most radiant freedom of the mind" (Das Elend hat eine Dehn-
ung der Grenzen zustande gebracht, die Spiegelbild der strahl-
endsten Geistesfreiheit ist). (See above, note 10). In this world,
favored by the intellectual egalitarianism of poverty, an amusing,
outrageous, or ridiculously bad writer had almost as much standing as a good one. Samuel Burshtein's "Anu, zumer lebn, kum
shoyn tsu geyn; Anu, vinter lebn, gey shoyn avek" (Well, summer life, hurry up and come; Well, winter life, hurry up and
leave) had as much value for this novelistic world as some line
from Mani Leib or Itzik Manger, especially since Burshtein exhib-
ited, in his rolypoly self-satisfaction, imperturbable vulgarity and
irrepressible randiness in middle age, all the contours of a personality, and as such was indistinguishable, in all respects but
quality, from a genuine genius such as Shlomo Schmulevitch. No
wonder, with standing to be obtained so cheaply, that everyone
wanted to be a writer. There was a genuine leveling in which the
low could share a certain height with the high. I will not attempt
to name all the poetasters who darkened paper during those
years. David Rome's anecdote about one of my mother's innumerable efforts to help struggling poets casts some light on the
circumstances. Calling a friend to assist in finding work for this
particular man, she is reported to have said: "He needs help, not
only because he is penniless and his family is falling apart, but
because he doesn't have a speck of talent." (In any case, of
course, her first principle was that help must be indiscriminate.)

Anthropology vs. History

The structure of the present account, which is a chronicle of
the Montreal Yiddish renaissance during the 1930s, will fall or
flounder between structures proper to anthropology and those
appropriate to history. (I could make my change of voice less
radical and abrupt, but I don't think that would help.) I know no
better review of the dilemma, the choice between writing a history and an ethnography, than that provided by Claude Lévi-
Strauss in the last chapter of La Pensée sauvage. History, he says,
provides the illusion of connectedness or continuity, whereas anthropology forces us to confront the disconnected variety of social
forms and of particular experiences; the subject of anthropology
presents "the appearance of a discontinuous system. Now, thanks
to the temporal dimension, history seems to restore to us, not
separate states, but the passage from one state to another in a

continuous form. . . . History seems to do more than . . . give us intermittent flashes of insight into internalities, each of which are so on their own account while remaining external to each other: it appears to re-establish our connection, outside ourselves, with the very essence of change" (*The Savage Mind*, Chicago: University of Chicago Press, 1968, p. 256).[12] As anthropologist, I, the author of the present chapter, may find that my subject matter can be dealt with best in the bizarre and erratic way in which I have been presenting it so far. As historian, though, should I not be able to pull myself as well as my subject together, and make something coherent and continuous out of what I am talking about?

But Lévi-Strauss goes on to mount a powerful argument against the supposed coherence and continuity of history. He begins by dissolving the historical givens: the notion of the fact, the notion of the set of events, above all, the notion of totality. "History, which claims to be universal is still only a juxtaposition of a few local histories within which (and between which) very much more is left out than is put in" (p. 258). A date, he points out (p. 259), is only a member of a class; therefore, it means nothing in relation to a different class of dates, and it would be impossible (as well as pointless) to fill in all dates to create a genuine continuity. "History is a discontinuous set composed of domains of history"(p. 261).[13] Faced with the choice between biographical and anecdotal history, which stoops below interpretation, and explanatory history, the historian oscillates between two forms of failure: the historian accepts either the loss of the material or the loss of the idea (pp. 261–262).

Without affording a justification for the irregular form of my presentation, this dilemma provides at least a pretext for it. Perhaps, also, I am drawn towards the anthropological pole of these alternatives in methodology because of a certain affinity between the community I am describing and those communities with which Lévi-Strauss concerned himself. Both evince some characteristics of what he called "la pensée sauvage:" praxis as "living thought" (p. 263), "a system of concepts embedded in images" (p.264),[14] in a word, a mythic self-consciousness in which the enacted lives of individuals are at the same time a significant story.

Through the contrast between anthropology and history I have attempted to approach, albeit obliquely, a major issue in the method of this chapter: namely, the respective values of anecdote and formal documentation. Again Lévi-Strauss provides a context when he speaks of internality versus retrospective schemes of interpretation. "I am not . . . suggesting that man can or should sever himself from this internality . . . wisdom consists for him in seeing himself live it, while at the same time knowing (but in a different register) that what he lives so completely and intensely is a myth"(p. 255). Then Lévi-Strauss adds a clinching aphorism: "All meaning is answerable to a lesser meaning, which gives it its highest meaning"(p. 255).[15]

Rather than try to determine exactly what Lévi-Strauss meant by this comment in terms of his own discourse, I should like to take it as license to promote the value of anecdotal history, even if that be deemed an oxymoron in my own project. The argument is perforce *pro domo*, since it is apparent that whatever contribution I can make to my subject must be primarily in the domain of anecdote or lived history. Not being in a position to give a panoramic review of the Montreal Yiddish renaissance, with a list of names, a chronology of events, and a judicious appraisal of the respective merits of all the cultural figures involved, I must fall back on what I do know: namely, how it felt to live in that world, as one who was immersed in the personal lives of its members, though not as a full-fledged participant in its cultural processes.

I must admit that when I read some of this chapter at a conference at the Jewish Library in Montreal I had, initially, some misgivings about presenting this kind of material, especially to an audience some members of which had known this world far better than I did, whereas others, as professional historians, might have found little value in private reminiscences. Can anecdotes, finally, stand on common ground with history? Is there any way in which private truth can become public truth? Should private truth, in fact, make any attempt to enter the arena of public truth?

Cardinal Newman and the Anecdote

I did finally come to terms with these questions, but in an unexpected way, and through the unlikely intervention of someone who was, incidentally, known as a virulent anti-Semite in his own day: namely, John Henry, Cardinal Newman. Interestingly enough, Ida Maza, I believe, translated Newman's "The Pillar of the Cloud": "Lead, kindly light, amid the encircling gloom" (Fir mikh, mater shtern, vuhin du vilst mikh firn;/A mider mentsch in payn shtelt zikh nisht antkegn) but I have not been able to find the remainder of the translation. With the help of Newman I came to the realization that the question whether personal memories should be presented as public history needs to be asked not because history may be demeaned by stooping to the level of anecdote, but rather because anecdote may be demeaned by contamination from history. Anecdote needs to be protected from history rather than accommodated within it. In some sense, anecdote stands higher than history.

As long as one remembers an "anecdote" by oneself it is an imaginative reality or myth; as soon as someone else remembers it it becomes nothing more than a fact. The confirmation of an event by someone else, rather than reinforcing it, robs it of its reality.[16] Someone else's memory is always either a critical memory or an irrelevant memory: it contradicts some aspect of one's own memory. The memory then becomes history, a shared abstraction; an occurrence rather than an experience: it becomes less true rather than more true. For instance: I remember the story of the woman who had lost her voice visiting us at the Desjardins' farm in Côte Henri. One day, it was said, her husband was reported missing in the woods, and, in her terror, she screamed his name—and recovered her voice, as well as her husband. If someone were to say to me, "Oh, yes, I remember that woman," the incident would lose its mythic value. Or what of that other woman, also at Desjardins' in Côte Henri, who wore a large hat and sat under a tree; she was said to be "posing." I wouldn't want the woman identified as some particular hapless individual who was insecure and needed to draw attention to herself. The same is true of my father's story of discovering a wonderful patch of wild strawberries deep in the woods and being terribly stung by wasps: the incident would dissolve into mere history if someone were to say to me "Oh, yes, I know that place." One knows and believes things in a different way if one holds one's knowledge and belief by oneself rather than in common with others.

Newman, in the *Grammar of Assent*, argued that there was a crucial difference between inference and assent. Inference, proceeding by logical processes, can only lead the way towards, but never produce, assent, which always requires a leap of faith and is psychological rather than logical in nature. (It is sobering to consider the possibility that some of our major ideas and opinions— and, therefore, some of our crucial decisions—are finally at the mercy of a principle that is both irrational and ineluctable). Furthermore, once we have assented to something, that assent is private and individual. It does not ask for confirmation from others. It is even, in some sense, anti-social. "Real assent . . . is proper to the individual, and, as such, thwarts rather than promotes the intercourse of man with man. It shuts itself up, as it were, in its own home, or at least is its own witness and its own standard" (*An Essay in Aid of a Grammar of Assent* [Notre Dame and London: University of Notre Dame Press, 1977], pp. 82–83. The speaker is that same Cardinal Newman who confessed to his disappointment on seeing the holy city of Jerusalem, for it turned out to be merely a real place; see p. 180). In a word, for Newman public truth is less true than private truth.

Although the initial context for Newman's arguments was the attempt to defend the concept of religious faith, the arguments themselves are applicable far beyond that area, and seem to me especially powerful in the branch of historiography that I have referred to. I repeat Lévi-Strauss's formulation: "All meaning is answerable to a lesser meaning, which gives it its highest meaning." The anecdote is something to which we have given our internal "assent;" it is, in Newman's terms, "its own witness and its own standard," and so can only become less real if "confirmed" by another.

In a related thought, a disciple of Newman's, Gerard Manley Hopkins, suggests that every word contains not only a public part (in his terms, the conception) but also a personal part. That personal or private part of the word is the image in the word; the image, which is physical, is an "inchoate word" within the word, "a word to oneself" (*The Journals and Papers of Gerard Manley Hopkins*, London: Oxford University Press, 1959, p. 125). The image part, the picture in the word, is for oneself. So too the anecdotal substance in history is for oneself. In *The Vocation of Man*, J. G. Fichte proposes the extreme view that such internally conceived images or pictures are in fact not just a dimension of language, or even a personal aspect of historical consciousness, but all we can know of reality. "Pictures are . . . the only things which exist, and they know of themselves after the fashion of pictures; pictures which float past without there being anything past which they float; which hang together by pictures of the pictures; pictures" (New York, Liberal Arts Press, 1956, p. 80).[17]

The relation of these various observations to the "événementiel" school of history, which also emphasizes the irreducible, implicitly specular particularity of the event, can be readily recognized. See, for instance, Paul Ricoeur, *Temps et récit* (Paris: Seuil, 1983, I, pp.

289–319). The historical point of view circles back to confront the subjective once more as "l'événement est restitué . . . comme résidu de chaque tentative d'explication" (the event is restored . . . as the residue of every effort at explanation)" (p. 312). Provisionally absorbed by history, the anecdote must finally be expelled again as an unassimilable element, or steal back out of its own accord, unabsorbed and unabsorbable. The very material of history, it yet eludes it.

More Images: 4479B Esplanade Again

I go back to my vignettes, and my chronicles, then; not necessarily with a clearer conscience, but with less of a nagging suspicion that a more thorough inquiry would necessarily yield a better approach.

I never thought that the apartment was crowded. We were four in my family: my older brother, myself, my mother, and my father; but my father, a traveling salesman who sold men's furnishings, was away most of the time. (By the way, it was he who composed the poetic epitaph on his tombstone in the de la Savane cemetery, not my mother, as is often assumed. It contains the striking line: "Groy in tifn shlof do rut mayn morgen" [Grey in the depth of sleep here lies my morrow]). For a year or so we rented out the double parlor or front room to Mrs. Ratner and her daughter Esther. That left, for the four of us, the bedroom (with two single beds), the dining room, and the tiny kitchen. There was a cot in the dining room.

One would never have guessed, from the furnishings and appointments of the apartment, that many of our friends were artists, or that it was a household that was largely concerned with the production and appreciation of beauty. My mother seemed to make not the slightest effort to transfer any of the aethetic values in which she dealt to her immediate environment. Apart from the pictures that hung on the walls, the rest was unrelieved 1930s ugliness; the notion of beautifying one's surroundings seemed to be entirely alien to her thinking. Poverty alone could not account for the cheap and shoddy quality of virtually everything in the house. Ornament was confined to a few dime-store trinkets. The interior decoration of our apartment was Depression style at its worst.

But we had lots of visitors. The coats hung from the row of hooks in the hall. Some of the visitors stayed overnight.

Fish-mongers would come up the stairs, to the third floor. Sometimes they had bunches of richly mottled fish overlapping, full-bellied perch, green spotted pike, sunfish with their brilliant orange gill covers that I was seeing for the first time, not having encountered them in the streams in which I fished.

The Cénacle

The telephone number was Plateau 2002. People rarely called before coming over. Most of them just dropped in when they felt like. There was, of course, always tea, eventually with the new-fashioned whistling kettle as the samovar. The writers, artists, etc. usually came in one at a time through the course of an afternoon; in the evening two or three would foregather after working hours. Other visitors were scattered through the day. Apart from my mother's own reading, writing, and correspondence, she ran what I can only call an ordinary poetry workshop. A friend would drop in with a poem; or somebody had a book in progress. Whether in extended tête-à-tête, or in group sessions, as I remember, the procedure was always the same; the participants would begin to wrangle over a word or a line. It was unusual, as far as I recall, for an entire poem to be put in question, or for structural changes to be recommended; the criticism almost always focused on detail. Perhaps the reason for this approach was that the poems being discussed were usually brief, and not very elaborate in structure. The poets who subjected themselves to this sort of criticism (and profited from it) were mainly members of a circle of close friends, people who were at the time of moderate to intermediate reputation: writers such as N. J. Gottlieb (1903–1967), Avraham Shlomo Shkolnikov (1896–1962), Sholem Shtern (1907–1990), Shapsi Perel (1906–1971), Moyshe Shaffir (1909–1988), Mirel Erdberg Shatan (1884–1982), Y.-Y. Segal (1896–1954), and so forth. Others such as Kadya Molodowsky (1894–1975), Melekh Ravitch (1893–1976), or Rokhl Korn (1893–1982) might read for my mother or for the group, but did not, I believe, submit themselves to its commentary; I think my mother, at least, would have considered it presumptuous to offer them advice. I don't recall visiting poets such as Y.-Y. Schwartz, Joseph Rolnick, or Nokhem Yud participating in these sessions either, even in those cases in which they remained for some length of time in Montreal.

The Old Library

The body of poetry produced by the cénacle, whatever its standing in the eyes of posterity, was the efflorescence of an intense general cultural activity. We lived in what could reasonably be described as a sauna of culture. The public baths, so to speak, were the Jewish Public Library and the Arbeter Ring. Public poetry readings and lectures by members of the group often took place at the latter. The library, around 1934, when I first knew it (we had just moved to Esplanade), had already been transferred from its original location on St. Urbain Street to 4099 Esplanade, near Duluth; it was there, under the guidance of Rachel Eisenberg (later Rachel Ravitch), that I learned to read extensively, wedged between the narrow stacks and taking down book after book. It was hard for me to tell whether our house was a satellite of the Library or vice versa. Later, the library moved, almost literally, next door to us, to the corner of Mount Royal and Esplanade; but when it was displaced to this larger, more public building, the personal and intimate qualities that it had when it was lodged in what had been a private house were immediately sacrificed. Instead of a beehive or ant-nest of a living culture, it felt like a monument to one that had just been anesthetized and might be presumed moribund. The busy, warm, individualistic atmosphere of the old library was part of what had fostered that culture; the new library was part of a new world, not a living context for its content but a box in which materials perhaps once vital were housed. I believe that my mother's Saturday morning readings for children went on, but the true link between the world of the library and the world of our apartment was broken.

Ida Maza

In any case, to speak again of the dense cultural atmosphere that surrounded us: the sheer quantity of reading, writing, corresponding, arguing, and lecturing that went on in this circle of friends is hard to imagine, above all for North Americans in our time. Every spare moment seemed to be devoted to some form of learning or cultural production. In the case of my brother it was manifested as an obsession with vocabulary and word lists; in the case of my father, as a kind of cultural crusade or mission to the remote outposts of Jewish survival, in the obscurest reaches of northern Ontario and Quebec. Of course I was most fully aware of this restless activity in my own family, but most of the people who passed through our house seemed to scurry about carrying the same preoccupation and passion with them in some form. My mother herself, along with the equivalent of a full-time job as social worker, placement officer, psychiatric counselor, and fund raiser, not to mention copy editor and literary agent, also contrived to read more than I did as a full-time student of literature, write literary criticism, lecture, do numerous translations, produce four books of poetry and an autobiography, send off about ten letters a day, and keep abreast of cultural developments in both the Jewish and the international domains. I found it a source of embarrassment as well as pride that on her deathbed she still knew her George Eliot better than I did, particularly since I happened to be teaching George Eliot at McGill at the time. She was also devoted to the English women poets from Christina Rossetti and E. B. Browning on. She had, I believe, not more than five grades of schooling. Russian and Hebrew she apparently acquired by listening in on the boys' lessons before she left Russia at the age of twelve. Academic learning was held in great regard in our household, and my mother was proud to be a correspondent of Watson Kirconnell and a friend of Harold Files, Greenshields Professor of English at McGill. Though still not fully convinced of it, I have come to accept the principle that there is no such thing as an uneducated poet, although, of course, the poet's education may have been acquired by unorthodox means. Certainly my mother had read enormously. No matter how late she went to bed, she always read before going to sleep, and she never forgot anything that she had read.

Some Artists

Her role as a leader of a literary salon, or perhaps "beys hakhakhomim" (house of the wise); entertainer extraordinary for traveling Jewish cultural figures; clearinghouse for information about jobs, visas, sources of funding, contacts, and publishing possibilities; in a word, overseer of a virtual crossroads of Jewish culture, from which she kept in contact by correspondence with every part of the world from Vancouver to Halifax to Montevideo to Warsaw to Tokyo: this large role must have developed gradually. I assume that it began after the 1931 publication of her first book of poems, A Mother, although I remember it as assuming its full-fledged form at the time of our move from Outremont to Esplanade Avenue around 1934. For some reason, I recall her first contacts with artists more distinctly than I do those with writers: in New York, Wallace Putnam; I believe Burliuk; the sculptor Gudelman; the Glicensteins; and peripherally, Chagall. In Montreal, Nekhemia Lerman; Beys Afroyim; Manievitch; Fainmell and his wife Paquette; of course Bezalel Malchi, whose bust of my mother is now in the Jewish Public Library (replacing the one by Fainmell that was destroyed by a vandal, possibly Moishe-Leib Hershenov, I was told); Louis Muhlstock; Bercovitch; Bornstein; and, later, Rita Briansky and Joseph Prezament; Jack Nichols (to whom I gave my easel, in recognition of his superior abilities); the fine portraitist Rapaport (who, I was told, was stingy); Harry Daniels (who, I was told, rarely washed); Malamud, who used to go up to Lamoureux' pension to paint the autumn colors; my own art teacher, Fritz Brandtner (from Danzig—now Gdansk); and Friedlander, who later moved to New York. I don't remember much sophisticated discussion of works of art in the early years, though I do recall the epithet "shablon" (Russian for "cliché") being applied as often to art as to literature. Friedlander, on the other hand, was an intellectual and capable of acute criticism; a criticism which tended to grow more acute in proportion to the success of his contemporaries.

The earliest memories I have of these people are, perhaps, imaginary; but I did, in fact, through a series of incredible coincidences, meet the semi-legendary Beys Afroyim again about a dozen years ago, and he actually put into my hands some pictures that I, as a five-year-old, had drawn to keep busy while he was painting my portrait. He had carried those scrawlings of mine throughout the world. I have them now. Each of these artists is marked in my memory by some significant detail. Wallace Putnam was very tall; I remember the smell of paint from the canvases in his studio, though I don't remember the pictures themselves. Lerman had a romantic, flamboyant air to go with his wide cloak. Malchi, a close friend, once rang the bell of our apartment and broke into sobs when my mother opened the door. He had just learned that his wife, Grune, would not be able to have children. My mother would remark that Bercovitch's cravat, above his broad front, was always stained with food. I once went down the hill behind the pension Lamoureux to the North River and found Bornstein wandering around stark naked with his little son; Bornstein wore his usual half-enigmatic grin. Standing behind the little boy, he would encourage him to urinate: "Makh a boygn," he said; "Makh a boygn!" (Make a bow!)

Music and the Spanish Civil War

Then there was the world of Jewish music in Montreal, mediated for me by my cousin, Marvin Duchow, the son of my Aunt Mollie; Marvin was later to become Dean of the Conservatory of Music at McGill University; the McGill music library is named for him. There were musical evenings in the 1930s at his parents' flat on Bloomfield Avenue near Van Horne (794 Bloomfield, third floor), with Alexander Brott and the fine violinist Izzie Gralnick, who was said to have committed suicide in New York not much later, at the very beginning of a highly successful career. This was about the time of the Spanish Civil War, when the question was always: to go, or not to go? Some went, and some—among them relatives, at least one of the Kassowatzky boys—remained there. Thirty years later Marvin still felt guilty that he hadn't gone, whatever the outcome might have been.

The Literary and the Pictorial

Unquestionably, the principal artistic activity in my environment was literary, yet it seems easier for me to talk about that environment through its painters and sculptors than through its writers, or through its musicians. This may be because of the tremendous emphasis on personality in that world, and personality has more affinity with the visual than it does with the verbal, at least with the verbal in written form. I take this to be true even though the tangible work of art, especially the portrait, grimaces in its inadequacy, somewhat as people themselves do: Novalis says that "A spirit appears to pass through every significant personality which is an ideal parody of his visible appearance" (*Blütenstaub*. Einen jeden vorzüglichen Menschen muss gleichsam ein Geist zu durchschweben scheinen, der die sichtbare Erscheinung idealisch parodiert). There is also the fact that my mother, though never considered a beauty, loved to pose for pictures and photographs, and she must have made an interesting subject, since there are dozens of likenesses of her, by almost every artist whose path she crossed.

The Visitors

It seemed to me that when anyone who had even the smallest role in the Jewish cultural world (and who did not?) came to Montreal, from anywhere in the world (and they did come from everywhere), their first port of call was my parents' house. On the other hand, David Rome has reminded me that the major dignitaries were usually entertained by the wealthier patrons of the arts, to spare them the discomforts of our crowded quarters. This may have been the case, but I have very distinct memories of Leivick's staying with us, for one. By that time Leivick was a vigorous cultural hero, who had come a long way from the chains of his Siberian exile, as well as from his cubicle in the Denver sanatorium. A handsome, distinguished-looking man, he nevertheless had certain mannerisms that made him seem, if no less distinguished, at least within the conceptual grasp of ordinary human beings. For instance, rather like Wordsworth, he would convey his food to his mouth with a single wolfish swooping gesture. Before a lecture he would take an hour or so to collect his thoughts. At that time, of course, public speaking still had greater importance for the life of anyone with the slightest cultural pretensions than we can possibly imagine now. Leivick was a master of the deceptive overture. He would begin his lectures in a quiet, conversational tone far below the acoustic potential of the hall. I have seen people, after straining for some time to hear what he was saying, turn to each other with raised shoulders that asked, "Is this what I paid for? I can't make out a word!" By the end of the performance, the hall could hardly contain his voice, as he strode up and down the stage with thrashing, peremptory gestures. The audience would sit transfixed, and creep out, awestricken, at the end. My father had some aspirations of his own to public speaking, and would comment first on the qualities of delivery of any lecture that he attended; the content might be assumed to take care of itself.

As people came from everywhere, books also came from everywhere. Hundreds of presentation copies that had been sent to my mother are now in the national library in Jerusalem. News of the Holocaust filtered through gradually, just as I myself was beginning to learn about German culture and fall in love with it, little thinking how very different the word "German" would sound a few years later.

As I try to recall the various visits of important poets to our house I realize that there is not a great deal of a genuinely literary nature that I can report on. My mother met them, listened to them, fed them, helped them sell their goods, solved their immigration problems. I remember Moyshe Nadir's scribbling a poem in our double parlor at great speed, and my mother's marveling at his fluency. But I remember even more distinctly my father's reporting that he had asked Nadir whether his success with women were attributable to some unusual physical endowment, and Nadir's assuring him that his appeal lay elsewhere.

Melekh Ravitch arrived as a war refugee, of course, in 1941. He soon moved into the apartment directly adjoining ours (his was apartment 5). My first distinct memory of him is connected with his having brought in *maté*, the South American green tea, which was drunk from a gourd through a tube, and, in its original domain, passed around from mouth to mouth around a table. (Here my memories begin to blend with details recalled from the artist Bezalel Malchi's accounts of South America, especially of Montevideo; he had been greatly impressed by the social services provided from the proceeds of the lottery there, and thought a similar system would have been of great benefit to Canada.) Being so close, Ravitch was a constant visitor in our apartment. Only later did I learn that he considered himself the first modernist in Yiddish poetry.

Y.-Y. Segal, though not properly speaking in place here among "visitors," may be considered in tandem with Ravitch as a fulltime poet and contemporary of Ida Maza's who was frequently in our apartment. His relationship with my mother was rarely calm. Since my mother was always laboring to help people in difficulty, she did not appreciate his interference, which she suspected often went well beyond an obvious tendency to jeer at people and insult them in public. Nevertheless she always seemed to find it in herself to forgive him; she apparently thought of him as a tormented person, at war with his own demonic urges. My mother's relationship with Joseph Rolnick, another particular friend, somewhat older than herself, always seemed (unlike her contacts with Segal) warm and mutually rewarding. They communicated over a great many years, both through an uninterrupted correspondence and in person.

Politics

During the war years, like Ravitch, the Erlich family—Sophie Dubnova Erlich and her sons Alexander and Victor with their wives—also came to Montreal as refugees. Olek and Victor were to become professors at Columbia and Yale, respectively, but could not find even part-time teaching employment in Montreal. None of this, of course, prevented them from arguing about literature. I remember a furious quarrel between my father on the one side and Victor and his wife Isa on the other over the perennial question whether D. H. Lawrence was a Fascist or not. My father, for once, took the common sense position, the affirmative. The venue was the veranda of the Joseph Boyer house, halfway between St. Sauveur and Christieville. The countryside reverberated to the ideological struggle.

This was, to be sure, not the only situation in which politics became an issue. There was the occasion on which one of my mother's children's poems was published by Sholem Shtern in the left-wing *Vokhenblat (The Weekly)*, I believe. Her line, expressing a mother's aspiration for her child's future, "May my child grow up to be tall, and kind, and rich" (Az mayn kind vet oysvaksn / Groys, un gut, un raykh), was altered to read "May my child grow up to be / Tall, and kind, and straight" (Az mayn kind vet oysvaksn / Groys, un gut, un glaykh), which in the original retains the rhyme, though it certainly alters the sense. Needless to say, its author was displeased. But in retrospect I sometimes wonder whether there was not, in fact, an implicit contradiction between the highly personal lyricism, not only of most of Ida Maza's poetry, but of most of the poetry of her circle, and the social commitment that was also taken for granted in that milieu. But this was not the only paradox. Not only did all the healthy poor have their hearts on the left side, but even the wealthy Lapitsky could be counted on to help a starving poet with radical leanings. Asked by my mother how he could reconcile his wealth with his belief in the Revolution, he replied (according to her sworn testimony) that it was hoped the Revolution would not take place in our time.

The Country

I have spoken of the subjective and lyrical quality that characterizes most of my mother's poems. To a large extent this mood is associated with natural surroundings. The opening of this chapter makes reference to Côte Henri, consisting at that time of two or three houses between St. Jérôme and St. Lin. Years before the major phase of my mother's activity as impresario for the Jewish cultural world of Montreal, a nucleus had already formed and re-formed in the various places we went to in the Laurentians. The Desjardins' hard-scrabble homestead in Côte Henri, the Lamoureux's pension in Mont-Rolland, and the Boyers' farm in Christieville were the principal locations for its activities. In the summer we were accompanied by my mother's parents, Shimon and Musha Zhukovsky. My mother would tell me, with respect, that her father had wept every day of his life as he recited the Psalms. This was before I learned that the regular recital of the Psalms had served as a kind of emotional therapy even in the Christian tradition, at least since the early Renaissance. On the night of the new moon my grandfather would lead us out on the "Vachok," the short walk in the field behind the de Repentignys' house, to greet the moon with a prayer, "Mekhabl zayn di levone."

We seemed to have as many visitors in the country as in the city. I remember my first sight of Mr. Pripstein, founder of the famous children's camp, with his persimmon-smooth, smiling face, crows' feet in the corners of his eyes, and thin, smooth, light-brown hair. He was coming down the road from the adjoining farm, the Jean-Baptiste Latour place, pulling a child's four-wheeled wagon behind him. It held the goods that he peddled from homestead to homestead. It was rumored that he did well enough the following year to buy a horse; I remember wondering where he stabled it in the winters. Among the subsequent visitors at the de Repentignys' were the Greens and their son Hymie, better known later as the actor Lorne Green[e]; the Dworkins, whose daughter, already a beauty, became the poet Miriam Waddington; and many of my mother's habitués.

For, despite the cultural vibrancy of our household in Montreal, we all escaped to the country at every opportunity, and it was there that much of my mother's poetry was written. It was not until a great many years later, when I met non-Jewish Slavic people on evening walks or picking berries in the Laurentians, that I realized these practices, as well as the maintaining of some sort of dacha, were not peculiar to Jews, but probably represented general East European cultural patterns.

When my father was away on the road I spent a good deal of time alone with my mother in the hills. We would go on walks on the back roads behind the de Repentignys', and she would sometimes send me away to stroll, pick hazelnuts, or amuse myself as best I could while she sat by a rill in the bushes at the roadside and composed poetry. Much later, in autumn or winter evenings at Lamoureux's in Mont-Rolland, I helped her to edit her work. She didn't think much of my judgment or taste in poetry, but acknowledged that I could be of some use in helping her select and organize her material. One thing that I could never understand, and that colored my opinion of her poetry, was her use of punctuation, which seemed crude and insensitive, clashing in the most incongruous way with the finely worked language of the poems themselves. It was not until decades later, when I began to study Russian, that I realized she must have been trying to use Russian punctuation, which seems strangely lacking in nuance to anyone accustomed to Western European notation.

The circumstances in which her first work, A Mother (A Mame, 1931), was composed I was, of course, not in a position to observe. It was written after the death of her first son, Bernard, at the age of ten.[18] She was sick at the time when she wrote her autobiographical novel, Dina, around 1937; it is a book in which I do not take great satisfaction, but it clearly excited her throughout the time when she was writing it, sick as she was. One cannot predict how one's autobiographical ruminations will strike someone else.

■

THE POETRY OF IDA MAZA

The following section, consisting as it does largely of translations, introduces an element that is not found elsewhere in this book. I have tried to deploy the material in a narrative fashion that illustrates the career of a communitarian/proletarian writer, but the large number of translations may still produce some sense of imbalance. Still, in order for an English or a Francophone reader to gain access to the poetry, a substantial amount of it had to be presented, and I have done what seemed necessary.

The first thing one hears, from the first poem in the first book, is that Ida Maza's poems are for the humble, and the lowly:

Nidert, nidert, mayne lider
In der nider, in der nider . . .
Vu a kranker, vu a mider,
Nidert, nidert, mayne lider

Go lower, now, my poems, lower,
To the lowest, to the lowest
. . . .
To the sick, to where the weak are—
Lower go, my poems, lower

□

Portrait of Ida Maza, circa 1930. Oil on canvas, by Nekhemiah Lerman.

□

The dining room at 4479B, Apt. 6, Esplanade Avenue, Montreal, circa 1940s. Pastel on paper, my work.

And, though the humility her poetry espouses is not primarily social in nature, it is true that most of Ida Maza's poems are intended for everyman, being accessible and straightforward in content and style. Initially one may also have the impression that the verse is somewhat singsong; that the sentiments are unelaborated and familiar. These are first impressions that change on reflection. For instance, as far as rhythms are concerned, one soon discovers that one is repeatedly caught off guard by an inversion, a hypermetric line, a displaced accent, a prose phrase in the midst of verse. Amid the apparent regularities we encounter a poetry of surprising metrical virtuosity. In *Vaksn mayne Kinderlekh*, p. 177, what one might call a dactylic tetrameter, "Mir hobn shoin matse, mir hobn shoyn vayn" (We now have our matzo, we now have our wine), unexpectedly produces, in the last stanza, the line "Un dos tsigele fun Khad Gadye iz dort oykh geven" (And the little goat from Khad Gadye was also right there) which has only the subtlest rhythmical relation to the dominant metrical pattern in the poem. Again, where one expects an emphatic stop, the concluding line of a poem will sometimes end on a weak syllable (*Vaksn mayne Kinderlekh*,[19]"The Wind," p. 82):

> Opgemostn, tsugeshnitn
> Tsugeknipt un opgeshorn
> Mit regn-nodl oysgetsakt,
> Ale pasike uzorn

> Measured off and cut to size,
> Buttoned up and snipped with scissors
> With rainy needle pointed up,
> Every pattern you'd consider.

In "The Child and his Grandfather" (Kind un Zeyde), a brilliant translation of Eugene Field's "Shuffle-Shoon and Amber-Locks," the verses open with an inversion that one usually expects only at the end of a poem, for emphasis or for summation:

> Zitsn kind un alter zeyde,
> Turems, shleser boyen beyde

> So sit the child and the old man,
> Since building towers they began

Translation and the Primacy of Rhythm

I have mentioned translation, and there is no doubt whatever that Ida Maza was an extraordinarily talented translator. A great many of her poems are translations, whether or not identified as such, many from children's poets such as Stevenson or Eugene Field, many from sources that I can no longer identify. The first principle of translation, for her, fidelity to the rhythm, was to be rigidly observed; if you have not captured the rhythm of the original, you have lost the poem. This rule of hers, I suspect, also reflects the deepest principle of her own style: she is above all a poet of music. That musical principle seems to reach out and settle over the unwary reader, catching him or her by what might be called the horn of music, and attaching him or her helplessly to the body of the poem. I am reminded of Shelley, who sometimes set down the rhythmic notation of a piece in "ni-na" syllables before he wrote the words themselves. It was as though the musical form of the poem preceded its verbal sense. Mallarmé once said that writing is only "la fixation du chant immiscé au langage et lui-même persuasif du sens" (the fixation of song mixed in with language and itself [the song] persuasive of meaning).[20] For Joseph Brodsky, the real data of poets' lives, not only of their writings, lie "in the way they sound," their vowels and sibilants, meters and rhymes (S. Heaney, "Brodsky's Nobel," *New York Times Book Review*, November 8, 1987, 1, 63–65, p. 63).[21]

If this is indeed the key to Ida Maza's poetry, it becomes apparent that it is not in the authoritative poem which proclaims its mastery that we should look for her characteristic achievement, but rather in the lurking melos always waiting to break out through the surface of the poetry. And there, in fact, she is a classic. The movement seizes us in the midst of apparently casual lines.

Shmeterlingen tantsn um,
Ze vi sheyn, ze vi fray!
Loz mikh nemen dikh baym hant
Der tog geyt bald farbay.

Butterflies go dancing past
See how free, look how high!
Let me take you by the hand
The day will soon go by.

Even, or especially, when a line doesn't seem to make sense, it will force itself into the memory (*Naye Lider*, p .6)

Nokh gut vos es iz dir dayn eygn harts azoy nont, azoy ibergebn.

It's a good thing that at least your own heart is so close to you, so devoted.

With some of the cradle songs, such as "See the Moon" (*VMK*, p. 143) or "Bright Morning" (*VMK*, p. 144), the refrain is so powerful that it subordinates the words of the poem; it is the carrier of the mood, and, finally, it becomes clear that it *is* the poem. The rhythm in these lullabies overwhelms the individual lines, the good ones even more surely than the weak ones. By the time the refrain has sounded for the third time the reader cares only about the beat in the poem.

> Shtark iz der shturem,
> Beyz iz der vint;
> Shlof ayn, mayn kind;
> Shlof ayn, mayn kind.

> Storm and wind,
> Angry and wild;
> Sleep, my child;
> Sleep, my child.

Pure nonsense, but entirely irresistible, is "A Bird Sings," in *A Mame*, p. 92, with the strictly traditional "Lullaby, my child must sleep" (Ay-liu-liu, mayn kind, shlof ayn) interwoven through its stanzas.

Partly because she is the poet of the fluid line rather than of the marmoreal stanza, and can be read with the "touchstone" approach that accepts the priority of the short passage over the entire work; and partly because her modesty as a poet does not forbid one to reshuffle her thoughts for one's own purposes, I have decided to organize my review of her poetry in a narrative vein that may violate both chronology and some basic precepts of critical method. Taking lines from any and every part of her work, at least up to 1954, the date of her last book, I will try to present an evolutionary portrait of her working life as it may have looked to herself. I will begin with the crisis that precipitated her turn toward poetry, the death of her child, go through the intermediate stages of love and devotion to nature, and conclude with the sober tones of a mature life, no longer playful, rich, or even hopeful, but ever more sure of its obligations.

Elegy

The mood of the early elegiac poems oscillates between the mild, submissive Pantheism of "Lullaby" (*Naye Lider*, p. 107):

> Grin der boym iber dayn bet,
> Di tsvaygn, shtile, vign

> Green the tree over your bed,
> The branches, quiet, swaying

and the bitter, denunciatory "Where From?" (*A Mame*, p. 41):

> Yedn tog der regn
> Grizshet oyf mayn tir;
> Yedn tog der troyer
> Nogt in harts bay mir.

> Every day the rain comes
> Gnawing at my door;
> Every day my sorrow
> Hounds me as before.

Not quite as terse, but in a similar mood, is "Such Joy" (*A Mame*, p. 15; translated with Irving Feldman).

> Dayn geboortstog haynt, mayn kind,
> Oon der tog iz aza shtiler haynt, mayn kind,
> Oon der tog iz aza vayser haynt, mayn kind.
> Iber shtiln tog,
> Iber vaysn tog,
> Flien kroen oom, tantsn kroen oom—
> Zekhtsn shvartse kroen in a kon.
> Dayne zekhtsn yor, mayn kind,
> In shvartsn ongeton.
> Tseyl ikh zekhtsn yor, mayn kind,
> In shvartsn ongeton.
> O-ho! Bin ikh a mame shoyn

Foon a zekhtsn yorik kind!
Vemen nor dertseylt men aza freyd?
Tsi dem shney, vos oyf dayn keyver,
Tsi dem shtiln tog,
Tsi dem vaysn tog?
—Aza freyd!

So today's your birthday, child;
And it's such a quiet day, my child
And it's such a pale day, my child
Over the quiet day
Over the pale day
Ravens hover round,
Sixteen sable ravens in a ring—
Sixteen of your years, my child,
Caught in a black wing.

So I am the mother
Of a sixteen-year-old son!
With whom can one share such a joy—
With the snow on your grave,
With the still day,
With the pale day?
—Such a joy!

But one often notices, in the very midst of the most somber elegies, a dominance of nature imagery; and it is as if that imagery reflects an underlying identification with nature that will eventually overcome, or at least subsume, grief itself. There is a pleasure attached to lyricism, and that pleasure is undeniably felt at such moments. The mother herself is startled to realize, at one point, that while watching over her child's grave she is also watching the moon ("My Hillock," *A Mame*, p.12):

Di luft do azoy gut un shtil,
Un veykh dos groz tsu lign

The air here is so good and still,
And soft the grass to lie on

But this is a cemetery, and she is among graves:

Nor bay mayn zayt dos bergele;
Dem bin ikh a mame.

But at my side a little mound:
This one, I'm its mother.

Durkh levonedike nekht
Bin ich do gezesn,
Levone-soydes oysgehert
Un hob zikh shir fargesn
Az nit di levone hit ikh do. . .

Here, through the moon-bedazzled night
I sat on turf untrodden
To moonlit secrets listening,
But almost had forgotten
It's not the moon I'm watching now. . .

But it is, in fact, the moon that she is watching, and that she is
in communion with: one kind of watching implies the other, or,
perhaps, even demands the other. In the poem "To Earth" (*A
Mame*, p. 18) we encounter some of her strongest lines:

Harts tsu harts mit dir
Farvig mikh, ziser shlof;
Ikh vel kholemen in dir
Mayn onheib un mayn sof.

Heart to heart with you
Embrace me, sweetest sleep;
In your warm arms I'll dream
How first and last can meet.

In the conclusion she calls on the rain:

Regn, fal oyf mir;
Kush mayne vies oys

Fall upon me, rain;
My eyelids need your love

and on earth, at last:

Du, erd, mayn harts shtil ayn.

Earth, set my heart at rest.

One soon notices that many of Ida Maza's poems are haunted by
sleep: sorrow, sickness, sleep, and the body are all closely allied.
The body comes into its own in sleep: even thought can then
proceed only in bodily form, in images. At its best, sleep allows
for a reconciliation of the mind and the body—but on the body's
terms (Volkelt), the only terms that can afford us rest. It is, indeed, the only time when the contradiction that seems to be our
destiny may be overcome.

Poems for and about Children

A *Mame* contains both poems of mourning and poems that
speak of living children. Without going into the order of their composition, I will follow the movement of recovery implied in the latter
sequence. The child's eyes open (*A Mame*, p. 72, "A Child's Eyes"):

Yedn tog azoy, bloie himlen tsvey

Each day it happens so—two blue heavens glow

and every night as well:

Yede nacht azoy, un yedn tog bazunder

Each night it happens so, and every day, unchanging

One of the most captivating of all of Ida Maza's children-poems
is the well-known "Flowers in the Rain" (*A Mame*, p. 70):

Orem iz mayn shtibele,
Mit an altn dakh,
Vaksn in ir kinderlekh,
Kleyninke a sakh.

Geyt in gas a regndl,
Vert in shtibl nas,
Loyfn mayne kinderlekh
Shpiln zich in gas.

Geyt in gas a regndl,
Geyt er zey antkegn;
Vaksn mayne kinderlekh,
Vi blimelekh in regn.

Crooked is my little house,
The roof is very thin;
Many children grow in it,
But they won't stay in.

A little rain fell in the street,
The house got very wet;
All my children ran to play
In the narrow street.

A little rain fell in the street,
To meet them out it came;
And my children grow in it
Like flowers in the rain.

The individual child, beloved as he may be, is hard to follow in his metamorphoses and his transmutations (*VMK*, p. 111, "I'd Like to Be"), from

Kh'volt veln zayn, Kh'volt veln zayn,
Kh'volt veln zayn a hoz

I'd like to be, I'd like to be,
I'd like to be a hare

to a hunter, a grandfather, an author, a

Kh'veys aleyn nit vos

I don't know what, myself!

Uncertain, not only of his identity, but even of his dimensions, (*VMK*, p. 42: "From Head to Foot") [he is]

Fun fus biz kop di groys

From head to foot's my size.

Maybe, if clothes can create a role, he is really his grandfather (*VMK*, p. 34: "Now I'm Grandpa"):

Dos iz mayn zeydns yarmulke,
Un dos, mayn zeydns shikh;

Un dos, mayn zeydns zshupitse,
Un ikh aleyn bin ikh.

This is my grandpa's yarmulke;
His shoes, you can't deny;
And this is grandpa's jacket, too
And I myself am I.

Whatever the vagaries through which he must be followed, the effort is well worth a mother's while. In a superb set of variations on Stevenson's "Farewell to the Barn," Ida Maza writes "All to Please My Little Boy" (*VMK*, p. 15):

Ikh for fun shtot in dorf aroys,
Feld arayn un feld aroys,
Alts tsulib mayn yingele.
Falt in dorf a shney aroys,
A vayser, vayser shney aroys,
Alts tsulib mayn yingele
Fun himl kumt di zun aroys,
A groyse, groyse zun aroys
Alts tulib mayn yingele.
. . . .
Poyer geyt in shtal arayn,
Shpant er ferd in shlitn ayn,
Alts tsulib mayn yingele.
Royter shlitn,royter ferd,
Gold un zilber oyf der erd,
Glin glon, glin glon, vayse velt,
Alts tsulib mayn yingele.

Our train has left the city now,
Past field on field it's going now,
All to please my little boy.

Now the sky begins to snow,
Big white flakes it's snowing now,
All to please my little boy.

The sun comes out now in the sky,
A great big sun is in the sky,
All to please my little boy.

The sun throws glittering gold on the snow;

Farmer goes out to his shed,
Horse is harnessed to the sled,
All to please my little boy.
Red, red horse and red, red sled
In smooth white snow the roads are spread
Ring on, white world, ring on ahead!—
All to please my little boy.

But the child's imagination, unsatisfied even by the fulfillment
and perfection of his immediate surroundings, reaches beyond it,
to the imperfection of fantasy: (*VMK*, p. 157: "Where do Stories
Come From?"):

Ergets vayt, ergets vayt,
Nit mit furen tsu derforn—

Somewhere far, somewhere far,
In a place not reached by travel,

There is a house that lights up on a certain night:

In a vinkl bay a shayn
Zitst a zeyde, lernt Toyreh,
Zitst a kind un hert zikh ayn.

In a nook, by lamplight's shine
A grandfather is reading Torah,
A child is listening, line by line.

In another corner,

Bay a koymen, bay a shpin-rod
Fun zayd di fedim, din un veykh,
Shpint a bobe sheyne mayses,
Un tseshikt zei mitn roikh.

Near a chimney, with her wheel, the
Thread of silk, so fine and soft
A grandmother sits spinning stories,
And with the smoke sends them aloft.

In its turn, the wind receives them (and)

Un teylt zey oys tsu yedn kind.

Sends them on to every child.

On Purim (*VMK*, p.171),

Es bakt die bobe homen-tashn
Un der zeyde fast a tones

Grandma's baking Haman's-pockets
And our grandfather is fasting

There is a hard truth, not to be forgotten, behind this cheerful celebration; not to be forgotten because, as another Purim poem tells us with laconic harshness, Haman is also here, now (*VMK*, p. 170, "Grager"—i.e., the noisemaker traditionally swung on Purim):

Grager, grager, gran, gran, gran!
Amol is geven a shlekhter man;
Amol geven, nokh itzt faran;
Gragger, gragger, gran, gran, gran!

Grager, grager, gran, gran, gran!
Once there was a very bad man;
He lived before, he still lives on;
Grager, grager, gran, gran, gran!

Finally, though, the child, in his mutations, his imagination, his fears, and his aspirations will be too much for even the mother to follow. As he changes form he decides, at one point, to become an eagle (*VMK*, p. 17, "My Little Bear"):

Un bald verstu an odler gor,
Un lozt zikh oyfn vint;
To vi zol ikh dikh nokhyogn
Mayn yingele, mayn kind?

So now you are an eagle,
Upon the wind you've gone;
Then how am I to follow you,
And where now find my son?

Part of the problem is that the mother herself is not altogether secure in her own role: even at this late date she is only partially committed to the adult world; even, in some strange sense, only partially committed to parenthood. In *VMK*, (p. 187), "Like a Child," she says:

Kh' bin a mame fun kinder shoyn groyse,
Un bin nokh aleyn vi a kind.

I'm a mother of full-grown children
And yet I am still like a child

Kh' derfrey zikh mit yedn frimorgn,
Ver umetik yedn farnakht:
Un shpil zikh arum mit mayn mazel
Vi a kind mit di oygn farmakht.

I grow happy with each sunny morning,
Grow sad at the coming of night;
I play with my fate in my blindness
Like a child with its eyes shut tight.

Kh' hob moyre baynakht in der fintster,
Un benk nor nokh alts vos iz groys;
Kh' hob azoy moyre far umglik,
Un kesseyder nor zukht es mikh oys.

I'm fearful at night in the darkness
And wish more adults were about;
I have such a terror of trouble
And it's always finding me out.

Nature Poetry

When the relationship with children finally fails or breaks down, there is still a continuity provided by the communication with nature that had been coupled with the love of children. That alternative remains available until life, bit by bit, crumbles the foundation from which she can speak to the natural world and be spoken to. But in "It's Nearly Spring" (*Naye Lider*, p. 67), the world has just begun:

Heyser gold fun zun
Shmeltst dem shney fun feld;
Luft, vi frisher durkhzikhtiker vaser
Fun horizontn kvelt

Un a ru aza. . .

Hot gold of the sun
Melts snow from the fields
Air, like fresh transparent water
From the horizon wells.

And a kind of peace. . .

There is a force to some poems of this middle period that is almost shocking.

In a lighter vein, having launched the world to such a powerful beginning, the poet may well say

Di velt vet aza sheyne zayn,
A khies far di oygn.

The world will be so beautiful,
New life for all our eyes.

Even in sorrow, to quote Shelley's "Stanzas Written in Dejection," despair itself can be mild (*Naye Lider*, p. 57, "Light"):

Es veynt mayn gemit haynt
Mit vareme trern;
S'vet likhtik mir vern,
S'vet likhtik mir vern.

Today my mood's weeping;
The warm tears fall on me;
Let light come upon me,
Let light come upon me!

On a day of rain (*Naye Lider*, p. 66, "Rainy Day,") she can watch white pigeon-wings cut through the gray, [and] see

Un vi di eydele vaser-shnuren
Tsien zikh fartroylekh iber mayn shoyb.

How the delicate water-threads
Creep trustingly across my pane.

One can count on the night, too ("So beautiful,: *Naye Lider*, p. 62):

Azoy sheyn azoy sheyn
Di nakht vet eybik azoy shteyn.
Dem gantsn himl farkhapt,
Mit milyonen shtern tsugeklapt
Azoy khokhmedik sheyn,
Di nakht vet eybik azoy shteyn.

Such bliss, such bliss:
The night will always be like this
The sky will still spin;
A million stars are hammered in.
Such wisdom in bliss!
The night will always be like this.

Night has, of course, its own religious beauty ("Silent, pious," in *Naye Lider*, p. 59):

Shtil un frum,
Shtil un frum,
Geyt di nakht
Azoy arum.
Nor di griln
Griln,griln,
Nor di shtern
Finklen shpiln
Nor in taykhn
Fun arum
Kvoken zschabes
Shtil un frum.
. . . .
Un di levone
in ir prakht
Shpant arum
Un hitt di nacht.

Silent, pious, pious, still
Night goes round and looks her fill:
Only crickets always singing
Only stars are playing, twinkling,
Only in the ponds around
Frogs that make their pious sound.
But soon the moon, with glorious light
Will sweep back out to tend the night.

One of the finest of the night poems is "Hills at Twilight": (*Naye Lider*, p. 65):

Es hobn barg tsoo barg zikh tsoogetooliet
Oon iber zey der vald
Hot zikh mit nakht fardekt
Oon ayngeshlofn.

In der vaytns ba a zayt,
Hot der himl tsoo der erd zikh tsoogerookt
Oon beyde hobn oysgehert
Di shtilkayt foon der velt.

Hill and hill nestled close
The woods there got under the night
And went to sleep.

To one side, far off,
The sky came down toward earth,
And they listened to the stillness of the world.
(Translated by Irving Feldman)

The personal world, though, is not always as peaceful as the visible one (*Naye Lider*, p. 126, "Alone"):

Grin di lonke,
Zat di ku;
Un ikh zukh ru,
Un ikh zukh ru.

Green the lawn, full fed the cow;
Give me peace now; Give me peace now!

Some of this restlessness, as one might guess, reflects a desire
for love (*Naye Lider*, p. 30, "Because"):

Derfar vos boym tooliet zikh tsoo boym,
Oon barg tsoo barg,
Oon groz tsoo groz,
Derfar beynk ikh nokh dir.

Derfar vos shtern shpiln zikh mit shtern,
Oon roymen aroom zikh mit zilberne soydes,
Derfar beynk ikh nokh dir.

Derfar vos nakht breyngt mit zikh khaloymes,
Oon viklt ayn di velt in tsiterndiker beynkshaft,
Derfar beynk ihk nokh dir.

Because tree touches tree
And mountain, mountain
And grass touches grass:
Because of this, I long for you.

Because stars play with stars
And sweep their silver whispers all around
Because of this, I long for you.

Because night comes with dreams
And folds the world in trembling longing:
Because of this, I long for you.
                (Translated by Irving Feldman)

One of the most achieved of the love poems, from which I have
quoted previously, is "See How Free" (*Naye Lider*, p. 34):

Shmeterlingen tantsn um,
Ze vi sheyn, ze vi fray,
Loz mikh nemen dikh baym hant,
Der tog geyt bald farbay.

Alts vert tunkl, alts vert groy,
Nakht kumt on fun umetum,
Zest dem kleynem shmeterling
Tooliendik zikh tsu a blum?

Loz mikh nemen dikh baym hant,
Red tsu mir mit libe reyd,
Biz di sho iz far unz nay;
Zog a lign; red fun freyd;
Der tog geyt bald farbay.

Butterflies go dancing past.
See how free, see how high!
Let me take you by the hand
The day will soon go by.

It's getting darker, turning grey;
Night comes on from everywhere;
See the little butterfly
Nestled in the flower there?

Let me take you by the hand;
Speak kindly to me; don't be shy
Let's make the old hour new, or try—
Speak happiness! So, tell a lie!
The day will soon go by.

Poems of Maturity

It is perhaps only through hindsight that I see the darkening
of her later life foreshadowed in some of the earlier poems (*Naye
Lider*, p. 128, "Ravens in my Way"):

Mide mayne shoen,
Shvere mayne teg;
Makhnes shvartse kroen
Flien durkh mayn veg.

Tired are my hours;
Difficult each day;
Hordes of swarthy ravens
Fly across my way.

At times she can say (*Naye Lider*, p. 53):

Ikh bin troyeriker fun alle harbstn

I am more sorrowful than any autumn.

She feels the season approach in disturbingly personified form
(*Naye Lider*, p. 137, "The Dream of Your Approach"):

> Es tsaytikt zikh in mir
> Der kholem fun dayn kumen;
> Dayn otem shtekht di luft. . .

> In my thought there ripens
> The vision of your coming;
> Your breath stabs the air.

An unimaginable sorrow closes off her way (*Naye Lider*, p. 123,
"Grief Like Night"):

> Troyer tif vi nakht
> Shnayt durch dayn eynzam gang;
> Shlefert ayn in dir
> Veytok un farlang.

> Grief with the weight of night
> Seals up your road again
> And puts an end in you
> To both desire and pain.

Beyond the personal, a darkness of another kind begins to
encroach as the content of the 1940s declares itself, and she finds
it necessary to say (*Naye Lider*, p. 92, "It's your World")

> Dem nomen mentsh fun mir mek op

> The name of man from me erase

As we begin to approach a point from which a retrospective
view seems appropriate in this survey of Ida Maza's working life,
it becomes natural to cast about for a poem that epitomizes her
own view of herself. Certainly, some lines from "Echo" (*Naye
Lider*, p. 114) are relevant:

> Ir lebn vi di vintmil-fligl
> In tog-teglekhn gedrey

> Her life was like the wings of windmills
> In their daily whirling round

When one thinks of her ceaseless work for others, these lines seem particularly apt; of someone else who also worked too hard she writes ("A Furrowed Face,": in *Naye Lider*, p. 143):

> Hent, tsvey shtile eydes
> Fun opgeton, un mid.

> Hands, two silent witnesses
> Of weariness, and done.

Something disturbingly opaque cuts across the line of vision in several of these poems that come closest to the quality of her experience; whether a crowd of crows, or a sorrow deep as night: something is suddenly there that was not foreseen. There is an interruption or an intervention: the demonic visitor whose breath stabs the air; the whirling windmill-sails that batter the sight; even the hands ("shtile eydes") that force us to pay attention to them by their immobility. There is often also something four-square and heavy, deliberately anti-lyrical, in the poems that seem most directly autobiographical. At times the timbre shifts towards bitterness (*Naye Lider*, p. 134, "If You Please"):

> Ikh bin di nit batsolte dinst,
> Vos tut ir arbet mit a shmeykhl,
> Un vil es zol gefeln zayn,
> Bite shoyn, un zayt nor moykhl.

> I am the maid who's never paid
> Who smiling puts you at your ease;
> "I hope that you are satisfied;"
> And "Please forgive," and "Pretty please."

In these lines there is an echo from one of the proletarian poems, "The Woman Who Washes Floors" (*Naye Lider*, p. 82), where the maid who faints at her employer's feet ends her lament abruptly with

> Antshuldik mir pani, itst ken ikh shoyn geyn.

> Excuse me, lady: I think I can go.

The last poem in *Naye Lider* (pp. 155–156), "A Woman's Prayer," is an appeal to God to let her rest at last. She has had enough of tears, love, and poetry:

Genug zol zayn, kh' vil shoyn nit mer!

Enough! I don't want any more.

the refrain is more or less the same from stanza to stanza:

Genug shoyn—ikh vil shoyn tsurik.

Enough now—I want to go back.

In absolutely prosaic language, shunning any hint of the melliflu-
ous, she tells us that she has had a life like anyone else's:

Ikh bin a froy vos hot a man,
Un shlept mit im dem shvern shpan.

I'm a woman who has a man;
We pull our load as best we can.

But hardest of all to accept is the brief circuit of

Ikh bin a froy vos hot geboyren,
Lebn gegebn, un tsurik farloyrn:

I'm a mother who's given birth
To life, and sent it back to earth.

We can understand why she says at last

Kum; makh di oygn mir tsu.

Come now, and close my eyes.

In her later life, what sustained her, when nature was no
longer a companion, was the memory of her parents, and especially of her father. It gave her the additional temporal dimension
that acted as a guarantor of meaning in an increasingly alienating
environment. In memory she hears her father's footsteps, that
comfort and steady her (*Naye Lider*, p. 109, "Your Footsteps"):

Fun mizrakh vant hern zikh dray shtile gemostene
klangen,

Dray shtile troyerike trit.
Dayne dray letste shtile trit
Fun shmone—esre oysgegangen.

From the eastern wall I hear three measured sounds:

Three sorrowful slow steps
The last three quiet steps
Of eighteen benedictions in your steady rounds.

She writes an epitaph "For Your Name, My Father, and for your Book of Prayer" (*Naye Lider*, p. 108), which is at the same time an epitaph for herself, for her poetry, and for Yiddish poetry as a whole:

Ivre-taytsh un yidish,
Shtam fun mayne lider:
Un zeyer goyrl, tate,
Der elnt fun dayn sider.

Hebrew lore and Yiddish
My poems and all my care:
Their fate, father, like that of
Your lonely book of prayer.

I remember a stanza of her very last poem, which was quoted at her memorial service by Melech Ravitch:

Ikh zits mit di hent farleygt
Un kon shoyn gornisht ton:
Nor zen vi der tog fargeyt,
Un zen vi di nacht kumt on.

My hands are folded: I sit;
There's just one thing I can do:
I can watch the day grow dark;
I can watch the night come, too.

Ironically, it echoes one of her early, playful poems, "It's All My Mother's Fault" (*VMK*, p. 36), where the child complains, similarly, that he can do nothing, because his mother is constantly saying

Tu nit dos, un tu nit dos,
Un rir keyn zakh nit on!

Don't do this, and don't do that,
Don't dare to touch a thing!

At the last point there is no one to blame for one's helplessness,
and no alternative to look to beyond it.

One cannot help feeling, though, in thinking back over Ida
Maza's biography, that, despite her later pessimism, hers was a
strongly affirmative life, in its end as in its beginnings. The quality
of devotion was never for an instant in doubt. This quality is
clearly recorded in the final poem of *Vaksn Mayne Kinderlekh* (p.
197), "Thank God."

Dank Got farn emes oyf kindershe lipn

Thank God for the truth on the lips of one's children,

she begins. There are things to be thankful for that still stand
outside time and human weakness; and there is still a standard that
is binding upon us and not subordinate to individual preference:

Dank got far der hant vos zeyt mit gevisn,
Vos du farzeyst dos zolstu shnaydn;
Die erlikhe erd tsolt bisn far bisn,
Dos guts vi dos shlekhts zol dikh nit farmaydn.

Thank God for the hand that sows with good conscience,
For as you have sown, so too shall you reap;
The honest earth pays back, mouthful for mouthful
As the good and the bad their tryst with you keep.

■

THE COMMUNITY AND THE INDIVIDUAL

If one were to sum up Ida Maza's achievement as a poet, one
would see at a glance that she did important work in four major
genres: the elegiac poem, the children's poem, the nature poem,
and the realistic poem of maturity. Nevertheless, she is not, as I

□

Yiddish poets Nokhem Yood and Y. -Y. Segal, in front of my parents' dwelling in Montreal, circa 1943.

□

The synagogue on St. Urbain Street, Montreal, behind my parents' dwelling. This synagogue has since been torn down. I painted this water color around 1936, when I was twelve.

have said, the poet of the achieved poem, the poem that is incontrovertibly complete and powerful. Rather (to repeat) she is the poet of an irresistible rhythm that carries one from line to line and that even leaps from poem to poem. But this characteristic is not inconsistent with a humble conception of her role as a poet. Again I return to the very first piece in her very first book, "To My Poems."

> Go lower, now, my poems, lower
> To the lowest, to the lowest
>
> To the sick, to where the weak are—
> Lower go, my poems, lower

Her poems are meant to contribute to a community rather than to set her apart from it. As she herself insists, they are the poems of a servant, not a master; the title of "The Unpaid Maid," "Di nit batsolte dinst," is one that can be worn with pride, not only with resentment. This is, perhaps, her greatest originality, and an attribute rare in modern poetry: she fulfills the ideals of her community while yet retaining her identity as an individual poet; she is a writer whose work, even at its most private, is subordinate to community. The poetic life that she led was a public life in private. Ida Maza was the "Gezelshaftlekher Mentsh," the "Public Person," of poetry, performing a role that is hard for us now even to imagine, in our totally individualized polity, in which corporate activity has infiltrated and saturated the social process, rendering more personal forms of grouping obsolete. She exemplified, in its poetic version, the principle that community itself, "with its systems of ideas, its institutions not separated from the body of community—is idea incarnate."[22]

Like the fish in the creek (see p. 49, above), each member of this community pursued a private purpose; but that private purpose would have been unthinkable and meaningless without the collective intention accompanying it. As far as Ida Maza's relation to her community is concerned, the point is not merely that her work reflected the interests or the preoccupations of her environment; that may be said, in some sense, of any artist. Whether consciously or otherwise, we all mirror and, of course, in the act of mirroring re-form, our world. In this case the public character of the work does not lie simply in the fact that the themes of the author's milieu find their way into the poetry; the point is rather that the public character of the life radiates back out from the poetry once written: we encounter the poet's responsibility to her group as the very essence of her writing. No doubt this is so in part because she was working in a minority language, which necessarily carries with it a high degree of group awareness; the matrix of her culture could not disappear from her consciousness as readily as it might have done from that of a poet working in the medium of the cultural majority. Her poetry functioned continuously on behalf of, as a representative of, the group's experience, even in the personal and/or "private" experiences of life, whether those connected with love, loss, joy, or the discovery of beauty in nature.

It is not difficult to see how such a process functions in three of the principal categories into which I have divided Ida Maza's poetry: the elegy, the children's poem, and the poem of maturity. All of these entail an immediate commitment to social responsibility and some form of engagement. It may be more difficult to understand how the poems of the fourth category, the nature poems, could reflect a communitarian attitude. Yet if we take some of them individually—"Hills at Evening," "Because," "The World Will Be So Beautiful," "Silent, Pious," "So Beautiful," "See How Free"—the connections soon become apparent. They are full of symbols of intimacy, joining, intertwining, full of face-to-face dialogues; they add up to a poetry of immediacy, of contact, of "tulyen" (leaning, nestling), of "I-thou" relations. This is a poetry of collectivity because it never loses sight of mutuality, even in its most personal moments. It never speaks for itself alone; that is why I have said that it does not entail disloyalty to the group, or violate a contract in which the values and needs of the group are always assumed to take precedence over personal needs.

If we compare this poetry, in this respect, with the nature poems of, say, the English romantics, we quickly recognize a difference. Keats's "Autumn" is never a personal figure; nor is his nightingale, nor is Shelley's skylark. Yeats turns nature to the purpose of his mythic theories.[23] The case of Wordsworth, where one might expect to find the greatest similarities, only serves to accentuate the difference. Nature, in Wordsworth, is *for him*; his view of nature is, in a sense, intensely selfish. None of this constitutes, finally, a *popular* poetry, whereas Ida Maza's is, in the truest sense, popular poetry. It draws everyone else after it; it is for all others of her world as they exist with her. It grieves with them, it exults with them, it experiences beauty or sublimity or fear with them, it never stands alone or puts itself on a separate footing. In her equivalent ("See how Free") of the round "Come, follow, follow, follow / Follow, follow, follow me" she appeals to us: "Come, let me take your hand," to go with her, so that we may all see what she sees and love what she loves.

It is, to be sure, often said that individuality is itself the product of a group.[24] But that is usually said of the kind of individuality which defines itself by opposition to its group and remains unconscious of its origins in that group. The individuality of which I have been speaking is, on the contrary, perfectly conscious of its dependence on the group and implies no rejection of it. It is not that a poet such as Ida Maza is attached to her community in the fashion in which Durkheim, Lévi-Strauss, or the socio-critics[25] would describe it, as a shadow-print of the society, or like a marsupial infant glued to the mother's body; she is, rather, like a mammalian infant, attached by an umbilical cord at one point only, and in a way which allows and in fact requires her to exist as an independent being.

In the first pages of this essay I spoke of the possibility that, in the Jewish Montreal of the 1920s and 1930s, the community could enter into and confer shape upon one's very death; perhaps it could even enter into the fashioning of one's moiety of immortality. To repeat: the community could not afford to have anything be merely private. This is, admittedly, an awkward concept to grasp. It is difficult to understand how, say, the act of thinking can be at the same time personal and public, though, once one thinks of ideas as implicitly dialogic, the possibility becomes more apparent. Then, as Judith Schlanger puts it, "le fait que ce soit quelqu'un qui parle lorsque quelque chose est dit, apparaît presque comme une complication retorse de l'intersubjectivité culturelle" (the fact that there is someone speaking when something is said appears almost as a distorted complication of cultural intersubjectivity).[26] Or (p. 144), "l'individualité connaissante est quelque chose comme un fragment culturel" (the knowing individual is something like a cultural fragment); subjectivity is (p. 149) the space of the "transcription directe des densités culturelles" (direct transcription of cultural densities).

Yet even after all these efforts at clarification some may still find it difficult to perceive how the composition of poetry can be thought of as being a public activity, or how the Romantic ideal of the artist who interpenetrates with her community can function in real situations (cf. Schleiermacher's *Monologen* [Leipzig: Felix Meiner, 1914], pp. 55–56). To set that point aside, I should like to go on to what is still, surely, the most difficult case of all to understand: namely, that of the person whose dalliance with death itself was experienced as not simply his own, but as something that everyone had to think through him. This, it seems to me (as to Bataille), represents the extremest form of communization: the communization of death.

This person then, Dimentshtein, whom I have mentioned earlier, while remaining an individual in his own right, served the community as a lens through which other people could contemplate his act of suicide. Significantly, no one seemed interested in his motives; in fact, to this day I have never heard anyone volunteer any opinion about the motive for his attempt. The most personal aspect of a suicide, the motivation, seemed irrelevant to the public identification of the act. In the process of its being appropriated through translation into a communitarian idiom, the issue of motivation simply slipped away. It was the mere fact that he had attempted suicide that was brought into focus, as a circumstance in which the community could see that potential of the human situation, the act of suicide as such; almost as if it were one in the catalogue of possible human experiences that the community had to know, and had had displayed and illustrated for it: the pure phenomenality of suicide.[27]

It would be appropriate to object at this point that the case of the suicide "adopted," so to speak, by a community, and the case of a poet who functions of her own will as an "outrigger" of the community, are not truly parallel: that, if both are difficult to understand, they are difficult in different ways, and therefore cannot cast light on one another. In the one instance what seems to matter is the group's perspective on the individual (the suicide), in the other, the individual's (the poet's) relation to the group. But, in fact, though the two cases may not be fully parallel, the same laws are at work in both, and that is what matters. If group attitudes had not prevailed in the lives of individuals as they did in this community, Ida Maza's role as that of a poet who was at once an individual and, so to speak, the vector of the group for the world of poetry, would not have been possible: it was not the kind of role that would have been available to her by a private choice alone.

Two Lives

As a matter of fact, the two biographies, that of Ida Maza and that of Joseph Dimentshtein, were not without their connection. Dimentshtein had been a lawyer in Europe, but, having contracted sleeping sickness during the great European epidemic of the 1920s, could no longer work.

The phrase "sleeping sickness" meant nothing to me at the time. Dimentshtein was a thin-faced, serious-looking man with glasses and a slight friendly smile that played on his face. He didn't look particularly sleepy, and he certainly didn't seem distinguishable from any of the other eccentrics and aesthetically inclined unemployables who haunted our cold-water flat near the railroad tracks. Described by Rachel Ravitch, who is full of wonderful anecdotes about him, as a "sensitive soul" (empfindlikher mentsh), he attempted various inappropriate jobs in Canada. His most improbable assignment was that of chicken farmer in Manitoba (cf. Henry Roth). Later, in Montreal, he tried to work as a dues collector for the Jewish Library when it was on St. Urbain Street, but, as he finally asked with some justice on giving up the attempt, was this a job for him? When all else failed, he was shipped off by my mother to marry the daughter of a Jewish merchant in Halifax. This gesture towards *Parnosseh* (making a living) was no more successful than the others, since he returned after six months with the query: "Was that a match for me?" After recovering from his attempted suicide he left for New York, married, and eventually died. A daughter of his may still be living.

But what of the suicide? Why should I, in particular, be concerned with it?

When I was five years old we were living in a second floor, coal-heated flat on Esplanade Avenue near Van Horne. One day Dimentshtein, who was a frequent visitor to our house, but whom I remember in that context specifically only on this one occasion, came by to see us. I believe he first talked with my mother, who was in the kitchen at the back of the flat, then came back to the living room, which had windows on the street. He sat down on the couch, with the light coming in behind him, and displayed for my twelve-year-old brother and me something he had brought in with him. It was a pistol. With his usual friendly, smiling manner he showed us the mechanism, opened it up, rolled the bullets in his hand, and, still his customary unhurried and amiable self, allowed us to play with the pistol and examine it. Then he left. A little later he shot himself, in the men's room or possibly the vestibule of Horne's restaurant, on Main Street near Duluth. He had put the muzzle of the revolver in his mouth, but the bullet had apparently passed out at the back of his neck.

Why he should have chosen our house in which to exhibit

what he intended to do I do not know, to this day. Why he should have wanted to present the instrument of his intended suicide in such a gentle, playful way, to two small children, is even more puzzling. But, above all, why my mother did nothing to prevent him or to notify anyone else who might have prevented him: that is the most mysterious thing of all. Perhaps she had the fatalistic attitude that someone who wants to commit suicide should not be prevented. She must have known that he was about to shoot himself; she must also have known what the reason was for his intention. Whether it was despair over some romantic attachment, or simply discouragement over his inability to function in a practical manner, nobody has ever told me. Strangely enough, I never thought to ask her, or, above all, to ask her why she was so strangely passive and impassive about the event; indeed I never raised these obvious questions even in my own mind until I began to write this chapter. During Dimentshtein's convalescence, we were told that he didn't want to see any of his friends, and that it was not uncommon for attempted suicides to reject their previous acquaintance. There is, in the Jewish Public Library's files, a note written by my twelve-year-old brother to Dimentshtein shortly after these occurrences: evidently my mother chose not to forward it.

> Dear Diamondstone,
> This as I suppose you recognize by the handwriting is Israel.
> As I can not go to see you, I have to send this with [my] my mother wishing you a speedy recovery.
> It really was a pity about the past event, and I really can't express how sorry I was, for you were my best friend after all. I suppose you had your reasons about doing this, and once you did it, I think you should have made a good job of it. Now it is all over with, and you are living. Now I hope you will get well, forget all about this affair, and start on a new life. I heard my mother say that
> ---------(*verso*)----------
> when you leave the hospital you will do it again, and make sure this time, but please don't for my sake.

But why did all this remain in my mind, and in what way did it remain in my mind? The experience was not in the least traumatic in the usual sense: I remember it, rather, as agreeable if inexplicable. Dimentshtein's friendly smile; the pleasant, airy daylight in

101

the room; the odd, compact appearance of the bullets in his palm; the pistol, with which I had no association of danger: merely odd.

Perhaps I attribute a mythical significance to this attempt at a self-inflicted death simply because of my own involvement with the event. I can understand that someone who had no such personal associations with it might well be at a loss to understand why I even mention it, much less devote so much time to it.

Again, the only explanation I can give for my attributing special importance to it, besides the fact that it had a place in both my mother's biography and mine, is that it seemed to be experienced by the community, including those who remember it to this day, as an event that concerned them, not merely the sufferer or protagonist. Death itself did not occur only for oneself. It was as though death was something too important to be left up to the one who was dying. Like all other matters, it was in the purview of, and fell under the responsibility of, the community.

As I have tried to explain, it is especially significant for me as a limit case: if public life was lived in private, and public death was lived in private, then it becomes easier to understand how something as private as the composition of poetry could also have a public dimension. In other words: if death, that most private of all events, could be assimilated to the experience of the community, surely poetry, which is less private than death, could occur as an event within community. This was clearly the case with my mother's poetry. To go further: one might even suggest that the review of her work solicited for the March 1988 conference on Yiddish in Montreal by that very Jewish Library which occupied so large a place in her private life was another instance of the community's reaching out, this time after an author's death, but now to shape for itself her subsequent identity, and to claim a role in determining her place in history.

A Remote Analogy

All of this is not quite unprecedented, though I am extremely hesitant about drawing the analogy that springs to my mind, for reasons that will soon be apparent. It has often been remarked that, in the Hebrew Bible, public lives are lived in private.[28] In carrying out their private lives, the characters in the Old Testament clearly are not doing merely that: the significance of everything is doubled. (It is as if the Hebrew Bible had been purposely conceived to show that the distinction between anecdote and history debated by Lévi-Strauss and Ricoeur is not genuine.) This is not Christian typology, in which comparisons between the past and the present, or between Old and New Testaments, impose their form on thought. This is an originary duality, in which everything that happens, the births, the deaths, the squabbles, or the battles, has public meaning at the same time, immediately and to begin with, not before and after. Every event is bivalent, and the more private and intimate the event, the more readily its public importance springs to view. Nothing is symbolic but everything is significant. What happens has the stark particularized realism of a courtroom report or a family record: but it is all happening under the aegis of a group process that is invested in each personal emotion and act. Call it a destiny, if you wish. In its own way, the Montreal of the Yiddish-speaking community in the 1920s and 1930s shared and illustrated that ancient process, and perhaps even some aspect of that destiny. It interpreted life in a manner that makes its history, in this respect, like a latter-day supplement to or, at the very least, a footnote to, our Book of Books.

3

Quebec

■

AGAINST NOSTALGIA

Language does not preserve moods; when one is in a different state of mind, the words appropriate to a previous experience will not bring that experience back. This limitation of language is not only unavoidable but probably also salutary: otherwise, our minds would be at the mercy of words, which could then force another mood on us in defiance of the current one. One cannot have one experience and another language: the two things have to be consistent. The language one may have brought back from an experience that one would later like to recapture is like the gold one produces to show that one has been in fairyland: to get more one has to go back to the source. The words of a different world will not of themselves give one access to their origin.

This non-transferability of language has always been recognized as particularly true of the beatific experience, as well as of some forms of sexuality. One cannot think or talk one's way back to such experiences: either one is there, or one is not.

We cannot know, when we are in time, that the alternative of eternity is available to us at all times: that hey presto, the barrier can be withdrawn, and suddenly one can love children; one can love not lust after women, stop writing, stop caring about making money, about achievement and success: any expression can become merely a byproduct of living in eternity rather than an end in itself. Ambition, distraction, uglification are the alternatives.

Nostalgia is what one takes up as a substitute for living in eternity. The two are antithetical: eternity does not lean on the past; but time seeks in the past a substitute for eternity. Since time cannot have eternity in the present, it must pretend that it can retrieve it from the past.

In view of these facts we may have to reconsider the whole tradition of the "spots of time," from Ramond de Carbonnières through Wordsworth to Proust. Eternity cannot be obtained again by replacing the present with the past, whether the past be sought after deliberately or recur spontaneously. There is no way to patch up the present. The "spots of time" are declivities rather than summits. They represent attempts to escape a dingy present by lapsing into moments of putative past eternity; they are not surges of eternity that arise and transform the present. The present, if it is to be redeemed at all, must be redeemed all in one piece.

What is wrong with nostalgia, then, is not that it weakens one's commitment to hard-edged, realistic experience; the problem with nostalgia is almost the opposite: it fails to provide access to a promised ideal. Nostalgia is substitutional, certainly, but it is a substitute, not for the real, the temporal, but for the ideal, the eternal. It will not transform the present, and nothing less will do.

What, then, is the content of the nostalgic moment, if it cannot be the integral experience of eternity, which is always an experience of currentness? It must be an attempt to create or recover or perceive in the past something that has its own integrity and is therefore uncontaminated by an inadequate present: something that is alive.

But if one is in eternity, one has the same sympathy for the past as for the present; for everything in the present: for the one who, in the present, tries to recover the past, and for the one in the past who tried so hard to keep his past. But for the reified past itself one cannot have sympathy, because the past is not separate from the present or of a different quality from it. To value the past as such one must have lost eternity. And, so, one writes: that is, one pasts.

In the following chapters I will attempt to deal, not only with the particular issue of the relation of identity to community in the work of Tremblay, but also with much larger social questions, among them the nature of prejudice, the character of the political process as such, and the meaning of both identity and community in themselves. I will then try to re-situate the specific topics of this book within this broader inter-pretive context.

■

LE RUISSEAU SAINT LOUIS
(SAINT LOUIS' BROOK)

One of the things that many of us still labor to recover late in life is the sense of place: the place in which one once felt comfortable: what some people call home.

In the previous chapter I remarked that my parents and their friends sought every opportunity to spend time in the country, which, for Jewish Montreal at that time, meant the Laurentians. When I was in my twenties I still knew exactly where I wanted to be. My most beloved place in the world was the hill, almost always (as I remember it) in stubble, folding down towards the creek, which ran through Jean-Baptiste Latour's land about a mile from Mont Rolland. Later I was told, or saw on a road sign, that the creek was called the Ruisseau Saint Louis: but secretly I believed (and still suspect) that the name was attached to it retrospectively and arbitrarily by some functionary when the road was paved, and it was thought that the bridge over the brook had to be a bridge over something that had a name. Certainly no one I knew ever referred to it as anything but "le ruisseau," "le crique," or "the creek."

I have trouble now experiencing again the love that I felt for that hill, traversed diagonally by the hay-road that led down from the farm before its crest. But at that time I still knew that some day I would come down over that hill again, plump down in the grass on the little flat area before the stream, and be home. I wanted to buy it. To own that spot would have been to own the world and paradise. That stretch of brook a quarter mile long, encompassing six or seven riparian formations, was all I wanted. There, and nowhere else in the world, could I be happy; nowhere else in the world was I sure that I would be happy.[1]

The broad pool at the top, where the brook came out of the

woods, held the occasional nine-inch trout. It had few bushes around it; the banks were unencumbered. Then (following the brook downstream, left to right, west to east) a longish very shallow run, with bright gravel and quick ripples. How could the brook suddenly be so shallow? Where was all the deep water from the pool? Then a dugout, or arrest: a biggish rock jutting out from the near bank had created a deeper spot before it, with a bit of eddy after a rain. Maybe nine feet long, it was sufficient for a single stroke, for those learning to swim. (I couldn't try; I had had rheumatic fever and wasn't allowed in the water. This was where I first saw a naked girl; it was from a distance; I inferred, from the fact that she didn't have any clothes on, that she must have been naked.) Then mixed pools and snags and riffles; then a beautiful spot, where cedar branches stretched out from the far side, cradle-shaped, low over the brook, growing from a group of small boulders embedded in the opposite bank; in full view, almost at our feet, trout would emerge unhurried from among those rocks and swim about, or go back.

Beyond was the deep part. The cedar-sheltered area of which I have just spoken was blocked at its downstream end by a large, sapling-studded boulder, which rose perhaps three feet above the level of the stream. Beyond that boulder was a quiet black pool, perhaps twenty-five feet long and eight feet wide, slightly puckered near the middle, closely surrounded by trees. It was here that the really large trout, such as we never aspired to catch with our bent pins, lived in dark retirement; the banks, thick with alder and cedar, were quite inaccessible to the fisherman, though in most of the other stretches the fields were either mowed to the water's edge or were naturally rushy and treeless. The only practical way to fish this stretch, or at least part of it, was from the little bridge (housing, in its hay-filled cracks, colonies of crickets on whose casualties the trout feasted, their fat white bellies stuffed with the brown and black sludge of crickets) that marked the downstream end. Here the brook narrowed; in the defile under the bridge a wary trout often lay, facing upstream, in wait for whatever might float from the west.

This bridge, the stream's narrow girdle, was sacred, so that I can still barely bring myself to talk about it as if it had been a mere thing or location, or to desecrate it with words at all. The bridge, with its few warped planks, was the secret place, the jewel at the waist, tucked in among the bushes and hard to see until one was almost on it, that one would come upon at the bottom of the long hay-road, slanting down the long slope from the south.

■

IN ANOTHER COUNTRY

It is awkward to have one's absolute home in someone else's country, or in a country that someone else regards as his or hers and not yours. "La Nation" is also in the Laurentians, perhaps sixty miles from Mont Rolland.

> I love that meandering road, . . . the secret valleys, steeped in intimacy and in a thousand memories of happiness. I also love that extreme landscape, where there is still room for me. When it will all be over, that's where I'll settle, in a house far from the road, not on the shore of the Ottawa River, but in that back country covered with lakes and forests that goes from Papineauville to La Nation. That's where I'll buy a house, right near La Nation, at the entrance to the great park of Lac Simon, that you can go up by portages all the way to Lac des Mauves and get to La Minerve. That house that I'll find between Portage-La Nation and La Nation, or between La Nation and Ripon, or between La Nation and Lac Simon on the road to Chêneville; I regret that I did not find it sooner. I'm horribly frightened that I'll die hanging from the bars of a jail-cell without having been able to return to La Nation, without having been free to go there and stretch out in the warm grass in summer, without having run alongside the great forests with their deer, without having watched the limitless sky above the home that I will have some day, and live quietly, without weeping. Where is that country that resembles you, the true, secret country of my birth, the one where I want to love you and die? This morning, this Sunday drowned in the tears of a child, I weep like you, my child, that I have not yet reached the sunny fields of that radiant countryside around La Nation, in the warm light of our rediscovered country. . . . A few hours would be enough for me to take route 8 at Saint-Eustache where our brothers died, to follow the Ottawa up through Oka, Saint-Placide, Carillon, Calumet and Pointe-au-Chêne, and from Pointe-au-Chêne to Montebello and to

Papineauville where I would take the road to La Nation, passing through Portage-de-la-Nation and Saint-André-Avelin. A few hours would get me to La Nation, near that house, safe from history, that I will buy one day.[2]

When Hubert Aquin wrote of his perfect place it was also a very particular place in Quebec, but in a Quebec that he felt belonged to him, or should have belonged to him more fully than it did. Of course, nobody can own land, or a place; the place is the same whoever claims title to it; Pascal and Rousseau remind us that it is only because we are fools enough to accept others' claims that they can say it is theirs. Yet for Aquin to lay claim to a place in Quebec was different from what it is, or was, for me: my place belonged to me only by right of my experience there; his belonged to him not only by right of his experience but by right of his group's experience there. He or his group might also choose to refuse me access to my place, no matter what my experience. No matter that I still have strong feelings for Quebec, the sense that this is uniquely where I belong, when I am confronted with the peculiar tangle of wildflowers characteristic of the Laurentians, or when I look over the St. Lawrence from St. Jean Port-Joli to Baie St. Paul. There can be no sequel, in reason, for me, to such moments. No matter that Aquin's title was also compromised in advance, not so much by the *force majeure* of political authority as by the self-undermining Hamletism of his hyper-intelligent stance, in which one's nationalism is asserted through the lucidity with which one sees through one's own pretenses. (His ideal place, after all, also had to be, like my own, somewhere outside history.) Even though Aquin may merely have been giving elaborate and circuitous expression to the truism that one can't go home again, the home to which he could not return was his in a way in which mine could not be. I cannot have the illusion of returning to it; he could at least have the illusion of having a place to return to. Cast out from the earthly Paradise, I am thrown upon the mercy of eternity, which must do the best it can for me; teach me not to lay claim to anything: to pray for those moments when time and eternity greet one another, and place can drop out of consideration: only a few minutes in a lifetime.[3]

None of these bucolic pleasures, by the way, is native to Michel Tremblay. Quebec is not Montreal, and when Aquin's protagonist sets out for La Nation it is on a road that leads steadily, west and north, *out* of Montreal. For all that the values of French-Canadian society are, or were until recently, founded in a rural culture—

Tremblay's family on the Rue Fabre had come from the village of Duhamel, not far from La Nation—Tremblay's hero, Édouard, is very much a city boy. Édouard, as a child, "n'avais jamais mis les pieds en dehors de Montréal et . . . me mettais à éternuer à fendre l'âme quand j'apercevais plus que trois marguerites en croix" (had never set foot outside Montreal and . . . began to sneeze frightfully when I saw any more than three daisies together p. 57). A belated nostalgia for the countryside does show up in Tremblay, though, in *La Maison suspendue*. Yet Tremblay's desire, too, is to find his place and the Rue Fabre again: to buy it, so to speak, as I wanted to buy Latour's creek and Aquin wanted to buy his house in La Nation. But for them, for Aquin and Tremblay, albeit in very different ways, the group's desire is what counts. It is through the group that the past is summoned: not just through the individual memory, not even through the so-called spontaneous memory, which is necessarily an individual's memory, dependent on the decision of the individual's past to spring into the present; but through recovery of the group and its experience, through the reconstituting of the group. Salvation must be collective if it is to happen at all.

I crave indulgence for making the following obvious distinctions, but I find it necessary to re-work through my own thoughts even the most familiar elements of my subject. Whatever its problems, then, French-Canadian literature, especially as represented by its fiction, and in particular by Tremblay's writing, does not suffer from the atonic loneliness that I find in much English-Canadian literature, whether in its naive form, as in Roberts, or in its sophisticated version, as in Atwood. French-Canadian literature, on the whole, especially in its fictional expression, embodies a strong social and communitarian impulse. No matter that French Canadians, as explorers, frontiersmen, and subsistence farmers, had even more intimate contact with the great wilderness than did English Canadians: their problem is not, by and large, a sense of inferiority and disorientation as individuals confronting an overwhelming alien vastness: their problems are such as Friedenberg thinks the problems of any great literature must be—the relations of people to each other within communities. Perhaps the French were fortunate in a way in having a hostile cultural, political, and linguistic environment to cope with: it forced them back upon the solidarity of community, and it may be that the political traditions of a peasantry still molded in the forms of the *ancien régime* made this continuity possible.

In any case, the point of departure from which the French-Canadian fiction writer goes out to deal with his or her world, whether it be the wilderness (as in the setting of *Kamouraska*) or the stage (as in *La Duchesse et le roturier*) is usually the community.[4] One does not feel the alienation one may find in much English-Canadian literature, vitiating it and making it seem incapable of gusto. In Carrier's *La Guerre, yes, Sir*, one is conscious not so much of the isolation of this tiny village on the lower St. Lawrence as of the uproarious life that goes on within it: it doesn't seem to be in the least aware that it is supposed to be a minute, desperately remote community stranded in nowhere. The same is true of Jacques Ferron's amazing villages. By contrast, Alice Munro's Jubilee and Robertson Davies's Deptford are flavorless, colorless, and without energetic core.

Of course, there are notable exceptions: for instance, in a related genre, Claude Jutra's film, *A tout prendre*, in which an individual's isolation, as artist, as friend, and as lover, is in fact the subject; and the movie ends with a drowning, one of the commonest themes in English-Canadian literature. Réjean Ducharme, a major novelist, is obsessed with alienation. It would probably be foolish to try to assimilate experimental prose, such as that of Suzanne Jacob or Louise Maheux-Forcier, to such categories as either communitarianism or isolationism. The same is even more obviously true of the proto-"language poetry" of someone like Claude Gauvreau.

Nevertheless, French Canada, embattled though it may be, has a tradition, and a tradition is a society: English Canada, to some eyes, seems to have neither, other than, as I have said before, the tradition of duty.

One might ask, though, whether there is not some compensation, at least for the intellectual if not necessarily for the artist, in feeling oneself to be without a fixed history. There is a curiously unfed quality to the English Canadian mind.[5] In the absence of a tradition, there is nobody to tell one that certain enterprises are inappropriate or simply beyond human capacity. It is difficult to have a style—one just produces words in dimensionless space—because there are no precedents. English Canadian intellectuals do, or at least until recently did, approach things with a kind of brutal innocence, and there was no telling what kinds of artifacts they might turn out. One of these artifacts, called Samuel Taylor Coleridge, was invented by Kathleen Coburn; another was William Blake, created by Northrop Frye; a third was the modern world, dreamed up by Marshall McLuhan. These discoveries feel like isolated events that took place without context, forays on one's own into a space with no fixed dimensions and without points of reference. The best ideas of this period in Canada seemed to come out of nowhere. Of course, this is not to say (far from it!) that the ideas themselves are not sophisticated, or that their authors are not well-read. In fact, if Arthur Kroker is right in *Technology and the Canadian Mind*, the problem has not been so much that Canadian writers lacked a past as that they lacked a future, and the space in which they functioned, far from being the space of innocence, was a kind of electronic "virtual space" *avant la lettre*. (Patrick Fuery, inspired, like Kroker, by Baudrillard, has analogous things to say about Australian identity. See "Prisoners and Spiders Surrounded by Signs: Postmodernism and the Postcolonial Gaze in Contemporary Australian Culture," in Jonathan White, ed., *Recasting the World: Writing after Colonialism*, pp. 190–207.) But whatever historians may later have to say about the cultural atmosphere that produced these intellectual phenomena, it did not, perhaps for the very reasons explored by Kroker, seem to reflect the character of a collectivity.

■

PREJUDICE

This part of the book will be difficult for me to write; nevertheless it will also be impossible for me to go on to my next topic without working it out. In order to proceed I will first have to confess to a major social failing. The fact that others have begun to acknowledge this vice and grapple with it in public view[6] does not make it any less embarrassing to talk about. Prejudice has been anatomized in numerous books, from Gordon Allport's *The Nature of Prejudice* (1954) through Barry Glassner's *Essential Interactionism: On the Intelligibility of Prejudice* (1988).[7] Some aspects of prejudice have been clarified: the fact that it is closely related to normal functions such as categorization, generalization, and prediction; that group stereotypes are readily formed by the exaggeration of minor differences;[8] and that it is easier to be prejudiced against a group rather than an individual because an individual often turns out to be much like oneself (Allport, p. 363).

The trouble with all attempts to describe, define, or explain prejudice is that no rational analysis can by itself cause an emotional reality to disappear. Like a trauma, prejudice cannot be dissolved by explanation, though its etiology may be easy to understand, especially for those outside its emotional loop. To take a cognate example which may cast some light on the situation: the English affection for domestic animals, which at times seems to approach worship, has been accounted for in rather simple sociological terms by Harriet Ritvo in her study of nineteenth-century British class structure, *The Animal Estate* (Cambridge, Massachusetts: Harvard University Press, 1987). Yet one is perfectly safe in assuming that the individual Briton's attitude towards animals has not been in the slightest degree affected by the information made available in such studies. This particular national characteristic may be regarded as benign: but more reprehensible attitudes, such as those expressed in fox-hunting, or in an inclination to riot at soccer matches, may be equally impervious to change through reason or explanation.

Because prejudice starts beyond rationality it can never be described exhaustively in rational terms; and, like any experience entailing pain or pleasure, it is best expressed by the person having that experience. For that reason I intend to start afresh in describing prejudice as I myself feel it. Even if such an effort ends up repeating what psychologists and sociologists have said in more systematic ways, my account will at least be imbued with the reality, if also with the confusion, of any lived experience.

It may be assumed, because of my prejudicial remarks about Britain, that I wish to explore primarily my prejudices against the British. This is in fact not the case. For reasons which are undoubtedly obvious to any political scientist, I actually identify more closely with English than with French Canadians, despite very substantial feelings of fear and hostility with respect to English Canada.[9] But in fact I have recently succeeded in developing some measure of prejudice against Britain itself as well, and that fresh feeling provides a field in which I can make at least one fresh observation, even though this is not the major prejudice that I want to probe.

Glancing through my notes for this chapter, I happened on an index card on which a reference that I have used earlier (with a mildly critical comment) was written. The card read as follows: "*Solitude. A Return to the Self.* Anthony Storr. New York: Free Press, 1988. Trash. British?"

I felt as if I had been caught in some indecent act, when I saw what I had written on the card: a sense of horror or at least of shame came over me. What if some British person were to see that card? What if I myself were to run across that card again? It appeared to express a dismissive hostility towards all of British culture. The inherent implausibility of prejudice seemed to be revealed at a stroke in this simple example. Why should I bother to single out the weaknesses in the book, if weaknesses there were, as particularly British? Whatever defects emerged as the dominant features of Storr's work, they were surely not the same as the most striking characteristics of a *King Lear* or an "Adonais." Nevertheless, I had apparently found it necessary to identify the defects in the book by placing it in a category that included many great works, which might then, by imputation, also be stigmatized or disqualified.

Storr's book seemed to me to be full of shallow and trivial thoughts, presented as if they were of great moment. What identified it for me as British? Probably the references rather than the style. But once I had surmised that it was British, I thought I knew why it breezed along with facile generalizations, making a virtue of avoiding close analysis, scholarly apparatus, or anything smacking of pedantry. It seemed to me bad in a specifically British rather than, say, an American way. Each culture has its style of defect (in this case, of superficiality): but to react to the style rather than the defect is the mark of prejudice. It may be reasonable to use the style as a criterion for identification, but not as a basis for condemnation. Why? First, because style is only one feature in the constellation of a culture, and goes with the good as well as the bad. Second, if style is bad, it is bad in itself, not as "representative" of anything. It is simply bad. A pedantic American book, concealing the shallowness of its content under thickets of reference or of Continental terminology, is bad because it is shallow and pedantic, not because it is American.

With the need to justify our hostility, we (or at least I) find it hard to resist picking a cultural manner rather than a universal criterion as a basis for rejecting something that we don't like. But a good deed or a bad one performed in a certain cultural style is no better and no worse than one performed in another style. Even if we were to find that certain good (or bad) deeds are more characteristic of one culture than another (see below), they would not for that reason be any better (or worse).

I will return to the question of the "style of a defect" shortly. But in general, as in all matters involving prejudice, the only way to answer the "reasonable hypothesis" defense of prejudice, for example, the argument that, one is justified in avoiding blacks because more of them than of whites are said to commit crimes—the argument from statistical probability—is to think of oneself as its target. There is no way to resist the wave of generalization that overwhelms one's identity when confronted with the force of prejudice. This becomes obvious to a Canadian who is a resident of the United States, when traveling in, say, South America. An Ecuadorean or Venezuelan may be pleased and hospitable when taking one for Canadian, but very uneasy on concluding that one is, after all, only another kind of American. Part of the reason for one's sense of confusion is that when one actually lives among people (in this case, Americans) one soon stops thinking of them as having any set of characteristics at all, and least of all of their all being either good or bad. They just are—the mass of people in the United States—they really have no identity whatever. If one really lives among them one has no generalization about them. Their characteristics as individuals seem much more noteworthy than any faint or vague traits that they are thought by foreigners to have in common, and that, in any case, if they did exist, would not constitute a cause for either praise or blame.

Yet, (to play Devil's advocate for a moment): why should we deny that groups do indeed have some distinct characteristics, or some "style of defect," as I called it above? We have no hesitation in attributing virtues to certain nationalities; nor do most nationalities hesitate to attribute virtues to themselves. When I speak with a particular colleague on the telephone I identify him as a British academic because of his polite, modest, self-deprecating manner. He is, I find myself assuming, a kind of academic who could have been produced only by the British educational system. Are his not British virtues? And, if there are specifically or uniquely British virtues, don't there also have to be corresponding specifically British vices? To take an intermediate example: we sometimes attribute characteristics that are not heavily weighted morally to a certain group, and have no hesitation about using them to identify that group. (After all, a group is a group because its members have something in common. They themselves may even think that they have something in common: witness the "negritude" movement.) For instance, it is sometimes said that sabras can be embarrassed by intimacy. A non-Israeli might not find such an observation particularly opprobrious (though a sabra might). It seems to be merely a reference to one of those innumerable features of behavior by which we distinguish some people from others. Must we expunge all references to group characteristics, whether good, bad, or indifferent, from our communications, in order to purge ourselves of prejudice, or of the imputation of prejudice?

The exact locus of prejudice on what might be called the psychological genome is hard to identify. It must be granted that more English people than Americans manifest an extraordinary degree of affection for animals; it is probably also true that a higher percentage of English people riot at football games than do, say, Swiss (though fewer commit murder!). But, of course, the point is different: if we have a prejudice against English people it is not because too many of them riot at football games, or behave in other objectionable ways: it is because we have fastened on those actions as being representative of their conduct, dismissing everything else about them, good, bad, or indifferent, as irrelevant—and also dismissing all those football fans who do not riot as "unrepresentative."

For what Kwame Anthony Appiah calls the "intrinsic racist," the prejudice slips between all specifiable blemishes, so to speak, to fasten on some essence that has nothing to do with the sins that one can name.[10] Does the "good" American, for instance, exist? Undoubtedly. But he or she is not "the type:" and having established the type, one proceeds to extract from each individual that which binds him or her to the type. When I was a child, among the French-Canadian families I knew there was one that I thought of as representing the lowest level of human evolution and another that I idealized. For whatever reason, though, I ended up identifying French Canadians not with the Desjardins but with the X family. Yet after observing the fact that I had identified one of the X family as "typically" ignorant, drunken, boorish, and uninterested in any other way of life, I would have been hard pressed to say what distinguished him from anyone of a different culture who would exhibit these same very common characteristics. In other words, what was really "typical" about him?

In every culture, each individual is affected by innumerable details of conditioning that produce preferences and aversions, attitudes that express themselves in the minute details of everyday life. For the most part these choices are morally neutral, but they add up to something that may be called, from the perspective of another group, a distinctive flavor. When one has developed a prejudice against a group, the flavor surrounding the actions one is objecting to is often the real target of one's hostility, although (as in the case I have just given) one may claim that one is protesting against some clearly defined defect. On the other hand, it is also possible to have a form of prejudice in which a generalization identifies the tone or flavor itself, real or imaginary, as the objectionable feature. Suppose one were to feel that Ontarians are smug, or that they are inclined to let themselves be bound by rules. (Only one's own group, of course, is ever normatively neutral.)[11] Accepting such a premise, one then finds that this characteristic suffuses and disqualifies the personality of every Ontarian: nothing more really needs to be known about the species. Such group stereotypes produce a much more sweeping rejection than the same criticism would if applied to an individual, since some non-Ontarian person who was smug or rulebound might readily be acknowledged to have other compensatory characteristics.[12]

But to return to the matter of flavor. If one speaks of a feature that is intimately characteristic of one culture—say, the French-Canadian—and not of another—say, the French—one is likely to be thinking primarily of the language. I find it easy to recognize the slightest French-Canadian accent in English, even in distant and unfamiliar contexts. Recognizing it, I assume that the speaker has certain attributes that align him or her necessarily with the X family; just as I assume that someone with a Southern accent in English is something like Bull Connor, or that a Yiddish speaker with a Polish accent is something like the fishwife who threw me down the stairs of her shop in the Kensington market when I was five years old because I was looking at her tank of carp. No doubt there are class assumptions at play in all this: ignorant people tend to be poor people, and who wants to talk like poor people? So, *mutatis mutandis*, my attitude towards French Canadians is no different from that of some cultivated Englishmen towards the lower castes of that society, readily identified by their language.

Of course, prejudice may be felt not only with respect to members of a lower class, or towards all people who are less privileged than oneself. It seems to be mainly where conflict, or the possibility of conflict, is involved that prejudice comes into play. Any group that threatens one, or that one thinks may threaten one, whether because it is superior or because it is inferior, readily becomes an object of prejudice. Unfortunately, this is such a universal condition, or so nearly universal as to be almost no specific condition at all, that it does not advance the understanding of prejudice very far. Above all, it does not help to distinguish prejudice from other forms of classification. Yet prejudice is clearly something more than just another problem in the relation of the general to the particular.[13]

Apart from technical distinctions that always seem to come out somehow insufficient, there is simply the fact that prejudice, like love, or anger, is an experience, not an idea. A prejudice is something that one feels is *right*; it is surrendered grudgingly, if at all, because it gives pleasure; perhaps, simply, because it satisfies the need to express hostility without self-judgment. It serves an emotional purpose, and, no matter how many times one may succeed in reasoning oneself out of it, one usually has to start all over again at the end of the demonstration, because it has merely been pushed aside by a sort of mental *force majeure*, not eradicated or replaced by a more appropriate feeling.

■

JOUAL

I have said that the flavor of a culture, whether one be favorably disposed towards it or otherwise, is carried in its most obvious and most accessible form by its language. My own relationship to the French-Canadian language of the Montreal region is, of course, confused and contradictory. I speak Joual on occasion, but never to French Canadians, with whom I use book French, no doubt as a way of making clear to them that I do not think of their culture as my own. I speak Joual mainly to myself; sometimes to my daughter (who has learned it from me). After all, it was the third language that I learned during my childhood (Yiddish and English were first and second). I don't remember ever having spoken it to other Quebecers, but I must have, since I don't remember having tried to Europeanize my French before I entered my teens, and I had used French a good deal before that. But at times I do speak Joual to myself, reveling in the juicy diphthongs, the harsh final consonants, the sententious phrases. Actually, as I have realized on reading Tremblay, to use Joual as a literary language would require great linguistic powers, for one would need to know both regular Joual, English, French, and a kind of encompassing or higher-order, ironic Joual embracing all three of those. (Compare Von Rezzori's description of the higher-order bastard

QUEBEC

Yiddish that formed a more flexible and expressive idiom than either Yiddish itself or German; this idea brings in its train, of course, all the issues raised by Gilles Deleuze and Félix Guattari in *Kafka: Pour une littérature mineure* [Paris: Minuit, 1975]).[14] In any case, I allow myself the private satisfaction of, I take pleasure in the private use of, a language that I would never be caught speaking in public—as though to use it were to violate my commitment to expressing myself "in the manner that I am accustomed to."

I remember Mr. Tanny, the pharmacist of Tanny's Drug Store on the south side of Mount Royal just west of Main, shortly after we moved from Outremont to Esplanade Avenue, around 1935. Mr. Tanny and his partner (I think his brother) were Jewish (Tannenbaum?) and Anglophone, but Mr. Tanny also spoke absolutely fluent, absolutely unselfconscious Joual. I remember both marveling at, and being horror-struck by, his voluble French, which he used with both his staff and his Francophone customers, as though he were performing some gruesome task with extraordinary virtuosity. If you're going to learn a foreign language that well, so that it's absolutely spontaneous, I seem to have thought, why learn *that*?

To be sure, I also speak the English that I choose to speak rather than some other form of the language that I would consider inferior: less copious in vocabulary, less complex in syntax, less finely tooled, poorer in tradition, given to solecisms: "ain't" is no different from "isn't," but I am more comfortable with "isn't," and I like to be free to use Latinate terms as well. Expressive as the proletarian language may be in some respects, it does not serve the purposes of the academic. Why, then, since I don't use hard-hat or blue-collar English, should I feel guilty about not using Joual? In the form in which I learned it, it was the language of the peasant and the laborer, not the intellectual, and the accent seemed inseparable from the limitations of what seemed, at least to an outsider, a crude and impoverished vernacular. When I studied music with Claude Champagne I found it hard to believe that this admired teacher had done major archival work in music history in Paris, Quebec accent and all. It was hardly to be thought, in the 1930s, that the Quebec language would eventually become legal tender in schools and universities, and a literary language to boot.

Or has it become a literary language? *Des nouvelles d'Édouard* is at least as much *about* Joual as it is *in* Joual: it is an exhibition of Joual *in* literature rather than simply the use of Joual *for* literature. In its confrontation with France and with European French it

119

reaffirms the borders of its own language while attempting to make those borders all-embracing. But Joual is not, after all, a language suited to all purposes; it has the limitations as well as the advantages of any vernacular. Primarily an oral idiom, it was formed by history mainly for face-to-face communication.[15] In fact, Tremblay's achievement in his novels and plays seems all the more remarkable because good dialect literature is notoriously rare. (One remembers Hubert Aquin's contempt for Joual as a literary medium, as well as Édouard Glissant's suspicions of Creole.) If one assumes that a well-elaborated tradition of some kind is necessary for the production of literature, then dialect literature (at least in prose) is at an obvious disadvantage, for, if it had such a tradition, it would not be dialect in the first place. Perhaps, indeed, dialect literature is limited (and eventually self-terminating) because it has strayed from its sources, repudiated its specifically oral tradition in order to become written literature. It can neither go on drawing on a tradition for any length of time (since its own production has, in a sense, brought the oral tradition to a close) nor establish one: all of which makes Tremblay's particular achievement, as I have said, the more remarkable.

In cities, the constituency of the vernacular is the neighborhood, even though it may be current far beyond those boundaries. It is meant to create and sustain a group, to forge it as well as to serve its individual members. (On the other hand, Jean Marcel insists there is no longer any social link that subtends the popular language of Quebec. See *Le Joual de Troie* [Montréal: Éditions du jour, 1973], p. 136.) In the countryside it provides linkage in what was, in Quebec, even within this century, a basically analphabetic population, exhibiting some of the features of a cult- or secret-society code, with values of exclusivity as well as cohesiveness: the language of a religion. At least, so it seemed before the fall of the Collèges classiques, the introduction of the CEGEPs, or junior colleges, and the diminution of clerical control, even in the life of rural Quebec.

■

FRANCOPHONE COMMUNITIES

To quote Édouard, "Partager, comprenez-vous? Chus venu au monde en gang et chus incapable de vivre et surtout de comprendre tout seul!"[16] (To share, do you understand? I was born in a gang and I am incapable of living and above all of understanding anything by myself!). Of course, the communal nature of French-Canadian life undoubtedly has much in common with that of other community-oriented societies, especially among immigrants such as the Italians. The similarities and differences, as I have said before, have no doubt been studied exhaustively by sociologists. Still, at least as they appeared to myself as an outsider, French-Canadian family and neighborhood life, especially in the countryside, seemed deeply cohesive.[17] There was much visiting of even remote family members on holidays, a tendency to keep aged and ailing relatives at home, children settling near parents, frequent adoptions, and a willingness to accommodate illegitimacies and social aberrations (drinking, adultery). Most of these characteristics, of course, are found in rural populations in general, and it is undoubtedly true that in the working-class neighborhoods of the city, more social disorder was apparent alongside the continuing generosity of family life. The native cohesiveness of the French-Canadian family sometimes seemed strained to the breaking point. Nevertheless, although grass on the other side of the fence always seems greener, the French-Canadian family and neighborhood did seem to have a spontaneous, almost a joyous cohesiveness. Marveling at this phenomenon himself, Tremblay's Édouard asks: "C'est-tu héréditaire, le fun, coudonc?" (Hey, do you think fun is hereditary?) (p.124). This made it quite unlike the cohesiveness born of necessity, and associated with a history of persecution, which I felt to be at the core of the Jewish group, both of the Jewish family and of the community. It was an obligatory as well as a natural coherence, not something that was simply there; and it could not afford a surplus of that enviable gaiety and joie de vivre that we find on Tremblay's Rue Fabre or in Roch Carrier's village on the St. Lawrence. Or at least so the two commonalties appeared, to a member of one of them.

■

THE JEWS AND THE FRENCH

The interests of the two groups were by no means coincident, except in their mutual fear and resentment of the cold, stenchy Anglos, the colonial superiors. Poor Jews aspired to be, not businessmen, as most would assume, but professionals; poor Cana-

diens aspired to join the managerial class, as far as I could see
(and as I say superciliously) and, with luck, to become technocrats. (How would I deal with all the exceptions—such as Tremblay himself?) Exactly where their needs conflicted I am not sure,
though the usual shopkeeper-laborer relationship was undoubtedly one of the areas of difficulty. In any case, anti-Semitism was
even more widespread among the French-Canadians than it was
among other groups,[18]encouraged by pulpit preachers as well as
by demagogues of the ilk of Adrien Arcand. Many disagreeable
incidents remain vivid for me. One may well ask: what is the
object in opening old wounds; surely it is better to forgive and
forget. But a trauma is precisely something that one cannot forget;
and it is only through anecdote that one can convey how people
actually felt during such hostile encounters. Since a large part of
my purpose is to communicate the actual atmosphere of mutual
prejudice, there is no point in my avoiding its raw material. Unquestionably there would be reciprocal anecdotes available in un-
limited quantity from the other perspective, if "equal time" could
be provided.

Until the early 1970s I spent all my summers in the Laurentians. In the late 1950s I used to rent a cabin from a family in
Mont-Rolland, and I often spent my afternoons in my rubber raft
on the North River, in the quiet water above the beginning of the
rapids, still-fishing for bass, perch, shiners, or whatever else
might come along. One afternoon, when I was anchored in one of
my usual spots, some young men launched a rowboat from the
west bank, and rowed at an angle across the river, crossing my
bow not far above me. (I thought they must be intending to land
on the east bank near a religious institution there, where I somehow had the impression that there was a seminary. Perhaps there
was.) I greeted them, and we exchanged a few words, to what
effect I do not remember; but I will not forget the last remark one
of them made, for which I was entirely unprepared: "Vous êtes
toujours ici sur la rivière à prendre les poissons—maudit Juif"
(You're always here on the river catching the fish—damned Jew).
And they rowed on. The hard, pointed tone of the young man—
clearly no *habitant*—remains with me as much as the content of
his remark.

The awareness of their endemic anti-Semitism certainly diminished the concern I might otherwise have felt about the national
aspirations of the French Canadians or the danger to their culture
represented by an Anglophone majority.[19] Perhaps native Cana-

dian groups have experienced a similar failure of sympathy for Quebec's political agenda, for comparable reasons.

The terre-à-terre quality of French-Canadian life, with its exclusivist, xenophobic overtones, could also at times create a broader anxiety in an intruder, an anxiety not strictly attributable to anti-Semitism. I was crossing the barnyard one afternoon at Lamoureux' farm on my way to walk in the fields when I saw one of the farmer's grown sons leading a white and orange cow into the barn, onto the barn floor in the hay mow. I paid little attention, crossed the fence at the far end of the yard, and went on to walk. On my way back, coming through the barnyard again, I was shocked to see the carcass of the cow hanging from a beam, the floor covered with puddles of blood. Seeing the expression on my face, the farmer's son stopped his work, and drove at me: "On aime ça, tuer, nous autres, les Canadiens!" (We French-Canadians enjoy killing!).

The remark could have been meant in several ways: as a reproof of the squeamish tourist who enjoys his meat but pretends not to know where it comes from; as a defiant assertion of the peasant way of life and its values; but to me it meant primarily "I would love to butcher you too if I could, you non-Canadien son of a bitch, you who come here among us, but with whom we have nothing in common."

4

La Grosse femme, Macbeth, and Des nouvelles d'Édouard

■

LA GROSSE FEMME D'À CÔTÉ EST ENCEINTE AND THE CONCEPT OF SOCIAL SPACE

I had intended to go on directly to a discussion of Tremblay's *Des nouvelles d'Édouard* at this point, but I cannot bring myself to proceed without first attempting to do justice, no matter in how limited a degree, to his *La Grosse femme*. Inappropriately pregnant in her forties, and confined to a bedroom in the apartment that she and her family share with her in-laws, the unnamed fat woman, with her irrepressible, fertile love, spreads grace through the neighborhood. She fills out the human spaces of her street. The novel consists of a going out and an ingathering, in which all the imperfect and the unhappy of the Rue Fabre, the children, the prostitutes, the adults, the old women, go out to the park separately on a spring day and return together in procession, redeemed. Appropriately, at the end of the day, they all eat together. The astringent allopathic alternative to La grosse femme is provided by the tomcat Duplessis, who, for all his toughness, lets himself be killed for love of the child Marcel but in recompense is transported to the cat heaven operated by the ghosts next door. His murderer, the dog Godbout, is still sniffing after him in irritable perplexity as the novel comes to an end.

It is a story without a story, and without an obvious intellectual exoskeleton, so it is hard to talk about except through expressions of admiration. Yet the automatic gesture of respect by which we show that we take a book seriously is not just that we praise it, but that we try to identify its philosophical implications. One might say that if you write well, others will find ideas in your writing for you; it's only if you write badly that you have to find ideas of your own.

So it is probably not the fact that there actually are ideas in a literary work, or that a work has meaning, which gives rise to the need to understand it. It is rather that, because we feel instructed by it in some obscure way, we search in it for ideas; these usually turn out to be the ideas that we already have. (That is one reason why older works often appear to us predictive of contemporary thought.)

One of the current ideas that *La Grosse femme* brings to mind, in its/her bodily fullness, its/her freedom from free intellectual radicals, so to speak, from the poisonous discrete quanta of thought, is that ideas themselves have a large component of physicality, of fatness, in them. The boldest formulation of this principle that I have seen is in an unpublished paper by Connie Schultz, who insists that once one has had an idea it has become part of one's body, and all subsequent ideas simply create more layers in a palimpsest. Recent pragmatist interpretations of the supposed idealist Kant by Étienne Balibar and Jean-François Lyotard tend to related conclusions: we know ideas only as they come home to us in our physical experience. After all, it was Kant who declared that truth lies only in experience ("Nur in der Erfahrung ist Wahrheit."[1] *Prolegomena to any Future Metaphysics,* "Supplement.") One could derive identical conclusions, in fact they follow *a fortiori,* from the writings of that still more extreme idealist, Fichte). As physical experiences, then, ideas become indelible parts of our body: a meaning never goes away. One cannot eliminate by hindsight what was once a meaning.

A few more references may help to show the currency that the union of the bodily with the abstract has in contemporary thought. For instance, Gerard Manley Hopkins's insistence that there is a bodily component (which he calls an image) in every idea (see chapter 2, text over note 17) comes back in Donald Phillip Verene's interpretation of Hegel.[2] The title of a book on eighteenth-century visual theory emerges as *Body Criticism.*[3] The first thing we are told in Michael Leyton's *Symmetry, Causality, Mind* is that memory, central to our function, is "always some physical object."[4] Everywhere

125

one finds the idea brought back to a relation with the physical.[5] One is reminded of the phenomenological tide that swept European philosophy—as well as American poetry—in the early twentieth century, except that now it does not seem to be so much a matter of "No ideas but in things" as "No idea without a thing somewhere in it."

The fat woman is the substantial core of thought. She remains in her room until the very end, when she comes out on the gallery and explains to the six other pregnant women of the neighborhood what their pregnancies are all about. But until that moment she is immured, like a broody hornbill or a queen bee: only her all-sufficient kindliness can issue through the doorway of her room.

The question is not so much, what ideas are in her, or in her book? but, rather, what are the ideas that are the emanation of her, or of her book? Of what ideas is she the physical center? What ideas does she attract?

Not inappropriately, they seem initially to be ideas of space: physical space and social space. (After all, a fat person occupies space.) I will develop this suggestion shortly, but initially I would like to deal with some secondary issues in order to clear access to the major ones.

First, we notice that the fat woman has no name. She is unnameable: hers is an essence that does not consort with names. All those around her—even the ghosts—have their names, but not she. Her fatness and her womanness are her only name. Too intimate for a name, she is also perhaps too real for a name. A name is an automatic demotion, a distancing: it is an instrument that can be used to control a person,[6] and there is too much unspoken devotion to the fat woman for one to want to limit or define her. In a contradictory way, a name can be de-humanizing. To attach a name to the fat woman would be to compromise her essence and to diminish her unique importance. It would be a way of preventing her from filling all spaces.

The fat woman is a kind of diagonal mother to all the other mothers. Hidden in her room, she can be present only in an indirect way, though she does reveal a public dimension at the very end; for it turns out that she cannot, after all, fit in her room. Hers is the marginal presence that provides a ground for all the others (not least for the author, perhaps her son).

In filling out everything around her, the fat woman seems to be telling us: this is all that there is in the world. Breathe this: there is no other breathable atmosphere: "that is all / Ye know on earth, and all ye need to know." But it is a world that can be known only in the act of being personally shared, and only to the degree to which it accepts one. It is the apotheosis of intimacy, and the creation of absolute community, perhaps even in the theological sense.

There are spaces in the book: in fact, it is organized around spaces. (I have said that the ideas one associates with *La Grosse femme* are initially ideas of space.) But how does one negotiate spaces in a world that is already filled to capacity by its central character? All the elements of a map are to be found in *La Grosse femme*: the bedroom, with its awkwardly conceived doorway; the window; the window sill; the flat; the gallery; the Rue Fabre and its markers (Marie-Sylvia's candy shop, the ghost house, the neighbors' apartments); the shopping area on Mont-Royal; the stretch of street leading to the Parc Lafontaine; and (in barely noticeable outline) the geography of Montreal; there is even mention of the Laurentian hinterland and some vague reference to the remoter reaches of Canada. But La grosse femme, the motionless counterweight to geography, is the sedentary magnet that informs and draws back to the center all the characters that surround her, in the systole of their springtime walk towards the park and the diastole of their return, when they gather in a reunion that is also in some sense a Last Supper; though we learn of the fat woman's death, appropriately, only much later, and incidentally, in *Des nouvelles d'Édouard*.

What happens, then, to all these topographical markers and geographical elements? Instead of an orderly grid, one gets a Piranesi-like landscape of cave-bedroom interiors and toppling staircases on the Rue Fabre, disjointed trajectories of dogs, cats, children, whores, and drunks, crisscrossing the street or hiding under the steps, making their erratic, fumbling way towards the park or returning in their triumphal parade from it. What happens is a disorientation of the familiar: or, rather, the familiar is itself a disorientation. How can one describe, or give directions in, what one knows too well? And how well oriented, after all, can one be in a world inhabited by spooks with names like Rose, Violette, and Mauve? And is not La grosse femme herself a kind of arch-spook hidden in her cave, a counterpart to Florence, the spook mother of the spooks next door? And, speaking of next door, who is next door to whom? Is it the spooks who are "à côté," or is it the fat woman? In fact, they are both "à côté" to each other, both forces in the margin, exerting their diagonal torque.

In a word, the geography of *La Grosse femme* is always in a state of incipient collapse. It is something that is played with, not a stable scene in which an outsider can establish coordinates for orientation and movement. This is no ordnance map. The sense is sometimes of a Braque-cum-Calder, a Cubist mobile, an impression of corridors and shifting spaces, of blocks moving. The book is a construct of spaces, a lecture on space, but also a lecture on disproportions in words and spaces. It lodges the dislodged in an unlodgeable space. There is a structure of overflow, as nothing can be contained in its assigned space. The fat woman continually overflows her room. Space becomes a syntax of excess. All the dross of sinew is squeezed out, and only the fat remains, filling everything with its tenderness.

The collapse of the map, then, of what had seemed to be a carefully built up spatial sense, is the result of space having already been pre-empted by the marginal figure that occupies the center. Spaces may be deployed in various ways, but there are no fixed priorities among them. All these errant and erratic spaces are meant to be collapsed, eventually, in a happy disorientation, and funneled into the scene of the Last Supper, which has its own space.

But does not each individual also carry around a space with him or her? I don't mean a "personal space" or zone of tolerance that is not to be transgressed, but, on the contrary, a space that constitutes the social sense, and invites interaction; what one might call a space of invitation. At times it seems to me that Sartre was wrong to divide the world up into the *pour-soi* and the *en-soi:* the distinction should have been between the *pour-l'autre* and the *en-soi.* The first coming-to-consciousness is in relation to another.[7] Reality (nowadays sometimes called referentiality) comes into being in relationship (nowadays sometimes called dialogue), or, better still, in desire; especially desire for another, the basic form of desire. Desire acts as an attractor; when one desires, the social and the real come to greet one, hand-in-hand.

As the various characters bounce or bustle, lurk or jerk, their way through *La Grosse femme*, making their discontinuous appearances, each one carries his or her capsule of desire, his or her space of invitation, or social space, with her/him. Their desire for each other, and the love that drives the whole, summons the social into being—for each one of them, if not quite collectively. This form of social space I propose to call *cellular social space*, in contrast to other forms of social space that I will mention later.[8] To put it in Deleuze's terms (*Kafka: pour une littérature mineure*, p. 116), "les investissements sociaux sont eux-mêmes érotiques, et inversement . . . le désir érotique opère tout un investissement politique et social, poursuit tout un champ social" (social investments are themselves erotic, and conversely . . . erotic desire produces a whole political and social investment, leads us into an entire social field"). It is as if the social came into being almost out of nowhere when summoned by desire, came to greet the individual, created by that person's desire, as space is created by matter. A momentary hospitality of polis to desire would constitute the only true polis, a cellular polis (see chapter five on "Identity and Community"). In *La Grosse femme*, the cellular community has responded to the individuals' acts of desire (of which the pregnancies are the sometimes grudging evidence).

La grosse femme herself acts from the cellular space of her crowded room, with its huge dresser, from each drawer or cell of which, according to the family mythology, a child has issued. Victoire, the fat woman's mother-in-law, is also confined and immobilized, largely because of her age. Marie-Sylvia, the storekeeper, is another cell-bound character, observing the world from her chair strategically placed between two counters, to see without being seen. Marie-Louise Brassard is only partially visible behind her curtain, but even she, in her self-imposed solitude, is always watching life from the cell of her living-room. She and her husband, who works at night, take turns sleeping in the same bed, and Léopold barely speaks with his fellow worker in the printshop, Gabriel, the fat woman's husband. Ti-Lou, the former terror of Ottawa, is now incapacitated and confined. Claire Lemieux' husband, Hector, is a kind of pallid whale who can't even go outside to get flints for his own lighter.

The point is not so much that many of the characters in *La Grosse femme* seem to be immured in physical cells as that they carry their own spaces with them when they move around, and set them down like teacups wherever they go: whether it be on a balcony, or in a bedroom. They have portable spaces. The fat woman asks her brother-in-law Édouard to act as go-between between her fixed space and the world, which means that he will bring her *his* world as it has journeyed through and reflected other worlds. The distinctness of their lives is accentuated by the crowdedness of their condition. When Édouard comes into his sister-in-law's room and sits down on the edge of her bed, he has not come in just to remove the breakfast dishes, but to bring her

as an offering the distinctness of his identity; that is the gift about which they confer in conspiratorial whispers. Édouard's is a separate, a *different* world; to call it the *gay* world is merely to find a name for his form of separateness. As a gay person he is already intermediate. Édouard acts as go-between at the table as well as for his sister-in-law, shifting spaces from his normal place, across from his mother, to various other positions, sometimes facilitating the communication among their separate centers of identity by impersonating other members of the family. He "often enjoyed changing places" (il s'amusait souvent à changer, p. 41) and passing from one camp, or group of family alliances, to another. In general, as Albertine complains of him (in *La Maison suspendue*), one can never know who is going to come in the door when Édouard comes to visit.

But Édouard is not so much a shape-shifter as a space-shifter, an articulator of spaces. I have said that the characters in this book have portable spaces. They are cellular without being insular. They do not bleed into a surround; they keep their distinctness yet they are not isolated. Their conditions, or at least the negative aspects of their conditions, are most poignantly expressed by Édouard, writing from Paris, when he says that on his return he will seek out his friends, and "Vous aurez jamais vu une solitude aussi bien entourée" You will never have seen such a well-surrounded solitude,) (*Des nouvelles d'Édouard*, p. 312). These people are together in their separateness, and distinct when together, even as children within families, even within the same bathtub,[9] even when, as happens to the cat Duplessis more often than he would like, one is cuddled in the warm lap of an adoring mistress.

To attempt once more the difficult transition from the analysis of mood to theory, I would like to go back to some of the other analytical structures proposed by Deleuze. There is a *besideness*, a diagonality, an *à côté* character in the operations of desire that make it always appear to stand in an oblique relation to law, justice, and society; of all of these it is nevertheless the driving force, although it is hidden, or seemingly incidental to the scene. There is "une *contiguïté du désir* qui fait que ce qui se passe est toujours dans le bureau d'à côté" (a *contiguity of desire*, which has the effect that what is happening is always happening in the office next door) (*Kafka*, p. 92). The bearing of all of this on *La Grosse femme*, and on her personal role in the book, is evident.

My thoughts on the subject of cellular social space first occurred to me as I was listening to Randy Prus lecture on *smooth* or *nomadic* space in *Hamlet,* at a NEMLA conference. The reference was, of course, to Deleuze's distinction, in the *Nomadology* (1975), between a smooth, undifferentiated, or continuous social space, which Deleuze calls nomadic, and striated or stratified space (a distinction that Nelson Goodman, in *Languages of Art* [1976] tries to apply to visual versus verbal art, the first being ungraduated or continuous, the second graduated or disjunct). At the risk of finding myself engaged in an excessively lengthy digression, I think it best to transcribe some of my notes and to comment on them, in order to give some idea of how the notion of cellular social space came to me.

Prus was arguing that *Hamlet,* with its absence or breakdown of societal systems, was a good illustration of smooth, undifferentiated social space. What I wrote at the time was, "But isn't there an alternative to both smooth and striated spaces that demands to be occupied? A space of one's own which at the same time has to be the polis?"

In *Hamlet* (according to my argument) there is little desire at work: therefore there is no summoning of cellular social space in response to individuals' impulses. In such a situation it becomes easy to talk about a smooth or undifferentiated social space. This I would call pure or abstract tragedy: a tragedy that does not depend on individual desire. (In this sense, if only in this sense, *Hamlet* may have something to do with Brechtian tragedy.) In *Othello,* of course, there is a great deal of individual desire, and, just as the layers of the Venetian state remain stratified, if profoundly disturbed, so the capsule of desire in which Othello exists likewise makes it impossible to claim a smooth or continuous social space for this play. Cellular social spaces are discrete but they are not stratified or striated. Othello's social impulse remains unfulfilled, but it never disappears, and it remains a force throughout. The play is caught among three incompatible needs, each of a different kind: that of Desdemona, that of Othello, and that of Venice; but it is out of the question for a smooth space to be achieved, for none of these needs is ever met, or dissolved away. Perhaps one could speak of *Othello* as illustrating the interaction of divergent cellular impulses, rather than merely the incompatibility of desire and the state.

To return to the "space of one's own which at the same time has to be the polis" in the passage that I have quoted above: this would be the site of reconciliation of the monadic and the social. Continuing with the Leibnizian model to which I have been implicitly referring, I would claim this as the locus for the combination of those two presumed incompossibles, the closed monad and the communal experience. We witness here the creation of that necessary impossibility, the social monad. Desire is what dislodges community from its virtual or Platonic presence and brings it into actual being, in the cellular frame of the social individual.

La Grosse femme provides an ideal field for observing this process at work. The discontinuous way in which the characters are introduced is not experienced as simply some routine novelistic device that catapults each one into the life of the street and of the work. They are very much separate individuals, but their need draws a social world into an individual cocoon or capsule around them. In the end, La grosse femme brings them together under the aegis of her divine sociality, as a kind of Leibnizian as well as Berkeleian God/dess who guarantees their social existence, who shows, to those who need to have it made explicit, that the commonalty of their existence makes sense. In these terms, Édouard's remark, "Chus venu au monde en gang" (see chapter 3, note 16) is perfectly reasonable. The embryonic human being, before it can know of the existence of others, has already claimed, through its need and its desire, the social space in which alone it can exist. It is the beauty of *La Grosse femme* that it makes that initial impulse manifest from moment to moment in the lives of its characters: its children and its adults.

■

NEWS FROM EDWARD

Before going on to a broader discussion of Tremblay I will try to give a summary impression of *Des nouvelles d'Édouard* for those who may not be familiar with the book. It is the fourth volume in the series of novels entitled *Chroniques du Plateau Mont-Royal*, beginning with *La Grosse femme d'à côté est enceinte*, in my view the best Canadian novel. In the first volume of that series, the unnamed fat woman provides a warmth and security that embraces and nourishes the family and indeed the whole neighborhood of the Rue Fabre. The wonderful disorderly group includes Édouard, the fat woman's brother-in-law, himself somewhat inclined to adiposity. He is a shoe salesman with aspirations to become a famous performer in the role of transvestite dancer. Apart from these incompatible pursuits he is best defined by his adoration of his sister-in-law, towards whom he feels far more than a familial affection, gay though he may be. The most moving moment in the tetralogy is the discovery that the fat woman has died, a fact of which we learn only in passing, in the most indirect way, and years after the event: but the shock of her loss brings with it the knowledge that everything that gave the world value is already behind us. After that nothing will matter very much, not even Édouard's own gruesome death, stabbed as a stale troublemaker, a has-been on the degenerate, tasteless cabaret circuit.

The bulk of *Des nouvelles d'Édouard* concerns Édouard's trip to Paris, as recorded in a diary that he keeps for his sister-in-law. As soon as Édouard finds himself aboard ship he has to deal with numerous forms of behavior that are incomprehensible to him, though he soon learns to maneuver among the exotica, as well as among all the pretensions and affectations. One of his fellow passengers is a lady from Outremont whose cultural tastes have kept her at a safe distance from the horror of East End vaudeville: Édouard tries to set her values right. He has intended to make an impression on Paris, but is instead overwhelmed by the city, with its strangeness, its weird familiarity, its literary associations, and all its mythic powers. He turns tail and runs, returning to Montreal far sooner than he had intended, and saying, yes, if I were with *you* I could deal with it all and love and enjoy it all, understand everything, but alone I can't. I can't understand anything alone.

The book is very funny, and beautiful in its report of the love between Édouard and La grosse femme, sexual in some emotional sense, though tender beyond sexuality. The whole latter part of the work is a distillation of what is best in *La Grosse femme*, the aroma, the purified quality of that book: in that sense, it is almost better than *La Grosse femme* itself. It is after all not primarily a political book, but it does have a political aspect, and it is the political aspect of Édouard's role in this as well as in other works of Tremblay's that concerns me here.

Édouard's is a redemptive degeneracy. There is a monstrous gap between the comical tenderness of his journal to La grosse femme and his gross railing in the scenes on the lower Main with which the book begins. Get that over with, the story seems to say, and get back to what still matters—the fun, the love that preceded all this. But both have to be reckoned with, and Édouard's campaign against the staleness and loss of verve of the later popular

□

The Rue Fabre in Montreal, scene of *The Fat Woman Next Door is Pregnant*.
Note: the neighborhood has been considerably gentrified since Tremblay
lived there, but is still typical of the east side of Montreal. Photo by Dr.
Ephraim Massey.

□

Another view of the Rue Fabre, giving some sense of what the street was like when it was part of a strictly working-class neighborhood. Photo by Dr. Ephraim Massey.

culture is an attempt to reinstate the life of the old. This is an effort in which he, in a spirit not utterly unrelated to that of Socrates, gives his own life. He offers himself, then, in a series of sacrificial roles, in each of which the nature and the purpose of the sacrifice are somewhat different. At his death, he sacrifices his life in the effort to restore vitality to the world of the Main. Refusing to discontinue his Jeremiad against the shoddy entertainment world that has replaced the vivid, imaginative milieu of his earlier years, Édouard is finally silenced by the knife of one Tooth Pick, purveyor of hormones, downers, and uppers for creating mechanical metamorphoses of the spirit. Earlier, he had sacrificed all possibility of an orderly, decent, or even tolerable existence in the hope that he might, whether in his role as apostle for the East End theater or as "La Duchesse de Langeais," help to gain recognition for that world. But first of all, he had sacrificed what little he had had in the effort to give status to his culture not only vis-à-vis the other French, whether of Outremont or of Paris, but vis-à-vis the Anglophone majority that had invested his culture. Édouard's militancy, though, is a militancy *à rebours:* by abandoning all dignity, by embracing a crapulous existence, he can assume the moral high ground of the prophet or the Greek cynic: I may be nobody: but who, Sir/Madam, are you?

Like the milieu of Ida Maza's work, the surroundings of Tremblay's literary world are dense with social values. The difference that strikes one immediately, though, is that, for all its grimness (*A toi pour toujours*), stifling limitations (the École des Saints-Anges), and grotesque self-humiliations (La Duchesse de Langeais), there can be, at times, as I have said before (chapter 3, "Francophone Communities") a gaiety or joie de vivre about the French-Canadian community that is foreign to its Jewish counterpart. The abandon, the sheer spirit of uproarious fun, that is available, at least from time to time, to the families of the Rue Fabre is something that Jews can never quite indulge in, shadowed as they are by a history that makes them eternally wary. It was a pure centripetal intensity, rather than a joyous cohesiveness, that marked the Jewish group of the 1930s in Montreal.

In any case: I will return to the characterization of Édouard and of his cultural- political strategy at the end of this chapter, but for now I wish to introduce another text, *Macbeth*, as casting a significant light on the stage that Édouard occupies, or, rather, that he deliberately ascends. *Macbeth* illuminates some aspects of political comedy that need to be seen clearly for one to appreciate what happens in any political comedy. For this reason I have decided to do a sufficiently thorough analysis of the play in its relevant aspects to serve as a propaedeutic for the subject of political comedy as a whole. I will then try to see how the characterization of Édouard relates to this scene. Hitherto, it has been *Hamlet* through which the dilemma of Canadian Francophone identity has been most frequently explored (Hubert Aquin, Robert Gurik); *Macbeth* provides another approach.

■

MACBETH

Setting the Stage for Ethics

The Glenda Jackson-Christopher Plummer version of *Macbeth* was presented in New York in 1988. The performance I attended seemed quite unsatisfactory. In fact, at moments it verged on the ludicrous, threatening to turn *Macbeth* into some sort of comedy. But as I thought about the performance I began to wonder whether Shakespeare's play did not in fact have something inherently comic about it after all. *Macbeth* is notoriously difficult to stage: perhaps it is so hard to perform because it is meant to demonstrate that performance is hardly possible.[10] As Richard Fly has put it, *Macbeth* is about the impossibility of representation.[11] Not only does Macbeth's playing at royal legitimacy fail to persuade, but every metaphor eventually runs aground in a shattering literalism. One can not very well expect this play itself, then, to function successfully as a representation, i.e., as a play: unless, perhaps, one take the subject of *Macbeth* to be acting itself.

The tangle of comedy, tragedy, representation, action, and politics that *Macbeth* contains seems relevant for me to the understanding of Tremblay's protagonist, Édouard. Édouard bears no resemblance whatsoever to Macbeth, but the performative predicament in which he finds himself, in its blend of the tragic and the preposterous, echoes significant tones in the Shakespeare play. Édouard infuses the political with the comic in a self-ridiculing way that makes him at once the martyr of his own posturing and a political hero. He sets aside the real in favor of the parodic, his real life in favor of his buffoonery, so that the buffoonery may bring others back to the real. The thought grows on one that the political, whether heroic or villainous, may finally be inseparable from the comic,[12] and that an awareness of the self-parodying undertow in *Macbeth*[13] might indeed help us to understand why Édouard set out to voyage on such treacherous seas. The collision of action with representation, which is one way of defining political theater, becomes a confrontation between the ethical (in either its positive or its negative valence) and the comic, inasmuch as the comic is, as Plato knew, an aspect of all representation. This confrontation begins to describe the world in which Édouard functions, or which he has constructed for himself.

The story of *Macbeth*, like the career of Édouard, is about the necessary failure of all acting, and at the same time about the impossibility of not acting. We are actors not because we *assume* roles, but because we are given them: to be human is to act. Yet in *Macbeth*, the roles that are distributed are not even proper social or dramatic roles, but arbitrary, random roles: wood to Dunsinane, King of Scotland, Thane of Cawdor; even the presumably well-integrated Banquo has to come back as a stage prop. Lady Macbeth herself is caught in the meaningless, repetitive role of the actor, endlessly rehearsing the washing of the stage blood from her hands. She too was an actress from the beginning, although she realized it only afterwards.[14] Nor can Macbeth escape role playing, step off the stage, or withdraw behind the arras. "They have tied me to a stake: I cannot fly, / But, bear-like, I must fight the course" (*The Riverside Shakespeare*, Boston, etc: Houghton Mifflin, 1974, V.7.1–2).

How does what I have just said pertain to the ethical element in the life of Édouard, and to the question of ethics in general? The answer is that *Macbeth* forces theatricality, both necessarily failed[15] and necessarily successful (successful in the sense of having to be acted out) on everybody, good and bad alike. In a sense, although it is a play about ethics, it levels good and evil ("Fair is foul" etc., I.1.11). But it is not so much anti-ethical as it is a prolegomenon to ethics: it clarifies the conditions under which ethical decisions are made.

Ethics involves the conscious grasp of the principle that Macbeth has eventually had forced on his understanding. By a deliberate choice rather than through blind necessity the ethical person (Édouard) seizes upon the rule of role playing, or, one might say, doubles that with a conscious choice: and that doubling constitutes (to coin a word) the ethicity of his or her experience. No matter that we are doomed to role playing: the ethical person dooms himself or herself to a second role playing that supersedes the first, and so renders the first, the one initially imposed, insignificant. A study of *Macbeth* suggests strongly that the integrated self is in any case a delusion; better, then, like Édouard, to give up the pursuit of that fantasy and accept, not merely a dramatic, but a metadramatic role.

However, before I can show that its special features are important for an understanding of *Des nouvelles d' Édouard*, I have to demonstrate that *Macbeth* really does have these particular features; that *Macbeth* is about the failure of theatricality as well as about the necessity of that failure. The play has to be understood as undermining its own ability to persuade an audience (as Édouard undermines his own performances) at the same time as it is all too convincing. Since this is not a view of the play that is universally accepted,[16] it should be argued in full, but I will have to limit myself to a few remarks.

Theater as Self-Parody

I will begin simply by tracing the scenes in *Macbeth* in which a comic or self-parodic element can be discerned, beginning with the witches. As witches, they have no presence; these witches are not meant to seem continuously convincing.[17] To the extent that they are presented as evil they are a joke, though as soothsayers they are overwhelming: perhaps all the more so because in their other role they seem so pointless.[18]

Immediately after the introduction of the witches, ten lines into the play, we get the bleeding messenger. The abruptness with which the blood appears makes it hard to ignore the fact that it is stage blood. We are put on notice that the blood in this play is always meant to be understood as at least partly a stage prop: the distance between the reality and the representation is emphasized as part of the effect, and actually becomes a contributing cause of the poignancy. Not only is fair foul and foul fair in this play, but real is noticeably unreal. The bombast of the messenger's speech, whether it be by Shakespeare or another, intensifies the sense of artificiality that the messenger's appearance had produced.

With the very first words of the witches to Macbeth, he is made to seem a fool, struggling to find meaning through language rather than pursuing the necessities of his life. Macbeth soon begins to sound as if he were reciting a playlet by rote (rather like Pentheus when entrapped by Bacchus). "And Thane of Cawdor too; went it not so?" (I.3.87). Banquo identifies the scene accurately as one in a play or ballad: "To th' self-same tune and words" (I.3.88). The witches have given Macbeth a little play to go over until he "gets it right." From the first we see Macbeth floundering; the script that has been thrust on him "cannot be ill; cannot be good" (I.3.131). He is disoriented from the very outset. "My dull brain was wrought / With things forgotten" (I.3.149–150). One begins to wonder, in fact, whether this disorientation is not there even before the beginning of the play, and whether the desperate deeds of heroism that are reported of Macbeth were not actually of the same quality as those he performs at the end. Even more than vaulting ambition or thoughts of regicide, sheer desperation, worthy counterpart to the destructive aimlessness of the universe, is fundamental to the character of Macbeth. Lady Macbeth helps him temporarily by forcing a direction on him, but that help must come to an end, and eventually all that he has left is the tedium of the actor who has to go on playing his role from one tomorrow to another, until "Returning were as tedious as go o'er" (III.4.137).

Lady Macbeth reading her letter is only somewhat more impressive. Very little of her speech is untainted by rhetoric. Why exhort herself to cruelty? Either she is cruel, or she is not. It must be difficult to speak many of her lines with conviction: they simply try too hard. The fact that her speech is strained may be a tribute to Lady Macbeth's character, but it detracts from the sense of her "fell purpose." Macbeth's exhortation to her to "bring forth men-children only" (I.7.72) recasts the whole previous exchange between them in a parodic vein that makes one feel she has wasted her most strenuous efforts.

The second act produces the scene with the imaginary dagger that I find particularly hard to take straight. An imaginary dagger is a stage dagger; Macbeth claims to be unsure of its status, but we are not. Soon the stage curtain falls on the staged nightmare: "and wicked dreams abuse / The curtain'd sleep" (II.1.50–51). Macbeth provides a running commentary on his own actions that could be a director's notes (II.1.51–55). It is not a satisfactory soliloquy; it is not what we imagine in the mind of a murderer, except perhaps a very literary one. Still less acceptable is the next scene. Enough that Lady Macbeth falls into the cliché of announcing that Duncan resembles her father (II.2.12–13); but Macbeth with the bloody hands is too good as visual dramatics not to be haunted by the ghost of farce. Macbeth also has the grooms wake conveniently in

140

the middle of the night and start to say their prayers, in order that he may find himself unable to say "Amen." Yet it is also in this scene that we get the strongest sense of Macbeth's helplessness: of his naivete and, in a sense, of his innocence.[19]

Apparently in perfect seriousness he asks, "But wherefore could not I pronounce 'Amen'? / I had most need of blessing, and 'Amen' / Stuck in my throat" (II.2.28–30). Again and again, as in this case, the play separates Macbeth from his role. ("To know my deed, 'twere best not know myself" II.2.70.) He is like a child who has learned to think of himself in the third person and has never found a way to reunite that person with himself. For instance, in the case of the "murdering" of sleep, everyone but he has murdered sleep: "Macbeth" has murdered sleep, "Glamis" has murdered sleep, "Cawdor" has murdered sleep; but there is no "I" who has murdered sleep—and therefore no one who could have prevented—or atoned for—that murder (II.2.39–40). Macbeth rarely speaks with his own voice, the forgotten voice of the one who has no assigned role to play: mainly at the end, when all the shows are struck. But neither does Macbeth believe in the role that has been assigned to him or, indeed, in any roles at all: he is too well aware that all the dramatic pageant of history has done is "lighted fools / The way to dusty death" (V.5.22–23).

There is no need to dwell on the knocking at the gate, since the comic element in that scene is explicit. But after it, the tormented bombast that characterizes much of the play soon resumes, in Lennox's speech (II.3.54–57). Macbeth has exactly the right response: " 'Twas a rough night" (II.3.61). Macduff's speech after seeing the dead Duncan is larded with lines not much better than Lennox's (II.3.66–69), and we cannot blame Lennox for being perplexed (II.3.70). It is very hard to distinguish such a style (or Macduff's in the next two lines) from the rhetoric that Macbeth summons up after he has murdered the grooms (II.3.113–114).[20] But from a merely noisy style we progress to a senselessness that I cannot imagine accidental in Shakespeare: what can one do but gasp at the idiocy of the report that, as a sign of the times, Duncan's horses went on a cannibalistic spree and ate each other up? (II.4.18).

The scene with Banquo's ghost is very hard to keep from the edge of comedy, particularly with Lady Macbeth's interposing "My lord is often thus, / And hath been from his youth" (III.4.52–53); to which Macbeth adds appropriately, "I have a strange infirmity, which is nothing / To those that know me" (III.4.85–86). But the weariness, the boredom that subtends all his actions makes nonsense as good as sense: "I am in blood / Stept in so far that, should I wade no more, / Returning were as tedious as go o'er" (III.4.135–137).

The scene between Malcolm and Macduff in IV.3 is pointless and stupid to a degree that makes it impossible to justify.[21] Soon after we have the opening of act five, with Lady Macbeth's hand-washing: "A little water clears us of this deed" (II.2.64). But why can't she get the blood off her hands in this new play staged by the gentlewoman for the doctor? It is because it is impossible to wash stage blood off the hands: imaginary blood is indelible. The blood is brought to our attention, as I said before, in the first minutes of the work, and it is forced on our notice repeatedly. But here, most of all, it is obtruded as if to make clear that in a play one is bound to theatricality. Just as Lady Macbeth cannot get the blood off her hands because it is not there, just so are we not allowed to forget that the blood could not have been there in the first place. This is doubly imaginary blood. Our hopelessly illusory state is being rubbed in, so to speak, by the rubbing of Lady Macbeth's hands.

In Macbeth's culminating speech, the self-dramatization that has been inflicted on him, or from which he has suffered, throughout the play, is projected as a universal condition.[22] "Life's but a walking shadow" (V.5.24); already double, an echo or shadow of itself,[23] the original of which can never be known. It is "a poor player, / That struts and frets [(exactly what Macbeth had been doing)] his hour upon the stage" (V.5.24–25). For all his desperate efforts to avoid becoming a bear tied to a stake (V.7.2.), a "Roman fool" (V.7.1), or "the show and gaze o' th' time" (V.8.24), Macbeth has been forced into the self-lampooning role that not only Édouard plays but that all of us are eventually forced to play, ending up as buffoons in a drama of someone else's making: one, besides, that does not work even as drama.

Compulsory Theatricality in Macbeth[24]

The action in *Macbeth*, then, is constantly seen, experienced, presented, or conducted as a dramatic performance—as Édouard conducts his own life—rather than as, simply, the action itself. The characters in the play—especially Macbeth—are forced to act, but in what for them is real life. They do not even have the option of remaining at the level of their own dramatic fantasies.

"In our desire to suppress pain, we are led on to action, instead of confining ourselves to dramatizing."[25] But, although the condition of these characters embodies a terrible deception, it is inevitably haunted by the shadow of the comic, since they are play-acting their lives to their own undoing.[26]

The disconnection of the visible from the actual, one more means by which the action ironizes and undermines itself, is emphasized again in the characterization of Cawdor: "There's no art / To find the mind's construction in the face" (I.4.11–12). The self exists only as the spectator of a self on stage, a self that is constantly eluding it, becoming with every real action something other than what it had just been observed to be. There is a continual slippage and syncopation.[27] The self that acts cannot be the same as the self that knows.

The play is full of images of non-coincidence and of recoil upon the self (for instance, I.4.51–53; I.5.64–65; I.8.81–82; II.2.73). Macbeth fears that what he will do, once it is separate from himself, will come back upon him (I.7.9–12). It becomes evident that the multiple dualities with which the play is infested ("Fair is foul" etc. I.2.11) rest on the duality between the dramatic role and action (I.7.27–28 again).[28] One acts only in order to see, to look upon, the consequences of one's actions. Macbeth has nothing within him pushing him to act spontaneously; but he must act, nevertheless, even if it be only to fulfill the conditions of a play.

Before returning to more specific issues, I would like to raise the general question whether, in acting upon a theatrical imagination, Macbeth is doing anything but acting under the necessary conditions of thought itself. Thought consists largely of dramatic scenarios: "personification" is merely a literary formalization of a fundamental and universal feature of the mind. It does not strike us as odd that English uses the same word, *act*, to express apparently opposite concepts: playing, and doing something real. What Macbeth does, or what Lady Macbeth says, is not remarkably different from what is done and said in the other circumstances of life, if action is always a byproduct of dramatic fantasy.

At the same time there is the fact of his being forced to take action, actually to do something.[29] But, again, as I have observed before, the action can only be seen, looked at, and viewed, afterwards, since it proceeds in a domain separate from thought. "To know my deed, 'twere best not know myself" (II.2.72) detaches thought from action in the most radical way.[30] As in the ironic roles that Édouard accepts for himself, the part of the mind that

143

has acted is incompatible with the part of the mind that has knowledge of that action; for Macbeth it is even less compatible with the part of the mind that judges that action. The action is independent; it is best known in isolation from the actor. That line (II.2.72) even implies that for Macbeth a knowledge of himself would make the act unintelligible, since it cannot be explained on the basis of what he is. The only place where one is not threatened by that rupture[31] is where one does not threaten to act: where Duncan goes (III.2.23 ff. "after life's fitful fever he sleeps well" etc.) or where Macbeth arrives ("I 'gin to be aweary of the sun" V.5.49).

The final scene, with Malcolm, builds another version of the theatrical into the play. In its stagey, official falsity it serves to underscore the unofficial, nomadic or outlaw theatricality of Macbeth. By that point, though, both actors, Malcolm and Macbeth, are being viewed from another vantage point; "the heavens, as troubled with man's act, / Threaten his bloody stage" (II.4.5–6). Every speaker, no matter what his or her circumstances, has been at all times on stage: "What's the newest grief? / Ross: That of an hour's age doth hiss the speaker" (IV.3.174–175).

∎

TREMBLAY: THE BUFFOON AS POLITICIAN

Tremblay, Bernstein, and Macbeth

It should be apparent by now that Édouard may be understood as a rectified version of Macbeth. Like Macbeth, he is a grotesque figure who seems confused and helpless. Nevertheless, despite his difficulties, instead of trying to avoid a political role and acting only on his own behalf, he embraces the political on behalf of both his culture and his group. Instead of trying to evade the tragedy in which he has been embedded by both history and his author, he recognizes that he has no choice but to be an actor both in life and on stage. And instead of trying to succeed in either role, he glories in the necessity of failure and turns it to his and others' advantage.

I will return to these comparisons later, but, at this point, I would like to reconsider the question in broader terms. What is there about *Macbeth* that casts light on the individual's relation to

the political process, not merely to the extent that Shakespeare
may help us to clarify Tremblay's work, but in general? Why is it
necessary to understand this play in order to have a full understanding of the political? I will attempt part of an answer now,
and somewhat more of an answer after the discussion of Bataille,
below. Provisionally, though, I will say this much: *Macbeth* sets
forth the conditions of the political, shows how Macbeth himself
fails to meet them, and, by implication, makes apparent the only
appropriate alternative: the ironic self-sacrifice of Édouard—or of
Socrates.

Was it Napoleon who said, "Tragedy is politics?" I seem to be
saying, "Comedy is politics." It is the terrain of theater, the faked,
that is deliberately adopted to convey the crucial political reality.
Theater must be taken as the place for dealing with the ultimate
problems of ethics because it cannot be taken seriously. It seems to
be saying: the questions that are being raised are wrong, but there
is no position from which any better ones can be asked. The blindness of action is our fate, and although a scenario is available to us
that will carry us as far as act five if we are fools enough to take it
seriously, at the end it will dump us in the original chaos where no
play matters. Who provided that scenario? It would be a mere
cliché to accuse the bad faith of narrativity, but I cannot think of a
more convincing answer.[32] Perhaps the tendency to narrative,
then, under the guise of which life presents itself to us automati-
cally as a consoling fiction, is to blame. Narrativity itself is the
seductive lie, and that lie, generalized, produces the structure of
the political. With the same gesture narrativity, in turn, summons
theater, because theater, a public act and an act of public consciousness, is political. It is, in a sense, a theodicy, a calling on the community to witness the injustices of narrative; it is also the initiation of
the polis, and it must acknowledge its wrongness, its fictionality,
its failure, as that inaugural act. It stands to, and doesn't stand to. It
is private, personal, universal, general, collective—in a word, political and, in a word, fraudulent: necessary, and necessarily
wrong. Perhaps that is why the buffoon, the one who is not meant
to be taken seriously, is its most appropriate representative.

In an essay entitled "Comedy and the Poetics of Political
Form"[33] Charles Bernstein argues, like Shelley, for the inherently
political and inherently revolutionary nature of poetry and of poetic form. What is different about Bernstein's argument is that it
emphasizes the self-parodic element in this revolutionary activity.
If it is going to be genuinely antinomian, it must disestablish even

its own rules of high art. Bernstein speaks of the poet as the confidence man, "deploying hypocrisy in order to shatter the formal autonomy of the poem and its surface of detachment; the sincere and the comic as interfused figure, not either/or but *both and*. For our sincerity is always comic, always questionable, always open to mocking" (p. 242).[34] Bernstein maintains that irony is too narrow a term to describe his program, which would allow for "a mix of comic, bathetic, and objective modes" (loc. cit.).

As spokesman for the group known as the language poets Bernstein is committed to poetry as performance: that is, as a form of theater. With his insistence on the political nature of poetry, performance poetry becomes, for him, political theater. Finally, if the most revolutionary poetry is a bathetic, comic, or self-mocking poetry, for Bernstein, the crucial poetry of our time is comic political theater. Bernstein's strategies for political theater (again recalling Tremblay's in some respects) are much like those advocated by the Canadian philosophers Arthur Kroker and Charles Levin, following Jean Baudrillard, for counteracting the force of simulacral culture: "ironic detachment," and a "hyper-conformist simulation. . . that moment of refraction when the simulational logic of the system is turned, ironically and neutrally, back against the system" ("Cynical Power: The Fetishism of the Sign," *Canadian Journal of Social and Political Theory* 15, nos. 1–2 and 3 [1991], 123–134, p. 133).

The linking of the futile, or the self-mocking, with political necessity reminds one of the existentialist attitude towards politics as expressed in works by Sarte and Camus. As I see it, there is a major difference: the existentialist attitude, for all its denial of the serious practicality of the political, is itself grimly serious in its devotion to an ideal, all the more exalted because it is an ideal that is, in a merely pragmatic sense, pointless. One would be hard put to it to construe "Le Mur" as a comedy.

In another writer from the same period, Georges Bataille, despite the fact that he owes much to the existentialist tradition, one does find passages that come close to what I have been saying about the connection between the political and the comic, in spirit as well as in matter. Bataille provides a natural context for discussing this theme in the forms in which it appears in *Macbeth* and *Des nouvelles d Édouard*.[35] I must preface my references to Bataille, however, with a caveat. I do not enjoy the continuously aggressive tone, the lack of modesty, of candid humor, or even of irony, not to mention geniality, that mark the whole French post-

Nietzschean school to this day. Yet to purge them of their extremism and extract the valuable marrow would be, at least in their view, to destroy the very source of the meanings that they pursue. Nevertheless, I think it is quite possible to employ some of their insights without participating in the bullying fanfare that often surrounds them.

Bataille, Macbeth, and Tremblay

For Bataille, drama is an offshoot of social authority; in a sense, it is even a form of oppression, since it reflects that aspect of community which functions by designating a victim.[36] It takes us out of our own individual selves, but at a price. Yet in the very act of submitting ourselves to collectivization and victimization by the dramatic, in an event that we have both called down upon ourselves and which we yet experience as forced on us (Bataille, loc. cit.: again, cf. Macbeth), we experience a reaction that Bataille calls comic. What develops, he says, is "an element of comedy, of silliness, which turns to laughter" ("un élément de comédie, de sottise, qui tourne au rire," Bataille, p. 26).

As I have suggested, Bataille's ideas on the evocation of comedy by the tragic spectacle owe much to Nietzsche and the Zarathustrean laughter, as well as (as Bataille acknowledges) to Kierkegaard (p. 27). But, derivative and murky as the ideas are, they seem to emerge from the same dense shadows as Macbeth. Some of Bataille's lines sound like comments on that play; a few even resemble lines from it. Laughter, Bataille says, tells us that our desire to freeze being is bad ("que notre volonté de fixer l'être est mauvais," p. 143). It points towards an abyss of emptiness: the inanity of being that we are ("Le rire glisse en surface le long de dépressions légères: le déchirement ouvre l'abîme. Abîme et dépressions sont un même vide: l'inanité de l'être que nous sommes," p. 143). Being in us is the desire to seize everything ("il est désir—nécessité—d'embrasser tout," p. 143), and the lucid awareness that all of that is just comedy changes nothing ("Et le fait de saisir clairement la comédie n'y change rien," p. 143). Like Macbeth, simply because we are human, we lack the means to renounce ambition ("L'homme ne peut, par aucun recours, échapper à l'insuffisance ni renoncer à l'ambition," p. 148). As long as he keeps up the battle, man can escape the play, by subordinating everything to the blind action into which he translates his will, and struggling to create vaster and vaster coherent configurations; but the moment there is a pause in the fight he is lost: devastated by his realization that he wants to be everything (p. 144). Bataille compares man to the bull who stops, at times, in the very midst of the corrida, and lets itself sink back heavily into its animal indifference ("tantôt s'absorbe pesamment dans la nonchalance animale," p. 144), but then, mad with rage, charges again into the emptiness that a phantom matador ceaselessly opens before it ("tantôt, saisi de rage, se précipite sur le vide qu'un matador fantôme ouvre sans relâche devant lui," p. 144). Man's only defense against that emptiness that, unlike the bull, he himself projects by his knowledge of it, is laughter.

We see Macbeth repeatedly tempted by the imaginary matador, but unable to realize that he is being drawn into a bullfight against a consummately evasive enemy, who is not Duncan, or Banquo, or Macduff, but the master of ceremonies himself who has elected him for mockery. The emptiness of Macbeth's gestures, which are serious enough to him, create a quasi–irony that contributes to the play's extreme sense of instability. We can't quite make fun of Macbeth *or* pity him, nor do we know where, whether, or in what way we are being called on to identify with him. For one thing, the emptiness that keeps sucking Macbeth into its maw is too well structured, too brilliantly deployed, to be mere emptiness; yet what else can we make it out to be? It is surely no tale told by an idiot; like a dream, it could not have been more expertly plotted. Yet for all that, it is emptiness; it has design, theatrical design, but it still does not signify anything. The wave of theater has picked Macbeth up and carried him (no doubt, even from before his birth), but it leaves him like driftwood on a shore. Failed actor, he is condemned to do; and what he does, alas, turns out to be real. But what, then, can be the purpose of the merely real?

Acting and doing, then, are both wrong; acting because it is just a play, and doing because it is real, and creates trouble because the real doesn't fit into any play.

But Macbeth has not seized the nettle of his nothingness with laughter. There are several ways to face a fate. What one might call the tragic way, the one that Macbeth chooses, is to fight the course as an individual, with the desperation of the animal at bay. A second way might be called the semi–individual: it involves assuming enough distance from one's fate as an individual to see the comic aspect of it, while at the same time recognizing that comedy is, by definition, supra–individual. (This seems to be

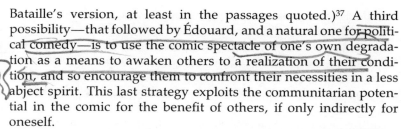

Bataille's version, at least in the passages quoted.)[37] A third possibility—that followed by Édouard, and a natural one for political comedy—is to use the comic spectacle of one's own degradation as a means to awaken others to a realization of their condition, and so encourage them to confront their necessities in a less abject spirit. This last strategy exploits the communitarian potential in the comic for the benefit of others, if only indirectly for oneself.

Instead of seizing hold of the comic nihilism that lies at the heart of political drama, then, Macbeth remains its target. He does not turn the commonalty of drama into politics with the spectacle of laughter; he continues obstinately fighting the nothingness of fate with nothing but the weapon of his own individual personhood. That strategy enables him to retain his authenticity; he has lost no battle because he has sustained the battle on the terms of blindness. To Macbeth every symbol must be real. A literalist, stubborn, he insists on taking each metaphor for brute truth: no distancing, no impersonality, no ironies for him. Because he is what he is, in the end his doublings do not cling to him (as they do to Malcolm). Reality may double-cross him, but he still falls back into his lone self.

What Bataille recommends, though, is to grasp the nothingness as nothingness and to stop filling it up, or allowing it to fill itself up, with the shapes of shadows. As Charles Bernstein would have it, and Tremblay's Édouard as well, "Man is comic to his own eyes if he is aware of it: he must therefore *wish* to be comic, for that's what he is by virtue of being man" (Il est comique à ses propres yeux s'il en a conscience: il lui faut donc *vouloir* être comique, car il l'est en tant qu'il est l'homme, Bataille, p. 143). Still more explicitly in the Bernstein-Tremblay vein, since both authors are deeply concerned with the political as a special form of dual identity, is Bataille's insistence that this choice "presupposes an anguished dissociation from oneself, a definitive disharmony and discord—accepted with vigor—without vain efforts to palliate them" ("Cela suppose une dissociation de soi-même angoissante, une disharmonie, un désaccord définitfs—subis avec vigueur— sans vains efforts pour les pallier" p. 143).

But to confront once more the problem: why, and in what sense, *Macbeth* is a prolegomenon to the political, and even to the ethical. *Macbeth* raises the first uneasy questions that surround all ethical action—even before the notion, or the issue, of the ethical has been formulated—Am I an individual? Can I act and, when I act, do I act for myself or for a group? And if for a group, or community, what can that mean before I can know what a community is, before there is one, before one has been constituted, whether by Bataille's "laughter" or by any other means? What would it have *meant* to act on behalf of a community if one *had* known what a community was? In a word, does the self precede the community?

By his behavior, Macbeth seems to show that he thinks that it does, or that he has not even thought of an alternative. He tries to deal with decisions about public matters as if they were simply private issues between him and his wife. Macbeth and Lady Macbeth are like children trying to play house, or castle, but with materials from the real world. *Macbeth* is acted out on the pre-political plane in order to show, by exposing the flawed nature of that effort, that one is still left with the political to deal with even if one has not even thought of its existence. Seeing the confused and contradictory jumble of Macbeth's career as an individualist, we, if not he, still have to pick through the debris to try to reconstitute, or constitute, the semblance of what a community might have been.

All the elements of a communal configuration are there, but scattered without logical sequence through the play, in bits and pieces, like tissue in a wen. It even teases us with the restoration of the communal ideal, like a mirage, in the reform of Cawdor, but at the point at which we can make least use of that example: at the very beginning of the play, just when the coherence of the world that surrounds Macbeth is breaking down. The work displays several phases of the political: the pre-political in Macbeth; the political itself, insofar as it can be retrieved from characters in merely defensive roles, in types such as Banquo or Ross; and what one might call the post-political in Malcolm.[38]

But Macbeth has missed all this. Not understanding that he must assume a public role, that it is his job to imagine a polis into being and, realizing that he is part of it, deal with it, he fails or refuses to take a dramatic distance on life. When, at the beginning of the play, he is confronted with things that "cannot be ill; cannot be good," blind to the fact that this is a description of the political condition as such, he can only think of that dilemma as it pertains to his own situation.[39] Macbeth's failure or refusal to take that distance on himself, however, does not help him in the least, since it is necessary to take that step, whether he likes it or not. The very fact that he is an actor in a play reveals that necessity, a necessity that is forced on him, since he fails to choose it and do it right himself. Macbeth first goes public as an actor; then, repeatedly, especially towards the end of the play, as an object of display (baited bear, etc.).

To be political, then, perhaps even to be at all, you have to be dramatic: either in the right way (Socrates's way, Édouard's way) or the wrong way—as a fool exposed on the stage, an unconscious rather than a deliberate buffoon.

Édouard

I said at the beginning of this part of my book that an understanding of the issues in *Macbeth* was an important preliminary to an understanding of Tremblay's Édouard, a character in a work in which the political, the dramatic, and the comic elements are deliberately confused. On the one hand, the differences in the two characters' situations are obvious. Macbeth does not set out to be anyone's martyr; nevertheless, he is pilloried on the hill of his own being, though he also stands free at the end as the unveiled eye of knowledge. That is his only reward. Macbeth achieves, rarely and belatedly, a few moments of pure, isolated selfhood: Édouard begins by setting all aspirations to selfhood of any kind behind him. Édouard is not interested in his personal salvation, either in terms of temporal power or spiritual clarification, and, far from being condemned by fate to the role of failed actor in a play set up for him by unknown forces, quite deliberately selects and carries out that role himself. Nevertheless, it will be apparent that *Macbeth*, especially if I am right in designating it as a pre-political play, lays the groundwork for political drama as some of the issues in it are grasped and made conscious. Macbeth, teetering between the personal, the predestinarian, and the political, topples into self-parody to become a figure of gruesome ridicule; Édouard assumes the political as his personal destiny and, as I have said before, takes up the instrument of self-parody as his strongest weapon. He wields his role rather than enduring it, even if it be the only role available to him.

Édouard makes a buffoon of himself, sacrifices himself together with any possible remnants of dignity, in order, as Stephen Daedalus puts it, to "forge in the smithy of my soul the uncreated conscience of my race." His act is ethical, not even artistic. This is the meaning of his being a transvestite. He by choice, like Macbeth perforce, is not at one with his role, and is not intended to be. An artist would be, but he is not. The higher act is not to do art: it is to do right. He admits repeatedly that he has no talent. To perform an ethical act on behalf of one's community is to be beside oneself, to set one's coherent, unified self aside in favor of whatever self one needs in order to carry out one's obligations.[40] He must abandon the very authenticity of which La grosse femme is the incarnation in order to become her perfect knight errant, the bearer of her ideals. To perform such an ethical act is to be dramatic, because it means to be not oneself but whatever it is necessary for one to be. In one sense, the luxury of a true self is something that the ethical actor cannot afford. The publicly ethical state is a denial of the real: it is a dramatic action. (That, again, is why Macbeth, which is about ethics, is about acting.) The ethical is a condition in which only a vestige of the true self remains attached to the dramatic self, as a poor relation, somewhat as an actor's true self remains, shadowy, mute, struck dumb behind his role.

To summarize once more, then, Édouard's enterprise: first, he (a.k.a. La Duchesse de Langeais) chooses the theater as his venue; then he goes on to act out the role of the pathetic buffoon, shoe salesman turned vaudeville queen, in a self-immolatory life that becomes a means of rescuing his culture from the very second-rateness that he seems to embody. Every weakness becomes a strength, every blemish a beauty, as Joual turns to language par excellence and the shoe vendor undergoes an apotheosis into a kind of divine salesman of French-Canadian culture on the Main. The hints of transfiguration in the Main Street arcade that we find at the end of Leonard Cohen's *Beautiful Losers* are carried further by Tremblay, to a sort of Joycean magnification, without the archaic echoes on which Joyce depended to transform bathos into sublimity.

Édouard and Altieri on Socrates

There is an obvious resemblance between the figure of Édouard and that of Socrates, that other ironic, self-mocking politician, who is similarly involved in strategies of self- making, self-unmasking, and state-making. These aspects of Socrates's role have been studied with subtlety by Charles Altieri in several essays, of which "Plato's Performative Sublime and the Ends of Reading" is representative.[41] Two questions relevant for the characterization of Édouard are addressed: why does Plato present Socrates's ideas in a dramatic form, and why does Socrates continually seem to undermine the seriousness of his own role? The first answer is that if we do not commit our physical presence to the act of communication, our ideas will necessarily lack ethical force: without our actual presence we do not share the dangers our audience faces in real life, and so we cannot be taken seriously, especially as exemplars of our own ideals. Dramatic presence can even entail risking a life, as becomes very clear in the case of both Socrates and Édouard.

The second reason for choosing the dramatic or, as Altieri prefers to call it, the performative mode for presenting ideas is that it tolerates contradiction. Performance makes it possible to combine the private with the universal, the real with the theoretical, the aesthetic with the abstract: at no point can one promote a principle that is not responsible to example, or confined to thought as such. Involvement with life is a condition of performance, and life is not the habitat of the disembodied. The acceptance of the living contradiction that is, in a sense, the very material of life, entails another acceptance: that of one's own inadequacy.

Performance, since it commits one to being physically present, exposes one to public view as a mere human being. There is no distance of writing to hide behind. At the same time, though, as it has the disadvantage of revealing vulnerability, it has the advantage of making identification possible. The performer forces the audience to recognize that it has something in common with him or her, so laying the ground for that identification. In order to make possible the fullest identification between the performer and the audience, the performer must reveal the fullness of his or her weakness, and accept the full range of human weakness as an essential attribute, the fullest abjection of which human nature is capable. Only so can complete humanity be revealed and complete trust be made possible. It is what the performer is shown to lack of perfection that counts, and that becomes the justification and the instrument for the self-transformation that he or she both seeks, and attempts to produce in others.

Beginning with the fact of abjection, the dramatic illusion of some alternative may begin to be constructed. As Altieri puts it, "the only example that will do is one that makes its own problems the basis of its authority" (p. 268). Beyond that, it is up to the performer: to the strength of the passion he or she possesses or is possessed by. But the demotic level, the layer of ordinary human identification is fundamental: as Altieri says, "Philosophers can be the educators of the race to the extent that they understand the

nebulous images of the good that lead people to imagine trans-
forming the self" (p. 269). So Socrates. So Tremblay's Édouard.

The dramatic has figured so largely in all of this: theater of the
mind, the only way we think; theater of the project, the only way
we do (though doing in itself be not theater); theater of self-
negation and the exaltation of the audience: the prophetic theater
of the martyrs. Can one find one's way back to more ordinary,
more level ground?

There is none: up or down: there are no horizontals in the
mind. Down we go, then, from drama to the uneasy purlieus of
statecraft, with its teasing images of a solution, of a horizontal
that flutters wildly on its way to collapse: but we must be prepared for the possibility that, after the mirage we have constructed has faded, we will be left with nothing but "The lone and
level sands" of Ozymandias, that "Stretch far away."

5

Identity
and Community

■

SOME OBSERVATIONS ON SOCIAL ORDER

Polis and Community

The ideal political role projected for Socrates by Plato, or for Édouard by Tremblay, is, paradoxically, one that sets the political hero outside community; it is a role in which he manipulates the public, for its own benefit, to be sure, but from a position external to it. That public itself may, but does not necessarily, constitute a community.[1] If one belongs to a community, one does so not by observing it from a reasonable distance but by immersing oneself in it: by one's blind side, through which one participates in processes that do not even always rise to the level of the individual's consciousness: whether by sharing in the opacities of the common language,[2] by simply taking part in the life style of the community (which may in fact, as in the case of Yiddish Montreal, encourage extreme forms of individuality), or by accepting and perpetuating its values, its fears, and its ideals. A difference, or even a contrast, then, may be identified between polis and community. The polis is, so to speak, the functional aspect of a group (whether one considers the group from the outside, as does the political hero, or from the inside, as does the citizen). The community is created by feelings of cohesiveness,[3] which make people want to be together and make them more comfortable with each other than with other people; it works by recognition.[4] Institutions may be generated by an interaction of community impulses with political forces. But, in principle, a polis is not necessarily a community. Some might even believe that when a polis is born, with its depersonalization and its processes of representation, community dies. In fact, one of the miracles of Jewish Montreal in the first half of the twentieth century was that it was able to function on a fairly large scale as a community without degenerating into a polis.

The distinction I am trying to make bears some resemblance to Charles Péguy's, between "mystique" and "politique," but it is probably closer to a sociological contrast that has been experiencing an extraordinary revival recently: that of Ferdinand Tönnies, between "Gemeinschaft" and "Gesellschaft." (It has been invoked once more as an organizing principle by Bill Martin in *Matrix and Line: Derrida and the Possibilities of Postmodern Social Theory* [Albany: State University of New York Press, 1992]). "Gemeinschaft" would have the major characteristics of community, with its elements of instinctual bonding and intimacy, while "Gesellschaft" would display the more intellectual features of a rational society. It is apparent that in talking about the individual's relation to the social group one should keep this distinction in mind, though governments routinely confuse the two, exploiting the craving for "Gemeinschaft" and turning it to strictly political ends. Perhaps we need to deal with both orientations, then, that towards community and that towards polis. For Georges Bataille, for instance, all that which creates genuine community—eroticism, sacrifice, ecstasy, laughter—is the expression of an impulse destructive of order. "La surabondance a pour conséquence inévitable la mort, seule la stagnation assure le maintien de la discontinuité des êtres (de leur isolement)"[5] (Excess has death as its inevitable consequence: only stagnation can assure the maintenance of the discontinuity between beings [their isolation]). It is not that community is unimportant: on the contrary, it is so important for humanity, whose defining characteristic is its incompleteness,[6] that the achievement of community warrants the destruction of the polis, if that should happen to be necessary. If the founding gesture of community is an act of violence, in the theater of sacrifice,[7] where our common destiny in transgression and death is experienced, the polis may come to be seen as a denial of both life and death, a kind of anti-dramatic principle: what Baudrillard might call the "obscene." In fact, if the moment of death provides the truest opening to the sense of community, when the strongest confirmation of community takes place, the entire organization of the polis would fade to a kind of dim Kandinskian sketch on the surface of the dying eye, where the real business of community is being transacted.

"La mort est indissociable de la communauté, car c'est par la mort que la communauté se révèle—et réciproquement"[8] (Death cannot be dissociated from community, for it is through death that community reveals itself—and reciprocally so). And "une communauté ne peut durer qu'au niveau d'intensité de la mort"[9] (a community can endure only at the level of intensity of death)—at the level at which the impossibilities inherent in the condition of mortality are always kept staring its members in the face. The true community has no work, no "oeuvre:" it is much too busy for that; nor has it any project. It is entirely defined by, and absorbed in, the act of being what it is: a community.

The Bataille-Nancy conception of community, for which the community is not only not a "polis" in the usual sense, but not even a society,[10] may seem exotic and extreme in terms of ordinary social science. Nevertheless, it falls into the broad category of open, aleatory models of human association that have proliferated over the past forty years.[11] It is difficult to say to what extent such models reflect current historical developments, and to what extent they are simply variants of traditional strains in social thinking. Obviously Bataille and Nancy owe much to de Sade, Nietzsche, and various schools of anarchist thought; on the other hand, a distinct if unintended topical relevance peeps through here and there. For instance, in Maurice Blanchot's commentary on Nancy's and Bataille's vision of human solidarity, *La Communauté inavouable*, published in 1983, Blanchot described the political movement of 1968 in France as having actually produced the ideal community, the "communauté désoeuvrée," of their fantasy. The interesting thing about his description of the 1968 crowd, though, and of its behavior, indeed of the whole spirit of 1968, is that it sounds exactly as if he were speaking of the events of 1988–1990 in Germany or Czechoslovakia. "Le peuple" *became* "la communauté désoeuvrée," an irresistible force because of its commonly felt though *undefined* purpose, its massive presence alone constituting the irrefutable argument for change; without a plan, without any structure, without intention

157

to outlast the moment or to set up instrumentalities for a polis or society of any kind: just a reaffirmation of community, which neither society nor politics can, whether by co-opting or by oppressing, finally, destroy.[12]

What I have called the open or relaxed models of society have kept pace, then, with the dissolution of empires, the immense growth in the number of independence movements, and above all with the repudiation of totalitarian political theory. I should be much surprised to learn that actual oppression of the weak by the strong in the real world has diminished, but it is practiced under different intellectual auspices, or under none. The French New Philosophers pulled the veil from Marxism well before the collapse of the East European Communist regimes, leaving the Left without ideals or even illusions to fall back on: and whether one think illusions are the only matrix of society (as Baudrillard sometimes implies), or that they are the very stuff of the totalitarian (as Lyotard sometimes implies), the world seems to remain without any political pattern to shape itself around. Lateralism (Deleuze's "rhizomatics"), post-modernism, and Nomadology offer simulacra of order in disorder, but it is difficult to extract a positive result from a negative model.[13]

In this atmosphere of free speculation, though, alternative concepts of social order, more flexible and better adapted to fluid political circumstances, have made themselves available or are being found relevant. Again, these range from the theoretical and abstruse to the genuinely practical. At the first extreme, Lyotard forces us to consider whether even something basic, such as the concept of "the public" itself, or the political "subject-victim," or "subject-spectator," is not as much a construct or a fabrication of the social theorists as are the systems they attempt to force upon society.[14] Local circumstances must be respected and allowed their full weight; generalizations cannot be trusted. An obvious consequence of this nominalist tendency in Lyotard and in other thinkers of his persuasion is that, in the absence of a logic of hierarchy, political topology quickly falls apart. Without models in which (for instance) bad groups do things to good groups, or the means of production determine political forms,[15] one is soon reduced to a picture of history that separates into vignettes of biography on the one hand, and huge systems interacting without human agency[16] on the other, as we see forces more abstract and mysterious than Hegel's own moving to occupy the Olympus of causality.

It is not surprising to find that Gilles Deleuze, as a committed Leibnizian, has produced a somewhat ambiguous concept of community. It has always been difficult to reconcile Leibniz's "windowless" monads even with a viable notion of intersubjectivity, much less of community or society. Leibniz's tendency to view the world as a splendid machine, but a machine nevertheless, is also reflected in Deleuze's thinking. The flexible, self-subsisting models or institutions of de Sade, which do not presuppose guilt or impose laws, provide the kind of societal context that Deleuze seems to favor.[17] The influence of Mikhail Bakhtin's literary theory of multivocality is likewise reflected in Deleuze's social thinking.[18] One form of "reticular" rather than hierarchical group process which Deleuze identifies is of course the one he calls "nomadic," and is associated with the extra-societal "war machine." Another, more obviously Leibnizian, is the Baroque concert of separate but coordinated monads, functioning under the guidance of an unseen conductor, who puts us through our paces in a voluntary yet deterministic ballet, in which we circle and pirouette like ghosts, not touching, but irresistibly moved to express our harmonious collaboration.[19]

Open Politics

Of course, as I have said, not all approaches to an open politics have been so radical or remained so theoretical as those projected by Lyotard or Deleuze. A good example of an intermediate position is that of Iris Young.[20] In her chapter on "Polity and Group Difference: A Critique of the Ideal of Universal Citizenship" she argues that all states should be required to provide formal political representation for minority interests (women's, native groups', etc.) within the official structures of government (p. 125), alongside structures of party or regional representation (p. 127). (For a critique of pluralist strategies see the work of the Canadian philosopher Louise Marcil-Lacoste).[21] Now that equality of rights has been acknowledged, she contends, the different needs of different groups must be confronted and negotiated (p. 129). Young does not accept the argument that "challenging the idea of a unified public . . . subverts the possibility of making rational normative claims" (p. 135). Her overarching argument, though, is that "rights and rules that are universally formulated and thus blind to differences of race, culture, gender, age, or disability perpetuate rather than undermine oppression" (p. 130), while "the political claim for special rights emerges not from a need to compensate for an inferiority . . . but from a positive assertion of specificity in different forms of life" (p. 132). On the other hand, "when participatory democratic structures define citizenship in universalistic and unified terms, they tend to reproduce existing group oppression" (p. 121). Young would like to see a society of mutual acceptance develop, in which "differences are publicly recognized and acknowledged as irreducible, by which I mean that people from one perspective or history can never completely understand and adopt the point of view of" others (p. 121). She is particularly opposed to the idea that "when they exercise their citizenship, persons should adopt a universal point of view and leave behind the perceptions they derive from their particular experience and social position" (p. 135). Stephen K. White, in *Political Theory and Postmodernism* (Cambridge, etc.: Cambridge University Press, 1991), adopts an even stronger position: societies need to foster, not merely tolerate, difference (pp. 117, 143–44).

I doubt that Iris Young's work will provide immediate comfort to Ireland, Azerbaijan, or other areas and polities seamed by histories of factional violence. Nevertheless, it represents a way of thinking that seems appropriate to the pluralistic world which we are now said to occupy, and it is certainly closer in spirit to the style of the Canadian "mosaic" than to that of the American "melting pot," to go back for the moment to those largely obsolete metaphors. The difficulties with Young's argument are easy to point out: how do we distinguish (and who is to distinguish) between a group with legitimate special needs (e.g., the elderly) and a "special interest group" (such as the National Rifle Association, the White Nation, and so on)? Furthermore, there have long been government instrumentalities for protecting some groups (child labor laws, old age pensions, etc.), but any formula for protecting us from the tendency of some to accumulate power over others still eludes us. Finally, if the Nagel-Olzak thesis on resource competition holds true (see Introduction, above), no rainbow coalition is likely to survive for long. Despite such serious objections, though, the reversal of emphasis achieved in Iris Young's work does create a sense of relief, providing as it does a fresh perspective on her subject, and the hope that new ways of thinking may develop.

Certainly it is encouraging to see that some of her ideas already enter into the discussion of real, tangible problems in Canadian society. A column by Robert Sheppard in *The Globe and Mail* (Monday, August 12, 1991, p. A 17) reads like an extended quotation from Young's work. Ethel Blondin and Len Marchand have been lobbying, Sheppard tells us, for "specific native seats in the Federal Parliament."

"It is an idea . . . whose time has probably come," Sheppard goes on to say. "The governments of Nova Scotia and New Brunswick are also studying the possibility of having special native seats in their legislatures (though possibly without full voting rights), and Ontario is being urged to follow a similar course. . . . Still, it is a difficult concept for many people to come to terms with, the idea of special constituencies, perhaps special status, for one distinct group of Canadians." Nevertheless, the still more radical idea of a separate judicial system for some groups of native Canadians is now being broached.

The Collapse of Complex Societies

It is hard to know how much of what we have learned about mixed societies in the past is relevant for the future, since economic forces, economic organization, information flow, and information management are so different. Just as no one foresaw the explosion of factional hatreds that has followed recent decreases in centralized control, so we are not likely to be prepared for the kinds of readjustment that will follow when things begin to settle down in their new patterns. A glance back at the ways in which previous societies have dealt with multinationality may be all that our capacities for applying the past to the future can warrant. Some social scientists, though, believe that there are trans-historical processes which will always have to be taken into consideration, no matter what the socio-economic situation. For instance, for Joseph A. Tainter, the recent collapse of the Russian empire or the potential collapse of the Canadian confederation would simply be instances of the phenomenon that he calls *The Collapse of Complex Societies*.[22] Increasing investment in complexity yields decreasing marginal returns (pp. 194–98), and so-called collapse is a rational economic solution to a managerial problem (p. 198); coherence or disintegration in a society becomes merely a question of cost-benefit ratios (p. 200). (For instance: would the smaller, and, in that sense, simpler administrative unit of Quebec be cheaper to operate than the same area under a Federal administration?) However, where no diminution of complexity ensues, there is no economic gain in collapse (p. 201), and in a world filled with complex societies, it is hard to see what form collapse could take, except a global, universal form (p. 214). Tainter does not appear to think that a reduction in the size of administrative units by itself produces a significant decrease in complexity. In the present situation, the so-called collapse of an empire or state would merely mean its absorption by another state, or its refinancing at an equally high level of complexity by a dominant power or international financing agency (p. 213).

If Tainter is right, then, the proliferation of nation states would simply raise the level of competitiveness and conflict in a situation in which no one gains. Yet it seems difficult for countries that contain divided populations, whether they identify their differences by color (United States), language (Canada), religion (France), or culture and traditions (e.g., Sephardic and Ashkenazic Jews in Israel), to control their centrifugal forces. Still, these same countries, in fact most countries, have had a long history of disputes along at least one of these fault lines, and have managed to hold together over long periods of time. We think of the United States as having developed its major ethnic oppositions recently, but in fact, as Andrew Hacker points out, it was already regarded in 1916 as "the world-federation of the most heterogeneous peoples under the sun."[23] Even European countries such as France, which presented the appearance of unity and coherence at the end of the nineteenth century, had achieved that condition only by the systematic suppression of local languages and the imposition of a centralized educational scheme. In a way, then, Switzerland, or Belgium, merely continue to display on the surface features that were only recently buried and still not quite effaced in many parts of Europe (such as England). The cacophony of what was Yugoslavia or Czechoslovakia, of Roumania, or of Moldavia, is a reflection of the normal multi-ethnic character of European nations and indeed of countries the world over. Even Switzerland had its embryonic civil wars during the 1830s and 1840s.

The Swiss Model

It is an almost irresistible temptation, in a time such as ours, to return to the study of Switzerland in the hope of finding the key to a peaceable and efficient multiculturalism. Unfortunately, the same hope has arisen in others in other times of conflict and has invariably met with disappointment. The impression one derives from reading commentators on the Swiss phenomenon is that its conditions are unique and not capable of being transplanted. Sometimes it is said that Switzerland can be harmonious because its multilingualism is not a result of conquest or the creeping imperialism of a dominant center, but of voluntary association among diverse ethnic groups seeking mutual support in the shelter of the Alpine terrain.[24] This contention may be qualified by the observation that it is only in post-Napoleonic Switzerland that the French and Italian regions of the country have obtained political equality with the rest.[25] At the other pole from attributing Swiss political harmony to either the personalities or the policies of the people is the view that Switzerland is merely an artifact created by its stronger neighbors, whether as buffer or as financial convenience, and that it consequently cannot be allowed to indulge its native centrifugal propensities.[26] By neither account, though, would the Swiss alternative be available to other troubled polities.

Another advantage that the Swiss are said to possess is a geographic pattern that prevents their differences from being mutually reinforcing; it is as though their maladaptive genes were never doubled. Thus, their different languages do not coincide with political (i.e., cantonal—and there are twenty-five cantons in this small country) or religious lines of demarcation;[27] the same is true of economic and industrial patterns in Switzerland.[28] It is conceivable that a government elsewhere, not already in the grip of a majority bent on preserving its hegemony, might achieve some such result by creative gerrymandering, relocation of industry, and so forth; but, even if such plans were practical, the initial will might well be lacking where minority languages are regarded not as contributing to the enrichment of a culture but as threatening the authority of the state.[29]

It is often suggested that Switzerland is in fact now as centralized as any other country, and that its federalist facade means little in real terms. Nevertheless, we have the undeniable fact that the Swiss are not in violent conflict over their language differences. It is hard to avoid being impressed, for instance, by the Swiss attitude towards Romansch, which, though spoken by barely 1 percent of the population (now even fewer), was accorded the status of a national language in 1938. One might have considered the Swiss justified if they had been a little less gen-

erous towards the Romansch activists who demanded that anyone settling in their area be required to practice his or her profes-
sion in the Romansch language, and who went so far as to raise
the cry of "maîtres chez nous" in their territory![30] Instead, the
Swiss went out of their way to try to reestablish the roots of the
language by launching an extensive program of kindergarten
classes in Romansch![31] It is as if they prided themselves on dem-
onstrating that a positive attitude towards cultural variety could
only strengthen their federation.[32] In this instance it is not incon-
ceivable that some other countries could actually follow their
example.

There are other important ways in which Switzerland has fostered dispersed and cooperative forms of control rather than centralized rule. One is the well-known referendum/initiative option
which, whether actually used or held in suspense, brings an element of direct democracy into the process of government that
makes power plays from the center an awkward option for any
ruling party.[33] The diversified composition—entrenched in law—
of the Federal Council also discourages autocratic inclinations.
Proportional representation is likewise generally understood to
militate against aspirations to Napoleonic (or even Reaganesque)
political careers, and evidently makes the development of political "machines" impossible or pointless. Perhaps for all these reasons, Bern, as Lionel Gossman suggests, has never assumed the
full status of a capital city.[34]

It is often remarked that the Swiss have not used their long
history of cooperation and accommodation to produce a great
deal that is of cultural value. On the other hand, it is equally often
said that a limitation on a country's creative potential may not be
too high a price to pay for the kind of harmony the Swiss have
maintained, at least for the past century and a half. (Similar
things, of course, are often said about Canada.) A glance over the
history of Swiss culture in our time also makes the first assertion
concerning the meagerness of the Swiss cultural contribution
seem rash; but the fact of Swiss harmony, at the very least at the
linguistic level, is incontrovertible.[35] I find it interesting that Max
Frisch, for all his mockery of Switzerland, describes his culture in
terms very similar to those I have used to characterize the immigrant Yiddish community in Montreal during the first half of the
century: "By culture we understand in the first instance civil
achievements, the community attitude more than the artistic or
scientific masterpiece of a single citizen."[36] The individual achieve-

164

ment is all very well, but the real question is: What does it do for all of us?

■

THE INDIVIDUAL AND THE GROUP

In contrasting, relating, or identifying the individual with the community we probably need to think in advance, not so much about the inexhaustible problem of what an individual is, as from whose point of view the question is being asked. To some extent the answer, or at least the kind of answer, one gets will be determined by the context that the questioner establishes. Even if one is only asking the question of oneself and about oneself, one may ask it from many different points of view and for many different reasons. If I want to demonstrate the crucial or primary importance of a creative self I will ask, what are the conditions that make possible the emergence of a creative self, and in what does that self consist? But, clearly, important as the creative (or the suffering, or the ethical) self may be, I am (as anyone else is) also at liberty to ask an entirely different question: for instance, what is the perceiving self? Setting up an epistemological context for the question will yield a different result. To attempt to reconcile two or more of these results may produce still another version of the self. To historicize or psychologize the questions—i.e., to ask, why do we frame our questions in a particular way, and so determine the parameters of the answers in accordance with our desires and preconceptions—is liable to lead to an infinite regress, but may also throw up still other concepts or constructions of the self along the way.

Given the nature of my subject, I cannot afford to become involved in a general effort to define the self or try to deal with all the difficulties that cling to such definitions once they have been reached (discontinuities in personal identity,[37] unity or duality or multiplicity of consciousness, the function of proprioception, the self as a byproduct of textuality, the possibility of having a personal self that is also an object of impersonal self-knowledge,[38] all come to mind). I will have to limit myself to a few ideas about the self that relate it directly, whether positively or negatively, to the idea of community. Of course, this is in itself a large field, and related issues, such as the role of the ethical in the construction of identity, cannot be entirely ignored. (See, for instance, Charles Taylor, *Sources of the Self: The Making of the Modern Identity,* Cambridge, Massachusetts: Harvard University Press, 1989).[39]

Do we know anything before we are socialized? Have we some crystallized awareness prior to language? Our struggles to introduce into language things that are not yet, or may never, be winched out into that area suggest that we do have an infinite number of pre-linguistic and possibly entirely extra-linguistic experiences, as adults as well as as children. But, of course, whether we still have extra-linguistic experiences or not after we enter the field of language, the moment we are involved in language we are involved in society, and there is no way of getting away from it again. From that point on, the self, whether considered subjectively or objectively, is a social entity.[40] The individual may behave in any number of private or anti-social ways, or even develop an idiolect, but the mere use of language, whether internal or interpersonal, stamps one as a dialogic and communal being.

If one grants that view, one may then go on to consider the various "states" of the individual—that is, of the individual defined, so far, as merely that conscious entity that participates in language. It is possible to consider the individual in terms of a sliding scale, on which he or she is seen as a more or less independent agent, as a participant in a group, or as someone whose behavior is almost entirely determined by society—as in the commonly held notion that "individualism" is itself a collective state of mind peculiar to certain societies.[41] In fact, it is sometimes suggested that the very notion of the individual is a by-product of specific economic conditions, such as the eighteenth-century situation in which superfluity (as well as large-scale debt) became a common feature of the financial scene; and Arthur Kroker implies that, under capitalism, the self is simply that which can possess something.[42]

There does certainly appear to be something wrong with what is sometimes called "methodological individualism," which seeks to reduce the behavior of groups to the actions of the individuals that go to make them up,[43] and tends to dismiss "societies" and "communities" as theoretical by-products of sociology rather than genuine entities. One can hardly have stood on a platform before a crowd of students in the late 1960s without knowing that a group has an identity which has very little to do with the characteristics of its individual members, even though they themselves, individually, have no awareness of participating in a trans-individual state.

166

In fact, it stands to reason that as social individuals (not really an oxymoron) we are at all times affected by the group forces in our lives, so that we live at the same time partly in ourselves and partly outside ourselves, though only certain elements of that "extra-territorial" self reach our consciousness.[44] It is not only that our society mysteriously signals to us that it is time to do certain things—for instance, to start to walk in a different way when we move to a different city, or to play our role in a groundswell of divorce[45]—but that we always live in two dimensions simulta-neously, so that, say, details of our most intimate sexual conduct will have both socially determined and personal components.[46] It is not just that our society is at all times influencing our behavior, but that we too are at all times alert to its background presence. We live, so to speak, with an eye on our society while we are doing other things, so that a trans-personal component enters into all our ac-tions. In other words, we are always to some degree members of that 1960s crowd.

To resist the influence or pressure of a society is not to step out of it: one participates in the social process as much by opposing a popular attitude or policy as by accepting it. To belong to a group is to interact with its other members, whether one do so positively or negatively. Differing with the majority does not make one an asocial being. The most individualistic program of behavior is still undertaken vis-à-vis a society, taking it into consideration while rejecting it. Even the solitary is solitary only with respect to the social world.[47]

One way of defining the self that preserves its autonomy while at the same time conceding its sociality is to make rational-ity its identifying characteristic or earmark. Here I am thinking not so much of "rational choice" sociology as of the mere fact that rational decisions are made—or revoked—by a process that requires both a collective and an individual contribution.[48] Para-doxically, though, the field in which the activity of the self as rational agent becomes most apparent is probably that of self-contradiction. When Mark Warren ("Ideology and the Self," p. 627) suggests that "beliefs that are integrated into the self in ways that *defeat revision* "are the mark of ideology," (italics mine) he seems to be pointing to beliefs that deny the self its character-istic function; and it may be, as Henry W. Johnstone suggests,[49] that that characteristic function is, precisely, the self's capacity not only for revision, but actually for self-contradiction. In accor-dance with this argument, self-contradiction may be thought of as the point at which the indispensability of the self for the prosecution of the rational process, no matter how great the contribution of culture, ideology, or historical moment, becomes apparent.

Still, this criterion may not be adequate to describe cultures in which what we call rationality is less consistently required, or even to describe those moments in which the individual is not engaged in a rational process. Consequently, the so-called micro-macro problem continues to elude solution, at both ends as well as in between (which is where Michel de Certeau would seem to want to place us), though some would prefer to dismiss it as a non-problem.[50] Allowing for all the differences, one could ask whether this conundrum does not share some features with other problems in systems analysis in which the relations of the part and the whole are at issue:[51] meteorology; the nature of the colonial animals, such as the sponges; taxonomy in biology; the body; the brain. If one objects that (unlike, say, the cell) the human participant in a society has the ability to fight against the authoritarian center or to make a contribution to the society that has not been specified by authority, it might even be proposed, only half-jocularly, that a Darwinian model could allow for some comparable process not only at the level of the species but even of the cell and the organ. My main point is, though, that without falling into mechanistic analogies one should recognize that the micro-macro issue in sociology shares the problems of a field that is hard to bring under control even at the level of physical description, besides being concerned with a species that is notoriously recalcitrant to a quantitative approach.[52]

Alberto Melucci, in *Nomads of the Present: Social Movements and Individual Needs in Contemporary Society,* has made an effort to examine the process by which small groups in contemporary society (which he sees functioning not as "characters" but as "signs," p. 75) are organized, maintained, and dissolved. He attempts to determine, for instance, how the "we" that is at the basis of collective action gets constructed (p. 64).[53] Movements live, he says, not in their organizational tactics but "in the everyday network of social relations" (p. 71).[54]

Melucci's work is interesting and valuable for its descriptions of the ways in which small groups function in complex societies, and of the respects in which modern group movements differ from earlier ones, especially from political movements.[55] However, despite his experimental and interventionist technique, which he attempts to communicate in some detail, he does not succeed in conveying to this reader how the individual relates to the group in even these small units. As usual, communitarian mechanisms are much easier to see at work and to understand in "primitive" societies, as in the striking example of the Guayaki that he cites (p. 113) from Clastres.

In the end, all I can add to the micro-macro debate is the suggestion of a compromise. The human being is clearly at the crossroads, or is the crossroads, of many forces, biological, social, individual, and historical; also, perhaps, even of forces that cannot be included in any such reasonable categories. We are shaped coercively to the convenience of the master ideology in our economy, but also by the positive needs of any society to survive on some terms: or, to put it differently, we are both Althusserian and Parsonian ("functional") characters at once.[56] We also respond to the explicit as well as to the occult signals that come to us from our society, and take rational, altruistic, egotistic, reactive, or other kinds of measures in dealing with them. We exist in a constant conscious and unconscious tension between the personal and the social. On top of that, we make our individual, unpredictable contributions to what is going on. No matter how far we push the theory of personality formation towards the rule of mass influence, no matter how much of our individuality we may attribute to conditioning, the fact remains that only to Mozart was it given to hear, among all the classical harmonies that he had inherited, the opening theme of the G minor symphony.

Conclusion

■

With this conclusion I seem to return to my initial position, developed in my chapter on Roberts: what is of value is centered in, or, at the very least, mediated by, an individual self. This opinion would appear to be incompatible with the nostalgic praise of communitarian values in my chapters on Maza and Tremblay, though in the instance of Maza I try to demonstrate that it is possible, in an exceptional case, to bridge the gap. In any event, I will attempt to show later that the apparent incompatibility is in fact not profound.

There may even be a connection (though, perhaps, a superficial one) between the contradiction adumbrated here (the individual versus the collective ideal) and the political attitudes implied in this book. On the one hand, the "relaxed" models of political function that I have sketched above would, if they worked, allow a "disunited" territory to be perfectly viable; its parts might function with considerable autonomy without violating its common purpose. Yet I myself probably also have an unstated neurotic nostalgia for the opposite ideal: for the family quarrel of unity in resentment, the bond of the familiar conflict (rather like that within Tremblay's "gang" on the Rue Fabre), which would want to keep the pattern of the Canadian tangle as it is now. But this book is not an attempt either to prescribe or to predict the political future of Canada, whatever implications it may have for that future.

I return, then, to the themes of community and individuality in the authors with whom I have been dealing. Some of the most useful research concerning contrasting attitudes on these issues between the English and the French has been done by Sheila McLeod Arnopoulos and Dominique Clift in *The English Fact in Quebec* (Montreal: McGill-Queen's University Press, 1980). Quoting Marcel Rioux, the authors point out (p. 35) that the English in Canada have traditionally been individualists, the French collectivists: the French seigneurial system lasted until 1854, and until that time land, since it belonged to the community, was not a marketable commodity that could be disposed of by an individual. The English, on the other hand, according to Arnopoulos and Clift, tend to see Canada not as made up of groups but of individuals with equal rights (p. 36). In the matter of schooling, for instance, the English defend the choice of language by a rationale of individual rights (p. 35). The whole issue of individual versus collective rights in the Quebec context is a major theme in the Autumn 1991 issue of *Philosophiques* (vol. 19 no. 2). Collective rights, however, notably as expressed in the right to bring class action suits, have actually been more fully recognized, on the whole, in American than in Canadian law (p. 38. It is interesting to observe that Israeli law, though not often invoked for this purpose, gives even more scope for the expression of group interests than does U. S. law. For a treatment of the identity-nationality issue on an international scale see Scott Lash and Jonathan Friedman, eds., *Modernity and Identity* [Oxford, U. K. and Cambridge, U. S. A.: Blackwell, 1992]).

As for Jewish communitarian feeling in Montreal, I have already attempted to describe the characteristics it displayed during the first part of the century; but there have been major changes in the later period. There is probably less tolerance for eccentricity and more institutionalization of cultural functions and social services; in general there is less of a participatory, grass-roots culture. The community has become more bourgeois, and at the same time perhaps somewhat more divided along secular/orthodox lines: the emergence of Israel has also produced a shift of focus: and Yiddish is no longer a lingua franca among various groups of Jews. It has certainly not been replaced by Hebrew in that capacity, and, even if it were to be, the situation would not be the same, for Hebrew is a language with a totally different set of associations, some archaic, most modern. Yiddish was brewed in the European world of the diaspora, a world of intimacy and poverty, and it is hard to imagine that a group for which that language was no longer available could retain its particular cultural flavor. The English and the French in Canada have suffered no such loss.

But to go back to the earlier period once more: I am struck, in retrospect, by the remoteness of Ottawa from the consciousness of the Jews of Montreal. Having lived in the United States, I know that Washington is an immediate presence in the lives of Americans, whether of recent or of older vintage. It is as if there were threads of communication that went directly from Washington to all the individuals in the U.S. To myself, and to those around me in my earlier years, Ottawa was not a presence: and the notion that it "represented" us, whether well or badly, was not even entertained. It was a place from which certain decrees emanated: how they were arrived at, or by whom they were framed (at all events, not by human beings), was not a question that crossed one's mind. Local politicians, on the other hand, such as Arcand, or Duplessis, could be uncomfortably real.

As for the French community, I do not know whether it has retained all of its instinctive solidarity, or whether some uncertainties have begun to reveal themselves in it as well. It may be harder to maintain a sense of unquestioning community in a group of sophisticated urban intellectuals and technocrats than in a rural or an impoverished city population with a largely religious culture. Certainly it seems a bit odd that Aquin, for all his revolutionary principles, should be so much more concerned with individual Angst than with group solidarity. Robert Schwartzwald maintains that, in fact, Canadian Francophone intellectuals in general suffer from a profound anxiety and uncertainty.[1]

But some of these issues, urgent as they are, already begin to appear a bit obsolete, because the context in which they now arise has changed so much. For instance, some of the premises of this book—that more cultures than the English and the French need to be taken into the purview of Canadian literature, or that it is important to identify differences in the internal dynamics of the three groups I have talked about—begin to seem only preliminary to a confrontation with the waves of change that are already upon us, the sweeping multiculturalist movements that both constitute and (some may think) threaten the fabric of Canada. Sometimes a systems analysis program (perhaps derived from engineering or from communications theory) for describing a field of cultures seems more relevant to the contemporary situation than an intimate exploration of the heart of each individual community. The period I have been talking about might be characterized by some as parochial: but whether ways of talking about that parochialism need to be old-fashioned and parochial, in keeping with their subject matter, or whether they should be hard-edged and critical, possibly with the result of relegating these obsolete phenomena to their appropriate and perhaps minor status, is undoubtedly open to consideration. Certainly a straight New Historicist reading would yield a very different Charles G. D. Roberts (no "Sir," either!) from the one I have produced (with the aphasia of his animals comparable to the subordination of the colonials' english to the real parent tongue,[2] etc.)

The fact is, these authors of mine do operate (or operated) in closed cultural conditions, less and less like those that prevail today. We may praise multiculturalism as a form of social organization, but Roberts, Maza, and Tremblay function in a context that is ethnically homogeneous, *not* multicultural, multiracial, or multireligious. Other languages and life styles do not make deep inroads into their worlds. "Joual" is not influenced by English: the more English words it includes, the less English it becomes. The same was true of Yiddish, which had been absorbing foreign words for four hundred years while becoming more Yiddish all the time. When it began to fail, it did so because of the virtual extermination of its speakers, not because it had absorbed too many Russian or Polish words. Authors such as Tremblay and Maza are not trying to regenerate Canadian literature by writing in broken English.[3] It hadn't occurred to them that they were writing in broken anything.

These authors, then, are old-fashioned because they do not really think macaronically; for them there is, or was, no question of adapting to another culture in order to function in the New World or in Canada. They do not confront the problem of the contemporary immigrant or even second-generation writer struggling to be himself or herself and someone else at the same time, so ably described by Barbara Godard.[4] They aren't concerned enough about Canada as such to think about it, or to pay that much attention to it. Above all, it would never occur or have occurred to them that they were writing for Canada. Canada for them is/was a place that may be or may have been a political entity, but it certainly had no culture to which one would address oneself. They wrote/write strictly for their own community, or for anyone else in the world at large, Canadian or non-Canadian, who might respond to their work. Tremblay has, of course, been widely translated; and one of Maza's books was published in Poland.

Roberts may have been old-fashioned for the opposite reason: because he seemed to have so few doubts about the manifest destiny of Canada, although he did "pipe for them that pay the piper"[5] too. But it is time for me to stop thinking about particulars, collect my thoughts, and consider the ways or the way in which the materials of this volume hang together.

One of the means by which a generalization might be attempted is by invoking the model of the polis-community opposition to which I referred in the preceding chapter. In these terms, one might venture the guess that Canada is marked by a separation of these functions: they simply do not unite. There are many communities, and there is a polis, but the two forms of social organization do not overlap substantially, much less blend.

Let me first consider the negative consequences of this situation. The sense of separation from the center is accompanied by fear, and by the awareness of not being included at the political level: of having little if any access to the decision-making process, even in theory. Every Canadian is a minority in his or her own country, if not in his or her own community.

As a rule, the last thing one would want to engage in would be invidious comparisons between the United States and Canada, but there are some aspects of Canadian political culture that are most easily brought into relief in this way. An American friend of mine who did his graduate work in political science at the University of Toronto has spoken to me of the growing sense of discomfort that he experienced during his years in Canada: at first he was full of enthusiasm, but gradually he become unhappy about something in the Canadian atmosphere. He used the word "community" in a somewhat different sense from mine, but, at the risk of creating some terminological confusion, I will repeat his remark verbatim. He spoke of his uneasiness with "repressive Canadian communitarianism," and of an opposition between "participatory and hierarchical senses of community." Evidently he missed the feeling of participation—even if it was only participation in chaos—that the United States provided. As I understand the problem of what he identified as "repressive communitarianism," it is that in Canada whatever form of unity exists is experienced as having been imposed by force, by a colonializing power that still makes its hegemony felt. This power may no longer be Britain, but the terms, flavor, and conditions of control and authority remain the same. "And the new Canadians dreamed and learned their place."[6] It may be something of this kind that Magdalene Redekop had in mind when she asked Joy Kogawa whether Japanese-American writers were not "less ghettoized than Japanese-Canadian writers, less obligated to write from inside that painful hyphen," and observed that Bharati Mukerjee felt "more free *there*."[7]

The notorious garrison mentality of Canada should, perhaps, be reconsidered in this sense. It may be that the garrisons need to be thought of as outposts that serve a central authority without participating in it, rather like the military settlements of Cossacks established in the sixteenth century along the river Don. The members of such a state are internal colonists, as much subservient to the ruling power as the inhabitants of any external colony. Where Northrop Frye says that the garrisons' need for inner cohesion comes from the confrontation with the immeasurable forces of Canadian nature, I would say that it comes from confrontation with a menacing central authority. (Louis Riel, as well as the rebellion of 1837 of course come to mind.) They must serve in order to survive, but they will survive only under conditions decreed for them from above.

Both Robertsian individualism or isolationism and Yiddish or French communitarianism are escapes from central authority. They represent living on the periphery, which is both the position that one has been relegated to and the one that keeps one at the greatest possible distance from the threatening miasma emanating from the center.[8] What they have in common is secrecy and privacy; both forms, individualistic and communal, create a childish sense of security, whatever other more significant values they may also provide.

For myself, Roberts is the most telling instance. He is at once the closest to me and the farthest from me of the figures about whom I have been writing. He is the farthest, first because his stories express an ethos of distance, and second because he represents the threatening, alien dominant culture (for all his being himself an "internal colonist," if I am right in my diagnosis of the condition which all individuals in a colonial polity endure). He is the closest because, as WASP, he did after all stand for the majority ethos of the culture I had been raised in, and that is the one that one internalizes most fully, like it or not. The animals in his stories perhaps acted as "transitional objects" to facilitate this process of assimilation and internalization for me.

Let me put the issues in their starkest form: if necessary, in an exaggerated form, to make my point clear. Canadians are somewhat cowed: they have taken authority into themselves, therefore they make a great show of rejecting it while remaining deeply conservative and obedient. Even the revolutionaries among them sometimes seem to be revolutionary in a patriotic and obedient manner, within reasonable limits. It makes me uneasy to come out once more where Friedenberg pointed the way, but I can't help it. When Robert Schwartzwald, among others, raises the familiar questions with regard to New Canadians, "integrate into what?"[9] I think the question is misconceived. It is a matter only of integrating into duty to an Emperor or Empress at large, not to any particular culture either local or national: a matter of, as Bruce Russell says, learning "their place," so that they may know exactly where they stand in the reception line and may aspire to have "almost as grand a time as if they were at Buckingham Palace itself."[10]

Sometimes I suspect that under the veneer of multiculturalism the colonial powers in Canada are, like bureaucrats in some of the recently totalitarian countries, still largely in control, and, in their stalest, most know-nothing form, still embedded in the heart of Canada's cultural institutions. When I was advised recently by a Canadian publisher to stick to the only thing I really know anything about—the Jews—I could feel myself slipping back into the same state of mind, helpless, defensive, and cringing, that I used to lapse into as a teenager when I had to confront official anti-Semitism at McGill. Even in this most benevolent of oligarchies, some things change slowly; some, it would appear, change not at all.

There is a rhetorical finality about that last sentence; besides, it is sincere. It has been hard for me not to succumb to the temptation of using it as the final sentence of the book. Yet the sentence is also captious, ungenerous, and radically incomplete. It would be as misleading to offer it as the last word on the Canadian experience as it would be to fall into the rhetoric of jingoism. At the risk of losing the impact of a strong negative conclusion, then, I will attempt to phrase an alternative, though the notorious Canadian diffidence makes it more difficult to praise than to criticize.

If my argument that Canada is marked by the dissociation of community from polis is sound, it still behooves me to consider what positive outcome this dissociation may have, especially since I have been saying that one's adjustment to any society is necessarily both adaptive and maladaptive. One of the useful things that the separation of the communitarian from the political functions does is make room for privacy. This may seem a minor benefit, but it is accompanied by some major advantages. It leaves one free to identify as strongly as one wishes with one's own group. At the same time, it does not preclude, at least for some, an occult, paradoxical patriotism.

In my own case, because it allowed me to identify more fully with my own community than with Canada at large, it permitted me to develop a style of writing that is marked by personal and communitarian values: a style that emphasizes the subjective and the individual; that always subordinates the impersonal, the objective, and the political to intimacy and emotion. It may also account for, if not necessarily justify, my feeling authorized to deal with intellectual problems in general, and even to write a book about Canada, in what may seem to some an inappropriately autobiographical vein. But for a Canadian critic, autobiography and abstract thought need not be in conflict: in the absence of the polis from the center of attention, the parochial and the universal can be at one.[11]

Notes

■

PREFACE

1. On the importance of the personal in literary criticism see my Introduction to the symposium on Particularism published in *Criticism* xxxii (Summer, 1990), 275–293, p. 288.

2. Sherry Simon, Pierre L'Hérault, Robert Schwartzwald, Alexis Nouss, *Fictions de l'identitaire au Québec* (Montréal: XYZ, 1991), p. 46.

INTRODUCTION

1. In a recent book John Naisbitt argues plausibly that the breakdown of the nation state is a simple consequence of new communications technologies. See *Global Paradox: The Bigger the World Economy, the More Powerful its Smallest Players* (New York: William Morrow, 1994), chapter I. An excellent review of multiculturalism in relation to the nation state is Joane Nagel's "The Ethnic Revolution: Emergence of Ethnic Nationalism," in Leo Driedger, *Ethnic Canada* (Toronto: Copp, Clark, Pitman, 1987), pp. 28–43. For an opinion at variance with my own see James Fallows,"What Can Save the Economy," *New York Review of Books* 39, no. 8 (April 23, 1992), 12–17, especially p. 14, as well as Robert Heilbroner, "Rough Roads to Capitalism," *New York Times*, Sept. 15, 1991, section 4, p. 17, and Paul Kennedy, in "Preparing for the 21st Century," *New York Review of Books*, 11, no. 4 (February 11, 1993), 32–44; but my position is reinforced by Catherine Arnst's article in the *Bangkok Post* for Nov. 27, 1991, "Western Computer Firms Crowd Soviet Market" (Post Database Section, p. 4). I quote: "Soviet regional manager for

the California computer chip maker Intel Corp Dimitri Rotow said the breakdown in government was not necessarily bad for foreign businesses, because it could mean less regulation and bureaucracy: 'The best thing the government could do from our point of view is get out of the way,' he said." And in "In Russia, it's Business as Usual," in *The New York Times*, March 29, 1993, D1, Kenneth N. Gilpin quotes an Otis Elevator executive on the irrelevance of central government for business in Russia: "Many companies have made their deals with regional authorities, so what happens in Moscow has little effect on them."

2. I have heard the head of Bechtel corporation quoted as saying that there are no countries, only companies. The Montreal *Gazette* for January 4, 1992, p. D 2, reports that 47 of the 100 largest economies on earth are corporations (up from 39 in 1980). The other 53 are political entities (countries). See also John Tomlinson, *Cultural Imperialsism: A Critical Introduction* (London: Pinter, 1991), p. 176.

3. *Social Problems* XXX no. 2 (December, 1982), 127–143. Some doubt is cast on this model, however, by Olzak's own work on Quebec. See her "Ethnic Mobilization in Quebec," *Ethnic and Racial Studies* 5 no. 3 (July, 1982), 253–275. For more doubts about the adequacy of the resource competition model see Donald L. Horowitz, *Ethnic Groups in Conflict* (Berkeley, Los Angeles, London: University of California Press, 1985), p. 104, and Crawford Young, "The Dialectics of Cultural Pluralism: Concept and Reality," in Crawford Young, ed., *The Rising Tide of Cultural Pluralism: The Nation-State at Bay* (Madison: University of Wisconsin Press, 1993), pp. 3–35, especially pp. 22–23. The ethnic resource competition model, especially as it applies to Canada, is dealt with again in Sarah Bélanger and Maurice Pinard, "Ethnic Movements and the Competition Model: Some Missing Links," *American Sociological Review* 56, no. 4 (August, 1991), 446–457.

The shift from state-as-empire to state as nation (see note 7, below) also weakens the position of minorities, exposing them to greater persecution and producing greater ethnic conflict. See Michael Banton's review of Hurst Hannum's *Autonomy, Sovereignty, and Self-Determination: The Accommodation of Conflicting Rights* (Philadelphia: University of Pennsylvania Press, 1990), in *Ethnic and Racial Studies* 14 no. 1, January, 1991, 112–114, especially p. 113. Seen from this perspective, the change in status from subject-of-empire to citizen-of-nation-state—i.e., the development of democracy—would be at best a mixed blessing for some segments of society. This issue becomes a major topic in Étienne Balibar's *Les Frontières de la démocratie* (Paris: Éditions de la découverte, 1992).

4. Craig Lambert, "Toward a Borderless World," *Harvard Magazine* (March-April 1991), 53–56, p. 54.

5. Ibid., p. 55. Ishmael Reed's "On the Fourth of July in Sitka, 1982" provides a wry comment on the concept of local management.

6. Joane Nagel (see note 1, above) is studying the influence of corporations on native American tribal groupings; her collaborator, Susan Olzak of Cornell, is interested in the relations between business and ethnicity in South Africa. One source of information on the interactions of business with native cultures is the journal *Cultural Survival*.

B. R. Roy Burman , in a review of a book on secessionist movements, goes so far as to ask whether the multiplicity of such movements does not begin to call into question, not only the viability of nationhood as a concept (cf. note 7, below), but of the state itself as an institution. See *Ethnic and Racial Studies* 14, no. 4 (October, 1991), 577–579, especially p. 579.

7. See Earl E. Fitz, *Rediscovering the New World: Inter-American Literature in a Comparative Context* (Iowa City: University of Iowa Press, 1991). Cf. Wlad Godzich's 1990 ADE address at the University of British Columbia, entitled "Multinational English Stateless Literature." On language-based rather than nation-based literatures see also Kenneth R. Lawrence, *Decolonizing Tradition: New Views of Twentieth-Century "British" Literary Canons* (Urbana and Chicago: University of Illinois Press, 1992), p. 15.

The opinion that the nation state, as successor to empire, is merely an artifact of nineteenth-century industrialism, is argued forcefully by historians such as Anderson, Gellner, Lloyd, and Wallerstein. This critique of nationalism, however, often leads to an analogous deconstruction of ethnicity (Eric Hobsbawm, Werner Sollors), leaving one wondering where the process will end. Such arguments can also be extended to the "national" literatures. I myself find more reasonable the common-sense view of Simon During, who insists that nationalism is no recent invention, but acknowledges that its meaning has changed profoundly over the centuries. (Cf. the concept of "Nature.") See "Literature—Nationalism's Other? The Case for Revision," pp. 138–153 in Homi K. Bhabha, ed., *Nation and Narration* (London and New York: Routledge, 1990).

8. In *All the Polarities: Comparative Studies in Contemporary Canadian Novels in French and English* (Toronto: ECW Press, 1986), especially in chapter eight, Philip Stratford has sketched a few of the contrasts that I will be talking about: I hope to deal with them in greater depth and detail.

9. Edited by Linda Hutcheon and Marion Richmond (Toronto: Oxford University Press, 1990). The summer, 1992 edition of *October* (no. 61) is entirely devoted to the question of political identity.

10. In "The Discourse of the Other: Canadian Literature and the Question of Ethnicity," *Massachusetts Review* 31 (Spring-Summer 1990), 153–184, p. 155. The problem of identity in French Canada is taken up in greater detail by Sherry Simon in *Fictions de l'identitaire au Québec* (Montréal: XYZ, 1991).

11. For a bibliography on multicultural studies in Canadian literature see William H. New, "Studies of English Canadian Literature," in *International Journal of Canadian Studies* 1–2, Spring–Fall 1990, 97–114 especially pp. 101–105. Some readers may wish to compare my analysis of differences in attitude towards society and the individual in Anglophone, Francophone, and Jewish Canadian literature with that of Roseanna Lewis Dufault in the final chapter of her *Metaphors of Identity: The Treatment of Childhood in Selected Québécois Novels* (Rutherford, Madison, and Teaneck: Fairleigh Dickinson University Press; London and Toronto: Associated University Presses, 1991).

CHAPTER 1

1. See John Colombo, "The Critical Period Concept," *Psychological Bulletin* XIC (March, 1982) 260–275. I would like to thank Professors Richard Abrams, Ann Colley, and Albert Cook, as well as Rachel Massey, for their helpful suggestions.

2. Madison: University of Wisconsin Press, 1984. It will be evident that I am working with a much more "minor" conception of "minor literature" than Gilles Deleuze and Félix Guattari in their important work, *Kafka: Pour une littérature*

mineure (Paris: Minuit, 1975). Still, they insist, almost as if they had Roberts in mind, that even an author writing in a major literary language must find "his own wilderness" (p. 33); in Kafka's case too, a "wilderness" largely peopled with animals. Actually, Renza could almost as well have used Roberts's own "Heron in the Reeds" as his example: its theme runs parallel to Sarah Orne Jewett's.

A recent work on marginality and "minor" literature in a Canadian context is Sylvia Soederlind's *Margin/Alias: Language and Colonization in Canadian and Québécois Fiction* (Toronto: University of Toronto Press, 1991).

3. Minneapolis: University of Minnesota Press, 1983.

In "A Penny Plain and Twopence Coloured" Robert Louis Stevenson testifies to the enduring influence of his childhood reading. See *Memories and Portraits* (New York: Charles Scribner's Sons, 1897), pp. 225–226. Further evidence of that influence can be found in Stevenson's own illustrated magazine, composed when he was sixteen, and now in the Beinecke Library at Yale.

4. Professor Charles Garton suggests the rhetorical term "hypallage" for this trope.

5. See p. 28 in Eleanor Perényi, "The Good Witch of the West," *New York Review of Books* 32.12 (July 18, 1985): 27–30. By the way, foxes are still being exported to the South for hunting. See Constance J. Poten, "America's Illegal Wildlife Trade: A Shameful Harvest," *National Geographic* 180 no. 3 (September, 1991), 106–132: pp. 108–109 concern the trade in foxes.

6. A classic sample of the stylistic matrix in which Roberts still worked was given on Canadian Broadcasting Corporation during a program on AIDS, on Sept. 22, 1985. A nineteenth-century historian of the cholera outbreak in the 1830s described the upper classes' callousness towards the sufferings of the poor during the early stages of that epidemic. Only when the wealthy realized that the living conditions of the lower classes were contributing to the spread of the epidemic in their own ranks did they respond, the scourge finally "wringing from fear what pity would not grant." This is a style that derives in turn, of course, from much earlier sources, some of them eminently respectable: "poscia, più che il dolor, potè il digiuno" (then starvation was stronger than sorrow). Dante, *Inferno* 33, 1. 75.

7. Bloomington: Indiana University Press, 1970.

8. See, for instance, Alec Lucas's introduction to Roberts's *The Last Barrier* (Toronto: McClelland and Stewart, 1958,) p. vii. Actually, the bees seem more consistent with the well-settled agricultural environment of Sackville, New Brunswick, (in which Roberts grew up) than do some of his wilder nature images, though he was, unquestionably, deeply devoted to the New Brunswick wilderness and chose to spend long periods in it during his later life.

9. *Selected Poetry and Critical Prose* (Toronto: University of Toronto Press, 1974), pp. 276–281. "the poetry of earth, or, in other words, the quality which makes for poetry in external nature . . . may work with equal effect through austerity or reticence or limitation or change. It may use the most common scenes, the most familiar facts and forms, as the vehicle of its most penetrating and most illuminating message" (p. 276).

10. Their enterprise has not grown any more practicable over the past two generations, if one is to judge by D. W. Harding's *Words into Rhythm* (Cambridge: Cambridge University Press, 1976) as compared with Morris W. Croll's *Style, Rhetoric, and Rhythm* (Princeton: Princeton University Press, 1966). See also Winifred Crombie, *Free Verse and Prose Style* (London: Croom Helm, 1987).

The name "Massey" had been bestowed on my father by an immigration officer who had difficulty in transliterating the original, a Hebrew acronym.

11. For passages in my text illustrating these features, see, respectively, p. 25, par.1 and, in the next paragraph: "At some particularly impressionable point. . ."

12. Cf.above, p. 39, par.1: the syntax of my first two sentences.

13. Cf. above, p. 31, the sentence beginning "As winter grows harsh . . . ."

14. Comte de Gobineau, Joseph Arthur, *Nouvelles II: Nouvelles asiatiques* (Paris: Pauvert, 1960), p. 337. It must be admitted, though, that, whatever the case for Gobineau's, Roberts's biography does not bear the stamp of moral authority. See John C. Adams, *Sir Charles God Damn* (Toronto: University of Toronto Press, 1986).

15. *Poetics Today* 5 (1984): 689–700.

16. Cf. Margaret Avison's "The presence here is single, worse than soul" ("Identity"). See chapter III, on literature and the monad, of my *Find You the Virtue* (Fairfax, Virginia: George Mason University Press, 1987). The title of Arnold Weinstein's *The Fiction of Relationship* (Princeton: Princeton University Press, 1988) suggests that the book should be relevant for this topic, but I have not found it very helpful.

CHAPTER 2

1. Two articles in English about Ida Maza are May Cutler, "Cutler's Last Stand," *MacLean's*, (December, 1974), 66–72 and Miriam Waddington, "Mrs. Maza's Salon," *Canadian Literature* no. 120 (Spring, 1989), 83–90. A less favorable semi-fictional account of the salon is Bella Kalter's "The Two Suitcases," which appeared in *The Atlantic* 1960/61 *Contests for College Students*, pp. 40–45.

For some background on the Jewish artists of Ida Maza's circle in Montreal see Esther Trépanier, *Peintres juifs et modernité/Jewish Painters and Modernity* (Montreal: Saidye Bronfman Centre, 1987).

2. Anthony Storr's *Solitude: A Return to the Self* (New York: Free Press, 1988) is concerned with some of these issues; unfortunately, I have not found the book very useful.

3. See Thomas G. Barnes, " 'Canada, True North': a 'Here There' or a Boreal Myth?" *American Review of Canadian Studies* XIX (Winter, 1989), 369–379.

Carolyn Masel remarks that Canadian authors are preoccupied with place— whether aboriginal, settlers', or immigrant place. See p. 162 in "Late Landings: Reflections on Belatedness in Australian and Canadian Literature," pp. 161–189, in Jonathan White, ed., *Recasting the World: Writing after Colonialism* (Baltimore and London: Johns Hopkins Press, 1993).

4. A similar point was made long ago by Mme. de Staël in *De l'Allemagne*. See also pp. 111–112 below, in my chapter on Quebec.

5. But cf. Safder Alladina and Viv Edwards, eds., *Multilingualism in the British Isles 2* (London and New York: Longman, 1991), p. ix: "The majority is not a community: community language refers to minority and migrant languages."

Some would argue that Stephen Leacock's stories about the town of "Mariposa," or Morley Callaghan's early work, are exceptions to my generalization about Canadian Anglophone literature. Of course, communitarian values cannot be used as a normative criterion in literature, especially since they often shade off into sentimentality or propaganda. One does not ask oneself whether the best stories of, say, Patrick Lane express communitarian values; conversely, Leacock's stories are not redeemed from mediocrity by their explicit communitarianism. For a useful recent selection of Canadian stories see David Lampe, ed., *Myths & Voices: Contemporary Canadian Fiction* (Fredonia, New York: White Pine Press, 1993).

6. In "Introduction," pp. 7–22, to J.M. Bumsted, ed., *Canadian Literature Supplement* no.1 (May, 1987), p. 17. *A/Part: Papers from the 1984 Ottawa Conference on Language, Culture, and Identity in Canada. La langue, la culture et l'identité littéraire au Canada.*

7. Ibid., p. 19.

8. A sucker is a coarse fish, something like a carp.

9. *Apprenticeship of Duddy Kravitz* (Markham, Ontario: Penguin, 1986), p. 310.

10. ". . . it has become apparent that the process of identity formation in feminist literature is crucially indebted to a concept of community." Rita Felski, *Beyond Feminist Aesthetics* (Cambridge: Harvard University Press, 1989), p. 155. See also Susan Wells, *The Dialectics of Representation* (Baltimore and London: Johns Hopkins University Press, 1985), p. 164, on feminist theory as uniting the private and the communal domains, with the slogan "The Private is the public." Felski repeats this argument (pp. 72,75).

In their essay on Naples, Walter Benjamin and Asja Lacis also describe conditions in which the individual life becomes the arena for the social: "What distinguishes Naples from all other major cities is what it has in common with the Hottentot-Kraal: every private attitude and activity has streams of communal life flowing through it. Existence, the most private affair for the northern European, is here, as in the Hottentot-Kraal, a matter for the collectivity" (Was Neapel von allen Grossstädten unterscheidet, das hat es mit dem Hottentottenkraal gemein: jede private Haltung und Verrichtung wird durchflutet von Strömen des Gemeinschaftslebens. Existieren, für den Nordeuropäer die privateste Angelegenheit, ist hier wie im Hottentottenkraal Kollektivsache). Walter Benjamin, *Gesammelte Schriften* (Frankfurt-am-Main: Suhrkamp, 1972—), 7 vols., vol. iv, part 1, p. 314. I am grateful to Ann Colley for pointing out this passage to me.

11. The argument that the creative moment, the moment in which the individual goes beyond the obvious and definable needs of the community, is the only moment when a true contribution to community is made, does not seem to have occurred to this collectivity: an interest in what one might call a transcendental concept of community, for which the individual's creative experience is crucial, awaits philosophers such as Bataille, Nancy, Bucher. See below, chapter 4.

12. "l'aspect d'un système discontinu; or on s'imagine que, grâce à la dimension temporelle, l'histoire nous restitue, non des états séparés, mais le passage d'un état à un autre sous une forme continue. . . . L'histoire ne se contenterait pas de . . . nous faire pénétrer par fulgurations intermittentes des intériorités qui seraient telles chacune pour son compte, tout en demeurant extérieures les unes aux autres: elle nous ferait rejoindre, en dehors de nous, l'être même du changement." *La Pensée sauvage* (Paris: Plon, 1962), p. 339.

13. The quotations from Lévi-Strauss in this paragraph run as follows in *La Pensée sauvage*: "Même une histoire qui se dit universelle n'est encore qu'une juxtaposition de quelques histoires locales, au sein desquelles (et entre lesquelles) les trous sont bien plus nombreux que les pleins" (p. 340); "L'histoire est un ensemble discontinu formé de domaines d'histoire" (p. 344); "les lacunes internes de chaque classe ne peuvent être comblées par le recours à d'autres classes" (p. 345).

14. "pour que la *praxis* puisse se vivre comme pensée" *La Pensée sauvage* (p. 349); "un système de concepts englués dans des images" (p. 349).

15. The quotes from *La Pensée sauvage* are: "Mais qu'on ne nous fasse pas dire que l'homme peut ou doit se dégager de cette intériorité . . . la sagesse consiste pour lui à se regarder la vivre, tout en sachant (mais dans un autre registre) que ce qu'il vit si complètement et intensément est un mythe"(p. 338); "Tout sens est justiciable d'un moindre sens, qui lui donne son plus haut sens" (p. 338).

16. Cf. Oscar Wilde: "A truth ceases to be true when more than one person believes in it." ("Phrases and Philosophies for the Use of the Young.") See below for the background of this idea in Newman.

17. *Johann Gottlieb Fichte's* [sic] *sämmtliche Werke* (Berlin: Veit und Comp., 1845; Nachdruck, Berlin: Walter de Gruyter und Comp. 1945), II, 245, in *Die Bestimmung des Menschen* pp. 165–319: "*Bilder* sind; sie sind das Einzige, was da ist, und sie wissen von sich, nach Weise der Bilder:—Bilder, die vorüberschweben, ohne dass etwas sey, dem sie vorüberschweben; die durch Bilder von den Bildern zusammenhängen, Bilder. . . ."

18. It was rumored (perhaps because typhus was the most virulent disease that the immigrant community had known in Europe) that typhus was what he had died of. It could have been for a child like him that Y.-Y. Segal wrote, "Death mixed its colors in your cool young blood" (In dayn kil yung blut/Hot der toyt zayne farbn gemisht).

19. Henceforth referred to as *VMK*. It will be evident that I have tried to follow Ida Maza's principles of translation in my own effort to render her poems in English. Whether I have also succeeded in preserving to any degree the communitarian quality that subtends that musical imperative is another matter.

20. Stéphane Mallarmé, *Vers et prose* (Paris: Garnier-Flammarion, 1977), p. 151.

Through the years various composers have set individual lyrics of Ida Maza's to music, but I do not have a record of these works, though I know the melody of one (the cradle song, "Zest di Levone"). There is at present a project in Toronto to set a substantial number of the poems to music.

21. Cf. Robert Frost to Robert Bridges, in *Selected Letters of Robert Frost* (N.Y., etc.: Holt, Rinehart, & Winston, 1964), p. 107: "The living part of a poem is the intonation entangled in the syntax idiom and meaning of a sentence."

For a communitarian poet such as Ida Maza the musical principle, " 'the kinetic melody' of writing" (A.R. Luria), is of particular importance. Oliver Sacks argues, plausibly, that music and community are virtually interchangeable concepts. See *Awakenings* (New York: E. P. Dutton, 1983), especially p. 248, but also p. 247 (where the quotation from Luria occurs), and pp. 249–50, 294–96, and 317.

22. Ferenc Feher and Agnes Heller, "The Necessity and Irreformability of Aesthetics," pp. 1–22 in Agnes Heller and Ferenc Feher, eds., *Reconstructing Aesthetics* (Oxford: Basil Blackwell, 1986), p. 18. About the difference between art that represents the *sensus communis* and post-communitarian art, Feher and Heller suggest that "There are no communities in bourgeois society and . . . the artist can meet the public only in the market place (i.e., only indirectly)" (p. 17).

Deleuze and Guattari, of course, make much of the communal nature of minor literature *(Kafka: Pour une litterature mineure)*, pp. 31–33), and, incidentally, of Kafka's involvement with Yiddish (pp. 46–47). More recently, Cary Nelson, in *Repression and Recovery* (Madison: University of Wisconsin Press, 1989), has emphasized the collective values of minor literature, as Louis Renza had done in "A White Heron," p. 17.

In "The Phenomenal Nonphenomenal: Private Space in *Film Noir*," Joan Copjec argues that the very concept of community has been rendered untenable by the demand that private pleasure be pursued as the essential civic duty (Typescript of lecture given at SUNY Buffalo, Spring 1993, pp. 26–27).

23. On Yeats's failure to create a genuinely popular poetry see Linda Dowling, *Language and Decadence in the Victorian Fin de Siècle* (Princeton: Princeton University Press, 1986), pp. 258–262, 280 ff., and, on the general question of popular and vernacular poetry, Dennis Cooley, *The Vernacular Muse: The Eye and Ear in Contemporary Poetry* (Winnipeg: Turnstone Press, 1987). See also Margery Sabin, *The Dialect of the Tribe: Speech and Community in Modern Fiction* (New York and Oxford: Oxford University Press, 1987), especially chapters one and two.

24. On this subject cf. Leonard W. Dean's book on Blake, *Conversing in Paradise* (Columbia and London: University of Missouri Press, 1983), pp. 1–12. Dean is concerned with the relation of individuals to mankind as a whole rather than to their specific community. Though there is some similarity of language, he and I are not really writing about quite the same issue.

25. On the derivative nature of individualism see Lucien Goldmann, *Structures mentales et création culturelle* (Paris: Anthropos, 1970), especially the first essay, "La Philosophie des lumières," pp. 113–114, 117–119 and *passim*, as well as Edmond Cros, *Théorie et pratique sociocritiques* (Montpellier: C.E.R.S., Université Paul Valéry, 1983), p. 9.

26. *Le Comique des idées* (Paris Gallimard, 1977), pp. 142, 144, 149.

27. On ways in which society can contribute to formulating the role of the suicide see Ian Hacking's "Making Up People," in Thomas C. Heller, Morton Sosna, and David E. Wellbery, eds., *Reconstructing Individualism; Autonomy, Individuality, and the Self in Western Thought* (Stanford: Stanford University Press, 1988), pp. 222–236, especially p. 235.

28. For an excellent treatment of this topic see Albert Cook, " 'Fiction' and History in *Samuel* and *Kings*," *Journal for the Study of the Old Testament* 36 (1986), 27–48, especially pp. 40 and 45.

CHAPTER 3

1. The most convincing description of this feeling that I know is the one quoted (with a few minor errors and omissions) by Charles Rosen in "Now, Voyager," from Ramond de Carbonnières. ("Now, Voyager," *New York Review of Books* 33, no. 17 [November 6, 1986], 55–60, pp. 58–59.) For the original see [Ramond de Carbonnières, Louis F.], *Observations faites dans les Pyrénées* (Paris: Belin, 1789), pp. 88–89. Actually, the end of the passage (pp. 89–90) seems to cast some doubt on Rosen's argument that science and reverie should not be thought of as mutually exclusive in the eighteenth century.

2. Hubert Aquin, *Prochain épisode* (Montréal: Pierre Tisseyre, 1965), pp. 78–79. (My translation).

3. Cf. "Un exilé qui dit 'Où?' " in Julia Kristeva, *Pouvoirs de l'horreur: essai sur l'abjection* (Paris: Seuil, 1980), pp. 15–16.

4. For some exceptions see my next paragraph. An extensive review of Francophone authors whose writing does not fit readily into the categories I have

been using may be found in the definitive work by Caroline Bayard, *The New Poetics in Canada and Quebec: from Concretism to Post-Modernism* (Toronto, Buffalo, London: University of Toronto Press, 1989).

5. Perhaps this is my equivalent to what some have called the sense of incompleteness in Canadian thought. See, for instance, Ian Angus, "Crossing the Border," *Massachusetts Review* 31 nos. 1 and 2 (Spring–Summer 1990), 32–47, p. 38. The quality I have in mind is rather like that described by Edmund Husserl in "The Origin of Geometry," where there are no precedents, and each problem has to be dealt with as if for the first time.

6. See, for instance, Gregor von Rezzori's *Memoirs of an Anti-Semite* (New York: Viking, 1981; originally *Memoiren eines Antisemiten*; München: Steinhausen, 1979).

7. On stereotyping and prejudice in a Canadian context see Donald M. Taylor and Richard N. Lalonde, "Ethnic Stereotypes: A Psychological Analysis," in Leo Driedger, *op.cit.*, pp. 347–373. On the varieties of prejudice see Elisabeth Young-Bruehl, "Discriminations: Kinds and Types of Prejudice," *Transition* 60 (1993), 53–69.

8. Gordon W. Allport, *The Nature of Prejudice* (Reading, Massachusetts, etc.: Addison-Wesley, 1954), p. 191. For an attempt at finding a value-free approach to classifying group characteristics see Kurt Lewin, *Resolving Social Conflicts: Selected Papers on Group Dynamics* (New York: Harper, 1948), pp. 3–33.

9. Michael Brown's *Jew or Juif? Jews, French Canadians, and Anglo-Canadians 1759–1914* (Philadelphia: Jewish Publication Society, 1987) attempts to account for the tendency of Quebec Jews to identify with Anglo-Canadians.

There is interesting material on Jews in a French-Canadian context in Sherry Simon, Pierre L'Hérault, Robert Schwartzwald, Alexis Nouss, *Fictions de l'identitaire au Québec* (Montréal: XYZ, 1991), pp. 34, 37, 64–69, as well as in Sherry Simon, "A. M. Klein: une esthétique de l'hybride," *Études françaises* 28, 2/3 (1992–1993), 93–104. On the defensive nature of Jewish communitarianism see Yaacov Glickman, "Anti-Semitism and Jewish Social Cohesion in Canada," pp. 45–63 in Ormond McKague, *Racism in Canada* (Saskatoon: Fifth House Publishers, 1991), as well as the various works of Raymond Breton on patterns of Canadian ethnicity.

10. "Racisms," in David Theo Goldberg, ed., *Anatomy of Racism* (Minneapolis: University of Minnesota Press, 1990), pp. 3–17; p. 6. For a Lacanian view of anti-Semitism see Slavoj Žižek, *The Sublime Object of Ideology* (London and New York: Verso, 1989), pp. 47–49.

11. Even this cautious generalization is not quite true either. There is also the phenomenon of prejudice against and within one's own group to be considered. It is familiar in the form of Jewish self-hatred, but is also widespread, as readers of Russian literature from Biely to Tolstoya will recognize.

12. For a similar argument see William Hazlitt, *Selected Writings* (Harmondsworth, Middlesex: Penguin Books, 1982), p. 465. The selection is entitled "Race and Class" and is taken from the article "Capital Punishment" in the *Edinburgh Review* (July 1821).

13. See Christopher Ricks, *T.S. Eliot and Prejudice* (London and Boston: Faber and Faber, 1988), p. 273. On the modern tendency to identify a community with a language (see above), Benedict Anderson's *Imagined Communities* (London: Verso, 1983), chapter 5, is illuminating.

14. Von Rezzori, p. 34, says, concerning his childhood friend Wolf Goldmann: "He used his mixture of bad German with Yiddish and Polish—in a word, he

'yiddled'—because this linguistic carelessness, rich in astute, colorful, and witty expressions, was more in keeping with his character, his swift, supple mind."

On the history of Canadian French see the collection edited by Noël Corbett, *Langue et identité; Les français et les francophones d'Amérique du Nord* (Québec: Les Presses de l'université Laval, 1990). Immigrants to Canada from northern France probably produced a more homogeneous French than France itself had until recently. The dialect of the Montreal region is called "Joual," for the vernacular pronunciation of "cheval;" it is marked by such features as the short "i" ("vite" is pronounced "vitt") and the long "a" ("bas" is pronounced "boh"); "dix" is pronounced "dziss." A vaguely international French was taught in the Montreal schools that I attended, but the debate over "standard" French continues to rage, especially among Francophones, in Quebec today.

15. On the whole question of "colonized" versus "official" languages see Ngugi wa Thiong'o, *Decolonising the Mind: The Politics of Language in African Literature* (London, etc.: James Currey, etc., 1986). I am grateful to Sumitra Mukerji for having drawn my attention to this work.

16. Michel Tremblay, *Des nouvelles d'Édouard* (Ottawa: Leméac, 1984), p. 300.

17. Cf. Yvette Longpré's list of guests at the birthday party for her sister-in-law in Tremblay's *Les belles soeurs*. For some discussion of this feature of Quebec life see Richard Handler, *Nationalism and the Politics of Culture in Quebec* (Madison: University of Wisconsin Press, 1988). On the historical tendency of French Canadians to think of themselves in collectivist terms, and for Anglo-Canadians to think of themselves in individualist terms, see Sheila McLeod and Dominique Clift, *The English Fact in Quebec* (Montreal: McGill-Queens University Press, 1980), pp. 35–42, 194–195, and passim. Philip Stratford points to the sense of solidarity with the community as well as with the reader that characterizes French-Canadian but not English-Canadian novels: see *All the Polarities: Comparative Studies in Contemporary Canadian Novels in French and English* (Toronto: ECW Press, 1986, pp. 101–102.) Jean-C. Falardeau argues that English-Canadian literature expresses a tension between man and his milieu, whereas the French-Canadian novel focuses on inner tension between man and himself. See *Roots and Values in Canadian Lives* (Toronto: University of Toronto Press, 1981), pp. 13–17.

18. See Lise Bissonnette, "Indications of Anti-Semitism." *The Globe and Mail*, Saturday, May 27, 1989, section D, p. 2, and the figures on Quebec anti-Semitism given by Irving Abella, as well as, more recently, by Esther Delisle. See also Robert J. Brym and Rhonda Lenton, "The Distribution of Anti-Semitism in Canada in 1984," in Robert J. Brym, William Shaffir, Morton Weinfeld, eds., *The Jews in Canada* (Toronto: Oxford, 1993), pp. 112–119. In "Le Québec ne doit pas se donner une constitution: il en a déjà une . . . .," *Philosophiques* 19 no. 2 (Autumn, 1992), 191–198, p. 193, Gary Caldwell asserts that there is no documented case of physical injury from anti-Semitic violence in Quebec. I was frequently stoned by the village boys when I went to pick up mail in Mont-Rolland; the fact that I managed to escape serious injury does not seem a sufficient reason to feel gratitude towards the society that indoctrinated my assailants.

19. Such associations have made me somewhat uncomfortable with remarks made by Tremblay about Jewish storekeepers at the beginning of *La Grosse femme*, as well as with the references to the "petites juives" in *La Duchesse de Langeais* (*Hosanna suivi de la Duchesse de Langeais* [Ottawa: Leméac, 1973.] First acted in 1969. The reference is on p. 87). By the time *Des nouvelles d'Édouard* was published anything even remotely redolent of anti-Semitism had disappeared or been expunged.

CHAPTER 4

1. Cf. the unimaginable reality of the father's heart being pierced in Rainer Maria Rilke's *Notebooks of Malte Laurids Brigge* (New York: Capricorn, 1952), p. 139. Nothing can be imagined beforehand, Rilke says: not the smallest thing. (For the German, see *Werke in drei Bänden* [Frankfurt am Main: Insel, 1966], III, pp. 254–255).

2. *Hegel's Recollection: A Study of Images in the Phenomenology of Spirit* (Albany: State University of New York Press, 1985), pp. 12–13.

3. Barbara Maria Stafford, *Body Criticism: Imaging the Unseen in Enlightenment Art and Medicine* (Cambridge, Massachusetts and London: MIT Press, 1991).

4. Cambridge, Massachusetts and London: MIT Press, 1992; p. 1.

5. Cf. Kafka's machine in "In the Penal Colony," which has no use for the officer because he is just a "reader," someone looking for a short cut, who thinks he can know directly, before experiencing through the body.

6. One thinks of the scene at the beginning of Diderot's *Le Neveu de Rameau*, where the usually irrepressible Rameau is quelled by the assembly at the dinner party, who shout his name in chorus. Rameau is another marginalized character who fills out all space.

7. A.T. Nuyen, in "The Fragility of the Self: from Bundle Theory to Deconstruction," *Journal of Speculative Philosophy* VI, no. 2 (1992), 111–122, pp. 112–13, reads Aristotle's theory of self in this sense. (I am grateful to Jerry Drost of Lockwood Library for bringing this excellent review of identity theory to my attention.) Cf. also the quotations from Emmanuel Levinas in Raoul Mortley, *French Philosophers in Conversation* (London and New York: Routledge, 1991), p. 16, as well as Francis Jacques, *Difference and Subjectivity: Dialogue and Personal Identity* (New Haven: Yale University Press, 1991), p. xii.

8. For references to the individual as social cell in Marx, Haeckel, and Norton Wise see p. 385 in Russell Ferguson, Martha Gever, Trinh T. Minh-ha, Cornel West, eds., *Out There: Marginalization and Contemporary Cultures* (New York, Cambridge, Massachusetts, and London: New Museum of Contemporary Art and MIT Press, 1990).

9. *La Grosse femme* (Montréal: Bibliothèque québécoise, 1990), p. 27.

10. Of the performances of *Macbeth* that I have seen in recent years the most convincing was the one directed by Meg Pantera and performed in a Buffalo bomb shelter.

11. One might say that, in this play, not only to represent, but even to signify, is a fraud: the only truth is what signifies nothing.

On the proverbial unluckiness of *Macbeth* in the theater see Marjorie Garber, *Shakespeare's Ghost Writers: Literature as Uncanny Causality* (New York and London: Methuen, 1987). I am grateful to Professor Richard Abrams of the University of Southern Maine for the reference.

12. Cf. Terry Eagleton, Fredric Jameson, Edward W. Said, *Nationalism, Colonialism, and Literature* (Minneapolis: University of Minnesota Press, 1990): "All oppositional politics thus move under the sign of irony." In Eagleton, "Nationalism, Irony and Commitment, " pp. 23–39 (p. 26). Cf also Stephanie B. Hammer's idea, in *Satirizing the Satirist* (New York: Garland, 1991) that the critic of society invariably ends up satirizing himself or herself. Simon Critchley argues that "The just polity is one that can actively maintain its own interruption or ironization as

that which sustains it" (*The Ethics of Deconstruction: Derrida and Levinas*, Oxford, United Kingdom; Cambridge, U.S.A.: Blackwell, 1992), p. 236. See also Georges Bataille, *L'Expérience intérieure: revue et corrigée* (Paris: Gallimard, 1954), p.153. (Another edition of *L'Expérience intérieure*, with a different pagination, was published by Gallimard in the same year.)

13. Cf. James Taylor, "*Hamlet's* Debt to Sixteenth-Century Satire," *Forum for Modern Language Studies*, 22 no.4 (Oct. 1986), 374–384, which argues for a popular satiric tradition underlying *Hamlet*.

14. On self-division and theatricality in *Macbeth* see H.W. Fawkner, *Deconstructing Macbeth: the Hyperontological View* (Rutherford, N.J. etc.: Fairleigh Dickinson University Press, 1990), pp. 8, 96–101, 184, 197, 208–214. As I have occasion to mention below, Fawkner and I start from different presuppositions, although our observations often converge. (See below, note 16, note 35).

15. In II.3.126–127, Banquo looks forward to the moment "when we have our naked frailties hid / That suffer in exposure." We act because we fear; but we are exposed in the end anyway.

16. See, however, Thomas Van Laan, *Role-Playing in Shakespeare* (Toronto: University of Toronto Press, 1978), pp. 190–197. For commentary on theatricality in *Macbeth* see Michael Goldman, *Acting and Action in Shakespearean Tragedy* (Princeton: Princeton University Press, 1985); James Calderwood, *If It Were Done* (Amherst: University of Massachusetts Press, 1986); and, especially, H. W. Fawkner, *Deconstructing Macbeth: The Hyperontological View* (Rutherford, New Jersey, etc.: Fairleigh Dickinson University Press, 1990). Although Fawkner and I start from different presuppositions, our observations often converge. Fawkner's point that *Macbeth* refuses to posit an ontological ground serves the same function in his argument as my suggestion that the play is not actable does in mine.

17. On the question whether Shakespeare himself believed in witches see, for instance, Henry N. Paul, *The Royal Play of Macbeth* (New York: Octagon, 1971). Paul's work is reconsidered in several of the essays in John Russell Brown, ed., *Focus on Macbeth* (London, Boston-Henley: Routledge and Kegan Paul, 1982).

18. For a wonderful defense of the witches' first scene see Robin Grove, "Multiplying Villainies of Nature," pp. 113–139 in Brown, ed., *Focus on Macbeth*, especially pp. 115–120.

19. Cf. E.A.J. Honigmann, *Shakespeare: Seven Tragedies* (New York: Barnes and Noble, 1976), chapter 8: "*Macbeth*: the Murderer as Victim."

20. During the confrontation with the knights after the murder, Macbeth conducts himself with a temporary composure and cunning that seem out of character.

For a subtle discussion of "Shakespeare's Bombast" in general see the chapter by that title in Charles Frey, *Experiencing Shakespeare: Essays on Text, Classroom, and Performance* (Columbia: University of Missouri Press, 1988). I am grateful to Richard Abrams for the reference.

21. John Turner, in *Macbeth* (Buckingham and Philadelphia: Open University Press, 1992), pp. 107–123, makes a reasonable case for Malcolm's being more of a villain than Macbeth.

22. Cf. Van Laan, *Role-Playing in Shakespeare* (note 16, above).

23. Philippe Lacoue-Labarthe, in his work on the concept of the political, *La Fiction du politique* (Paris: Christian Bourgois, 1987), refers to the second part of our century as it reflects the first in terms that are curiously reminiscent of Macbeth's career: "entre cauchemar et parodie" ("between nightmare and parody,") p. 21.

24. In the first chapter of *Find You the Virtue* (Fairfax: George Mason University Press, 1987) I discuss some of the issues that arise in this section with respect to *Hamlet*, in the context of the word-image problem. *King Lear* is the Shakespeare play in which the incompatibility of knowledge and vision is most often pointed out. For an extension of this idea to historiography see Reinhart Koselleck, "Standortbindung und Zeitlichkeit," in Reinhart Koselleck, W.J. Mommsen, J. Rüsen, edd., *Objektivität und Parteilichkeit in der Geschichtswissenschaft* (München: Deutscher Taschenbuch Verlag, 1977), pp. 17–46.

25. "Dans la volonté de supprimer la douleur, nous sommes conduits à l'action, au lieu de nous borner à dramatiser." Georges Bataille, *L'Expérience intérieure: Édition revue et corrigée*, p. 27.

26. Macbeth often seems to be viewing a play in his own mind: "That suggestion / Whose horrid image doth unfix my hair / And make my seated heart knock at my ribs" (I.3.134–136). When he asks "What hands are here?" (II.2.59) we are not quite sure what the answer should be: they are his hands, but they are also hands that have been prepared for an audience to see. Even the famous candle at the end—"Out, out, brief candle!" (V.5.23)—is a stage prop.

27. For related ideas on dramatic fantasy preceding action, as well as on the disconnection between imagined prospect and actual subsequent event, see William Hazlitt's "Essay on the Principles of Human Action" in P. P. Howe, ed., *The Complete Works of William Hazlitt*, 21 vols. (London and Toronto: J.M. Dent & Sons; vol. I, 1930. Vol. 21 is 1934). Hazlitt sums up the position memorably if enigmatically with the pronouncement, "I am what I am in spite of the future." The quotation is on p. 48 of vol. I.

28. As in I.7.7., "We'd jump the life to come," there is no way to cross the unbridgeable gap, the unscalable wall, between thought and action.

29. Is he, after all, a closet Hamlet? Cf. Calderwood, *op.cit.*, pp. 16–21, and Fawkner, p. 38.

30. For related lines see IV.2.18–19 ("When we are traitors / And do not know ourselves") and IV.3.164–165 ("Alas! poor country; / Almost afraid to know itself").

31. On the conflict between theatricality and meaning in *Macbeth* cf. Fawkner, pp. 45, 88, 215–216.

32. It is not so much that Macbeth rises to the challenge of narrativity, as Jonathan Culler (*The Pursuit of Signs: Semiotics, Literature, Deconstruction* [Ithaca: Cornell University Press: 1981]) says of Oedipus (pp. 174–175), but rather that narrative is the only game in town; it is not only a temptation offered to Macbeth, but the only way for anyone to deal with the threat that life confronts one with, even if one is not offered such temptations. In a sense, in fact, the temptation makes things easier for Macbeth, since he does not have to concoct his own narrative, but can simply fall into one that is thrown in his way.

Yet it has been suggested that narrativity is an imperative only in modern Western cultures. See David Carr, *Time, Narrativity, and History* (Bloomington: Indiana University Press, 1986), pp. 177–185. For a recent text that reaffirms the centrality of narrative in the construction of the self see Owen Flanagan, *The Science of the Mind* (Cambridge, Massachusetts and London: MIT Press, 1992, second edition), pp. 352–361, "The Self as the Center of Narrative Gravity." Paul Ricoeur has also developed a concept of narrative identity in the middle chapters of *Soi-même comme un autre* (Paris: Seuil, 1990).

33. Charles Bernstein, ed., *The Politics of Poetic Form* (New York: Roof Books, 1990), pp. 235–244. On the political centrality of humor see also Renato Rosaldo,

"Politics, Patriarchs, and Laughter," in Abdul R. JanMohamed and David Lloyd, eds., *The Nature and Context of Minority Discourse* (New York and Oxford: Oxford University Press, 1990), pp. 124–145, as well as Deleuze and Guattari, *Kafka: Pour une littérature mineure* (Paris: Minuit, 1975), pp. 76–77.

34. Both Musset's *Lorenzaccio* and Büchner's *Danton's Death* (not to mention *Wozzeck*), also political plays, show elements of this attitude. On the tragicomedy of political self-sacrifice as a theme in more recent theater see Paul Hernadi, *Interpreting Events: Tragicomedies of History on the Modern Stage* (Ithaca: Cornell University Press, 1985).

35. Fawkner has seen the relevance of some of Bataille's categories for *Macbeth*; however, he uses almost exclusively Derrida's interpretation of Bataille's concept of laughter (pp. 177–178), which is distinct from Bataille's own, and also draws different conclusions from mine about the ways in which Bataille's "le rire" pertains to *Macbeth*.

36. Georges Bataille, *L'Expérience intérieure*, pp. 25–26.

37. On laughter as community in Bataille see *L'Expérience intérieure*, pp. 141, 151. I will not attempt to deal here with the broader aspects of Bataille's concept of community.

38. Like Turner (note 21, above) I find myself moving to the view that Malcolm, rather than Macbeth, is the villain in the play, the one who threatens the human compact most directly. (I find it significant, for instance, that it is he who thinks of the disguise of Birnham Wood.)

39. As I write this I begin to realize that there are similarities to Jonah's situation in what I am attempting to describe.

40. For Bataille this dissociation of the self appears as a by-product of the duty to be comic (see above, p. 149), which is an absolute or existential duty rather than a political one.

41. *New Literary History* XVI no. 2 (Winter, 1985), 251–273. See also "Plato's Masterplot: Idealization, Contradiction and the Transformation of Rhetorical Ethos," in Brian G. Caraher, ed., *Intimate Conflict: Contradiction in Literary and Philosophical Discourse* (Albany: State University of New York Press, 1992), pp. 39–74.

CHAPTER 5

1. It is interesting that Thomas McFarland, in his essay "Individual and Society in Shakespeare's *Coriolanus*," refers to community as such only once, and in passing. (See Peter Baker, Sarah Webster Goodwin, and Gary Handwerk, eds., *The Scope of Words: In Honor of Albert S. Cook* [New York, etc.: Peter Lang, 1991], pp. 111–134; the reference is on p. 133.) Coriolanus asserts his individuality vis-à-vis a public, rather than a community.

2. Suggestion by Steve Martinot at the IAPL conference, Montreal, May, 1991.

3. "Solidarity" and "significance" are the key communitarian values picked out by David B. Clark in "The Concept of Community: A Re-Examination," *Sociological Review* 21 no. 3 (August, 1973), 397–416.

4. Defining "community" is a difficult enterprise. The problem is dealt with in a serious spirit by Raymond Plant in "Community: Concept, Conception, and Ideology," *Politics and Society* 8 (1978), 79–107. I am grateful to Professor Monroe

Eagles of SUNY at Buffalo for the reference. In *The Moral Commonwealth: Social Theory and the Promise of Community* (Berkeley, Los Angeles, Oxford: University of California Press, 1992), pp. 357–386, Philip Selznick likewise attempts a definition of community.

It is noteworthy that the concept of community is attracting a great deal of attention at a time when the very idea of the social is under attack: whether by those who claim that it has been undermined by the simulacrum (Arthur Kroker and Charles Levin, "The Fetishism of the Sign," *Canadian Journal of Social and Political Theory*, vol. 15, nos. 1–2 and 3 [1991], 123–133, pp. 129–130), or by those who argue that it has been destroyed by the transformation of private pleasure into public duty (Joan Copjec, "Film Noir," typescript).

5. *L'Érotisme* (Paris: Minuit, 1957), p. 111.

6. *Le Coupable*, in *Oeuvres complètes* (Paris: Gallimard, 12 vols., 1970–1988), 5 (1973), 235–392; the reference is to pp. 262–263.

7. "Le Collège de sociologie," *Oeuvres complètes*, 2 (1970), pp. 364–374: "La déchirure du sacrifice ouvrant la fête est une déchirure libératrice. L'individu qui participe à la perte a l'obscure conscience que cette perte engendre la communauté qui le soutient . . . il est difficile de savoir dans quelle mesure la communauté n'est que l'occasion propice à la fête ou la fête et le sacrifice le témoignage de l'amour donné à la communauté" (p. 371). (The rupture of sacrifice that begins the festival is a liberating rupture. The individual who participates in the loss has a dim awareness that this loss brings into being the community that sustains him. . . . It is hard to know to what extent the community is just the useful occasion for the festival or the festival and the sacrifice are the expression of love towards the community). For Michel Maffesoli, it seems to be collective sexuality that founds society. See, for instance, the recent English edition of his best-known work, *The Shadow of Dionysus; A Contribution to the Sociology of the Orgy* (Albany: State University of New York Press, 1993).

8. Jean-Luc Nancy, *La Communauté désoeuvrée* (Paris: Christian Bourgois, 1986), p. 39. I am reminded of Jules Romains' *Mort de quelqu'un*, and even of Michel Tremblay in his "unanimist" moments (e.g., *Le Premier quartier de la lune* [Ottawa: Leméac, 1989], p. 147.) See also above, chapter 2, on the attempt of the Jewish community to experience a suicide collectively.

9. Nancy, op. cit., p. 43; here Nancy is quoting Bataille. It can be seen why some fear that in its practical application such a philosophy might reveal affinities with Fascism.

This conception of a community that reveals its reality only in crisis or in death should be contrasted with Royce's caveat that "the lives of communities cannot consist of miraculous crises. A community, like an individual self, must learn to keep the consciousness of its unity through the vicissitudes of an endlessly shifting and often dreary fortune." *The Philosophy of Josiah Royce* (New York: Thomas Y. Crowell, 1971, p. 379). For Royce and Mead consciousness itself is a communal condition.

10. Maurice Blanchot, *La Communauté inavouable* (Paris: Minuit, 1983), p. 24.

11. Typical is Pierre Clastres' *Society Against the State* (New York: Urizen Books, 1977), which tries to prove that "primitive" societies deliberately exerted themselves to prevent the formation of states. The French title is *La Société contre l'état* (Paris: Minuit, 1974).

12. Blanchot, pp. 55–56. Cf. George Konrád, *Antipolitics* (San Diego, etc.: Harcourt Brace Jovanovich, 1984). A problem for Westerners is that, although they

have (unlike, say, the Czechs) been allowed to be unpolitical when they choose to be, that option in itself has not reduced the damage brought on by the actions of their governments (as in the case of the massacre of the Bosnian Muslims).

Bernard-Henri Lévy has tried to find a way out of the dilemmas produced by the rejection of activism in his *Éloge des intellectuels* (Paris: Bernard Grasset, 1987).

13. But see the chapter on "Penser le négatif" in François Châtelet, Gilles Lapouge and O.R. d'Allounes, *La Révolution sans modèle* (Paris, etc.: Mouton, 1975), pp. 172–174. I am grateful to France Giroux for the reference to this prescient work.

14. These arguments are summarized in Geoffrey Bennington, *Lyotard* (Manchester: Manchester University Press, 1988), p. 14, pp. 1–7. See also Jean Baudrillard, *Les Stratégies fatales* (Paris: Bernard Grasset, 1983), p. 107. Lyotard's position is ridiculed by Terry Eagleton in *Ideology* (London and New York: Verso, 1991), p. xiii.

15. For a denial of the latter principle see, for instance, Pierre Clastres, *La Société contre l'état*, pp. 172–173. The relevance of the whole "production paradigm" is also, now, questioned at times; in fact, it was already under attack in the nineteenth century. Robert Louis Stevenson's quip would be hard to improve on: "He believed in production, that useful figment of economy, as if it had been real like laughter;" *The Amateur Emigrant* (London: Hogarth Press, 1984), p. 36. For a defence of the production paradigm see Bill Martin, "Conceiving Postsecular Socialism," (typescript), p. 5.

16. Cf. Gilles Deleuze, *On the Line* (New York: Semiotext, 1983), pp. 79–80. See also the methodology of Niklas Luhmann and Friedrich Kittler as described by David E. Wellbery in his "Foreword" to Friedrich A. Kittler, *Discourse Networks 1800/1900* (Stanford: Stanford University Press, 1990), pp. vii–xxxiii.

17. Gilles Deleuze, *Présentation de Sacher-Masoch* (Paris: Minuit, 1967), pp. 79–80.

18. Gilles Deleuze and Félix Guattari, *Rhizome: Introduction* (Paris: Minuit, 1976), e.g., p. 25.

19. *Le Pli: Leibniz et le baroque* (Paris: Minuit, 1988), p. 93, p. 181 ff. See also p. 155, on the intermediate domain between statistical agglomerations of people and dispersed individuals: this area is "interindividual and interactive rather than collective" (Il est interindividuel et interactif plus encore que collectif).

20. For instance, in *Throwing like a Girl and Other Essays in Feminist Philosophy and Social Theory* (Bloomington and Indianapolis: Indiana University Press, 1990).

21. Alberto Melucci, in *Nomads of the Present* (London: Century Hutchinson, 1989) proposes a program similar to Iris Young's, with what he calls "public spaces" reserved for minority group interests within the political process (pp. 172–173, 228–229). See also Raymond Plant, "Community: Concept, Conception, and Ideology," p. 101. An essay on pluralism by Louise Marcil-Lacoste, "The Paradoxes of Pluralism," may be found in Chantal Mouffe, ed., *Dimensions of Radical Democracy: Pluralism, Citizenship, Community* (London and New York: Verso, 1992), pp. 128–142; see also Charles Taylor, *Reconciling the Solitudes*, pp. 125, 133.

For an interesting treatment of the relation betrween individual and group in a working-class Italian community see Herbert J. Gans, *The Urban Villagers: Group and Class in the Life of Italian-Americans* (New York and London: Free Press and Collier Macmillan, 1962), especially pp. 98–99. I am grateful to Peter Grieco for the reference.

22. Cambridge, etc.: Cambridge University Press, 1988.

NOTES TO CHAPTER 5

23. The quotation is from an article by Randolph Bourne. See Andrew Hacker, "Trans-National America," *New York Review of Books* 37, no. 18 (November 22, 1990), 19–24, p. 24.

24. Emil Egli, *Switzerland* (Berlin: Paul Haupt, 1978), p. 212. J. Christopher Herold, in *The Swiss Without Halos* (Westport, Connecticut: Greenwood Press, 1979), p. 240, points out that Switzerland has ignored or rejected possibilities for expansion.

On the relevance of the Swiss model for Canada see pp. 454–455 in the article by Bélanger and Pinard cited above (Introduction, note 3).

25. J. Murray Luck, ed., *Modern Switzerland* (Palo Alto: Sposs Inc., 1978), p. 326. From the chapter on "Swiss Federalism in the Twentieth Century" by Max Frenkel, pp. 323–338. Separatism in the Jura remains a problem, though. See, for instance, "Attentato separatista a Berna," *Corriere della Sera* (January 8, 1993), p. 8.

26. See, e.g., de Tocqueville (*De la démocratie en Amérique*), who is notorious for his denigration of Swiss federalism as mere anarchy, though he saw some hope for an increase in centralization after 1848. See also Herold, p. 4.

27. Egli, p. 215.

28. Luck, p. 327: not all rural areas are Catholic, nor are all industrial areas German.

29. There is, for instance, little possibility of applying Swiss techniques or Swiss attitudes in the United States, where Spanish is associated with impoverished immigrants, rather than (as in the case of, say, Swiss Italian) with an indigenous community of more or less the same economic standing as the others.

30. Robert Henry Billigman, *A Crisis in Swiss Pluralism* (The Hague, etc.: Mouton, 1979), p. 190.

31. Ibid., p. 334 ff.

32. Cf. C. D. Minni's claim that the assertion of ethnicity makes people more Canadian. "The Short Story as Ethnic Genre," in Joseph Pivato, ed., *Contrasts* (Montreal: Guernica, 1985), pp. 61–76, especially p. 74. A curious but highly significant feature of Swiss linguistic culture is its deliberate restriction of German to the written form of the language: what is spoken in so-called German-speaking Switzerland is another language: Schwyzerdütsch. This avoidance of spoken German by the ethnic majority in the country provides encouragement for the other ethnic groups to maintain their linguistic autonomy as well. It implies that the majority chooses to distance itself from a powerful neighbor, to avoid being confused with it. At least so it seems to an outsider.

On the extraordinary number of languages recognized in the city state of Singapore see Els Witte and Hugo Baetens Beardsmore, eds., *The Interdisciplinary Study of Urban Bilingualism in Brussels* (Philadelphia: Multilingual Matters, 1987), p. 2.

33. This system is in the process of being introduced, though with extreme reservations on the part of some political scientists, in British Columbia.

34. "Success Story," *New York Review of Books* 36, no. 16 (October 26, 1989), 56–59, p. 56. The EEC is, of course, beginning to challenge Swiss isolation and to produce pressures for consensus in order to enhance Switzerland's economic competitiveness.

35. The "Gastarbeiter" problem and the recent refugee problem are perhaps at last presenting some challenge to Swiss cultural harmony. See Hans Joachim Hoffmann-Nowotny, "Sociological, Legal and Political Aspects of the Situation of Immigrants in Switzerland," *Research in Race and Ethnic Relations* 2 (1980), 73–95.

Time also points to other social problems ("Switzerland," August 19, 1991), 38–40, among them the highest incidence of AIDS in Europe (p. 40). On the plight of immigrant workers in Switzerland see Barbara E. Schmitter, "Immigrants and Associations: Their Role in the Socio-Political Process of Immigrant Worker Integration in West Germany and Switzerland," *International Migration Review* 14, no. 2 (summer, 1980), 179–192, especially pp. 189–191.

36. Quoted by Gossman in "Success Story," p. 59. On the communitarian nature of Swiss law see the excellent book by Jonathan Steinberg, *Why Switzerland?* (Cambridge: Cambridge University Press, 1976), p. 90.

37. This problem does not begin with Hume's *Treatise*: see Christopher Fox, *Locke and the Scriblerians* (Berkeley, etc.: University of California Press, 1988). In fact, I suspect that much in Hume goes still farther back, to medieval nominalism.

It would also take me too far to try to deal extensively with those philosophers who reject the notion of self as such, as well as those who consider the concept of the subject a product of ideological forces. For further references on identity theory see chapter four, note 7, above, as well as Paul Ricoeur, *Soi-même comme un autre* (Paris: Seuil, 1990). In his fifth and sixth chapters Ricoeur also deals with the relation between identity and narrativity, discussed in my fourth chapter. Kenneth J. Gergen's *The Saturated Self: Dilemmas of Identity in Contemporary Life* (New York: Basic Books, 1991) considers the impact of modern and postmodern experience on the self. Gerald N. Izenberg has revived the familiar argument that the early Romantics were responsible for the modern conception of the self as autonomous agent. See *Impossible Individuality: Romanticism, Revolution, and the Origins of Modern Selfhood, 1787–1802* (Princeton: Princeton University Press, 1992). For a brief review of twentieth-century theories of identity see Scott Lash and Jonathan Friedman, eds., *Modernity and Identity* (Oxford UK and Cambridge USA: Blackwell, 1992), pp. 3–7.

38. Charles Altieri has stressed this difficulty in some of his recent work.

39. See also David L. Norton, *Personal Identities: A Philosophy of Ethical Individualism* (Princeton: Princeton University Press, 1976). Max Stirner, on the other hand, once offered a defense of extreme individualism. For further references on individualism see Mark Warren, "Ideology and the Self," *Theory and Society* 19 (October, 1990), 599–634, p. 632, as well as Elizabeth Frazer and Nicola Lacey, *The Politics of Community: A Feminist Critique of the Liberal-Communitarian Debate* (Toronto and Buffalo: University of Toronto Press, 1993), chapter 2 and Eva Kushner, "History and the Absent Self," pp. 27–37 in Katalin Kurtösi and József Pál, *Celebrating Comparativism: Papers Offered for György M. Vajda and István Fried* (Szeged: publisher unidentified, 1994).

40. On the subjective self as merely that which an ideology forms and defines as such in order to achieve its specific purposes, see Warren, "Ideology and the Self," p. 603, citing Althusser.

For an earlier debate, in an ethnographic context, on the subject of identity, see Claude Lévi-Strauss, ed., *L'Identité* (Paris: Presses Universitaires de France, 1977). It should be remembered that concepts of the self vary so widely from culture to culture that an universally valid definition of the self seems very difficult to conceptualize. See, for instance, Augustin Berque, *Vivre l'espace au Japon* (Paris: Presses universitaires de France, 1982).

41. David Lloyd goes so far as to say that the very concern for uniting the individual with the general is merely a reflection of bourgeois problems. See *Nationalism and Minor Literature* (Berkeley, etc.: University of California Press,

1987), p. 17; also Ben Agger, "The Micro-Macro Non-Problem: The Parsonization of American Sociological Theory," *Human Studies* 14.2 (1991), 81–98, p. 92.

42. Peter de Bolla, *The Discourse of the Sublime* (Oxford: Basil Blackwell, 1989), p. 14; Arthur Kroker, *The Possessed Individual: Technology and the French Postmodern* (New York: St. Martin's Press, 1992), p. 6.

43. See K.J. Scott, "Methodological and Epistemological Individualism," in John O'Neill, ed., *Modes of Individualism and Collectivism* (London: Heinemann, 1973), pp. 215–220; p. 215. Mark Warren argues that even Max Weber, who is sometimes considered the founding father of methodological individualism, is not really as one-sided in his thinking as is usually assumed. See "Marx and Methodological Individualism," *Philosophy of the Social Sciences* 18 (December, 1988), 447–476, pp. 466–467.

 Alberto Melucci also attempts to work out an intermediate position in *Nomads of the Present*: we must reject "the assumption of collective action as a unified datum. Only then can we discover the plurality of perspectives, meanings and relationships which crystallize in any given collective action" (p. 25).

For a sophisticated attack on the philosophical presuppositions of methodological individualism see Cornelius Castoriadis, "Individuality, Society, Rationality, History," pp. 233–259 in Peter Beilharz, Gillian Robinson, John Rundell, eds., *Between Totalitarianism and Postmodernity* (Cambridge, Massachusetts and London: MIT Press, 1992).

44. Frank Paci speaks of the pleasure experienced when the barrier between the two breaks down: "that total joy when all the separations of our being—the secret you and the social you and the religious you—merge into one rapturous being." "The Stone Garden," in Linda Hutcheon and Marion Richmond, eds., *Other Solitudes: Canadian Multicultural Fictions* (Toronto: Oxford University Press, 1990), pp. 219–228; p. 227.

45. See above, chapter II, text below note 10.

46. Philip Wexler, in *Critical Social Psychology* (Boston, etc.: Routledge and Kegan Paul, 1983), puts it rather harshly. Intimacy, he says, "is a particular historical and structurally regulated process by which specific aspects of the relations of the totality are segregated out and given a special designation, one which is then experienced phenomenologically by the participants as a private dyadic matter" (p. 144). He adds, "The nature of intimacy depends on the specific sociohistorical contradictions of a given society" and develops the thesis that intimacy sublimates social contradictions (p. 151).

47. See the discussion of solitude in chapter one, above.

48. On the group contribution to individual rational thought see Mary Douglas, *How Institutions Think* (Syracuse: Syracuse University Press, 1986), e.g., chapter 5.

49. *The Problem of the Self* (University Park, Pennsylvania: Pennsylvania State University Press, 1970).

50. See Ben Agger, "The Micro-Macro Non-Problem: The Parsonization of American Sociological Theory," especially p. 85, p. 95. *(a donne)*

The micro-macro problem is also dealt with by Michel Seymour in "Aspects de l'anti–individualisme," *Philosophiques* XIX no. 2 (Autumn, 1992), 63–77, but primarily as a preamble to a defense of nationalism, and of Quebec nationalism in particular.

51. For an excellent treatment of this whole group of issues see Anthony Appiah, "Tolerable Falsehoods: Agency and the Interests of Theory," pp. 63–90 in

Jonathan Arac and Barbara Johnson, eds., *Consequences of Theory* (Baltimore and London: Johns Hopkins University Press, 1991).

52. I am in possession of a photocopy, the provenance of which I cannot determine, entitled "Chapter 2. Identifying Dimensions of Communities: Factor Analysis." It is an extensive statistical study of certain features of communities, with a view to determining the underlying "dimensions, or factors, of communities" (p. B-41). It examines variables such as population stability, industrialization index, aid to dependent children, housing construction, unemployment, mental illness, and so forth. It is paginated from B-41 to B-70, and carries the caption "B Statistics Guide" in the margin.

53. See the chapter entitled "From I to We" in David Carr, *Time, Narrative, and History* (Bloomington and Indianapolis: Indiana University Press, 1986), pp. 122–152, for an attempt to deal with this problem in general philosophical terms.

54. According to Melucci a major contribution of such small movements is that they help make the symbols of power visible. On small group culture see also Michel Maffesoli, *Le Temps des tribus: le déclin de l'individualisme dans les sociétés de masse* (Paris: Meridiens Klincksieck, 1988).

55. Perhaps there is less point nowadays in organizing politically, when political foci are no longer the centers of power. See my argument concerning the replacement of governments by multinational corporations as centers of influence in the Introduction, above.

56. Donald L. Horowitz hints that political theorists often reduce all social motivation to economic self-interest because they themselves come from a culture in which economic ambition is the supreme value. See *Ethnic Groups in Conflict* (Berkeley, Los Angeles, London: University of California Press, 1985), p. 120.

I have not seen much mention of de Maistre and Tolstoy in my readings for this chapter, but, clearly, many of the current issues are still the ones that they debated.

CONCLUSION

1. "Fear of Federasty: Quebec's Inverted Fictions," in Hortense J. Spillers, ed., *Comparative American Identities* (New York and London: Routledge, 1991), pp. 175–195.

2. Perhaps his "colonial" condition helps to account for the hint of wistful impotence in Roberts's well-known letter about Canadian prose: "we do not seem to be seized & compelled by our subject matter; . . . we are not quite sure what we want to write about" *The Collected Letters of Charles G. D. Roberts* (Fredericton, New Brunswick: Goose Lane Editions, 1989), pp. 466–467. On colonial mutism cf. Dennis Lee, "Cadence, Country, Silence: Writing in Colonial Space," *Boundary 2*, 3 (fall, 1974), 151–168, p. 156. For general background see also Abdul R. Jan Mohamed and David Lloyd, eds., *The Nature and Context of Minority Discourse* (New York and Oxford: Oxford University Press, 1990), as well as Coral Ann Howells and Lynette Hunter, eds., *Narrative Strategies in Canadian Literature: Feminism and Postcolonialism* (Philadelphia: Open University Press; Milton Keynes, 1991). On the specific topic of animals in a post-colonial context see Eric Cheyfitz, *The Poetics of Imperialism: Translation and Colonization from* The Tempest *to* Tarzan (New York: Oxford University Press, 1991).

Of course, one might also choose to interpret Roberts's preoccupation with animals in the opposite sense, as a rebellious "deterritorialization" (Deleuze). Like all general themes, the animal lends itself to both local/political and psychological/universal readings.

3. See Barbara Godard, "The Discourse of the Other: Canadian Literature and the Question of Ethnicity," *Massachusetts Review* 31 (Spring-Summer, 1990), 153–184, pp. 182–183. Giuseppe Turi, in *Une culture appelée québécoise* (Ottawa: Éditions de l'homme, 1971), p. 53, also insists that a language can absorb a large amount of material from other languages without losing its own identity.

4. See the previous footnote.

5. "The Poet is Bidden to Manhatten Island."

6. Bruce Russell, "True North," *Massachusetts Review* 31 (Spring–Summer 1990), 81–85, p. 82. Some of the historical background for the sense of political subordination/alienation expressed in this poem, as well as for the generally uneasy relations between center and periphery in Canadian politics, is given in R. Kenneth Carty and W. Peter Ward, eds., *National Politics and Community in Canada* (Vancouver: University of British Columbia Press, 1986). See especially Gordon Stewart, "The Origins of Canadian Politics and John A. Macdonald," p. 15–47, and David E. Smith, "National Political Parties and the Growth of the National Political Community," pp. 80–93. Frank Davey, in *Post-National Arguments: The Politics of the Anglophone-Canadian Novel Since 1967* (Toronto, Buffalo, London: University of Toronto Press, 1993) also addresses some of the concerns that I have raised in this book about the nature of the Canadian polity and the sense of community in Canada. I am obliged to my colleague Deidre Lynch for this reference.

7. Linda Hutcheon and Marion Richmond, eds., *Other Solitudes: Canadian Multicultural Fictions* (Toronto: Oxford University Press, 1990), p. 99.

8. I find it interesting that Canadians are more likely than Americans to be offended if people mispronounce their names: they are more assertive about their ethnic identity, but also more anxious about being subordinated to a center or majority.

9. "an/other Canada. another Canada? other Canadas." *Massachusetts Review* 31 (Spring–Summer, 1990), 9–27, p. 23.

10. "True North," p. 83.

11. This conclusion has some relation to the problem of reconciling the communitarian with the objective discussed by Richard Rorty in *Objectivity, Relativism, and Truth* (Cambridge, etc.: Cambridge University Press, 1991), vol.I, pp. 21–34 ("Solidarity or Objectivity?") See also David Rasmussen, *Universalism vs. Communitarianism: Contemporary Debates in Ethics* (Cambridge, Massachusetts and London: MIT Press, 1990) on related issues. On the reconciling of the parochial with the universal cf. Hubert Aquin, "La fatigue culturelle du Canada français," *Liberté* 4, no. 23 (May, 1962), 299–325, p. 324; and J. Michael Dash, "Introduction" to Édouard Glissant, *Caribbean Discourse: Selected Essays* (Charlottesville: University Press of Virginia, 1989), pp. xi–xlvii, p. xxxix: "Universality paradoxically springs from regionalism."

Index

■

Erlich, Sophie Dubnova, 66–67
Erlich, Victor, 66–67
Evans, Mary Ann (pseud. George Eliot), 62

Fainmell, Charles, 63
Falardeau, Jean-Charles, 187 n.17
Fallows, James, 178 n.1
Fawkner, H.W., 189 nn.14, 16, 190 nn.29, 31, 191 n.35
Feher, Ferenc, 184 n.22
Feldman, Irving, 12, 75, 86, 87
Felski, Rita, 183 n.10
Ferguson, Russell, 188 n.8
Ferron, Jacques, 111
Fichte, Johann Gottlieb, 12, 58, 125, 184 n.17
Fiedler, Leslie, 29
Field, Eugene, 72, 73
Files, Harold, 62
Fitz, Earl E., 180 n.7
Flanagan, Owen, 190 n.32
Fly, Richard, 132
Fox, Christopher, 195 n.37
Freud, Sigmund, 30
Frey, Charles, 189 n.20
Friedenberg, Edgar, 43, 46–47, 110, 176
Friedlander, Isaac, 63
Friedman, Jonathan, 171, 195 n.37
Frisch, Max, 164
Frost, Robert, 184 n.21
Frye, Northrop, 111, 175
Fuery, Patrick, 112

Gans, Herbert, 193 n.21
Garber, Marjorie, 188 n.11
Garnett, David, 35
Garton, Charles, 181 n.4
Gauvreau, Claude, 111
Gellner, Ernest, 180 n.7
Gergen, Kenneth J., 195 n.37
Gever, Martha, 188 n.8
Gibbon, Edward, 40
Gilpin, Kenneth N., 179 n.1
Giroux, France, 193 n.13
Glassner, Barry, 112
Glicenstein, Enrico, 63
Glickman, Yaacov, 186 n.9
Glissant, Édouard, 120, 198 n.11

Gobineau, Joseph-Arthur, Comte de, 41–42
Godard, Barbara, 23, 173, 198 n.3
Godzich, Wlad, 180 n.7
Goldman, Michael, 189 n.16
Goldmann, Lucien, 185 n.25
Goldmann, Wolf, 186 n.14
Goodman, Nelson, 131
Goodwin, Sarah Webster, 191 n.1
Gossman, Lionel, 164
Gottlieb, N. J., 60
Gralnick, Izzie, 64
Greene, Lorne, 68
Grieco, Peter, 193 n.21
Grove, Robin, 189 n.18
Guattari, Félix, 119, 180 n.2, 184 n.22, 191 n.33
Gudelman, (first name unknown), 63
Gurik, Robert, 137

Hacker, Andrew, 162, 194 n.23
Hacking, Ian, 185 n.27
Haeckel, Ernst, 188 n.8
Haman (Biblical), 82
Hammer, Stephanie B., 188 n.12
Handler, Richard, 187 n.17
Handwerk, Gary, 191 n.1
Hannum, Hurst, 179 n.3
Hardenberg, Friedrich Leopold Freiherr von (pseud. Novalis), 64
Harding, D. W., 181 n.10
Hazlitt, William, 186 n.12, 190 n.27
Hébert, Anne, 111
Hegel, Georg Wilhelm Friedrich, 125, 158
Heilbroner, Robert, 178 n.1
Heller, Agnes, 184 n.22
Hernadi, Paul, 191 n.34
Herold, J. Christopher, 194 nn.24, 26
Hershenov, Moishe-Leib, 63
Hershman, H., 53
Hobsbawm, Eric, 180 n.7
Hoffmann-Nowotny, Hans -Joachim, 194 n.35
Honigmann, E.A.J., 189 n.19
Hopkins, Gerard Manley, 58, 125
Horowitz, Donald L., 179 n.3, 197 n.56
Howells, Coral Ann, 197 n.2
Hume, David, 195 n.37
Hunter, Lynette, 197 n.2

McGill 176

INDEX

Van Laan, Thomas, 189 nn.16, 22
Verene, Donald Phillip, 125
Virgil (Publius Vergilius Maro), 38, 45
Volkelt, Johannes, 78

Waddington, Miriam (née Dworkin),
    68, 182 n.1
Wallerstein, Immanuel, 180 n.7
Ward, W. Peter, 198 n.6
Warner, Sylvia Townsend, 35
Warren, Mark, 167, 195 nn.39, 40, 196
    n.43
Weber, Max, 196 n.43
Weinstein, Arnold, 182 n.16
Wellbery, David E., 193 n.16
Wells, Susan, 183 n.10
West, Cornel, 188 n.8
Wexler, Philip, 196 n.46

White, Stephen K., 160
Wilde, Oscar, 184 n.16
Wise, Norton, 188 n.8
Witte, Els, 194 n.32
Wordsworth, William, 65, 97, 105

Yeats, William Butler, 97, 185 n.23
Young, Crawford, 179 n.3
Young, Iris, 159–160, 161, 193 n.21
Young-Bruehl, Elisabeth, 186 n.7
Yud, Nokhem, 60

Zhukovsky, Musha (mother of Ida
    Maza), 68, 91
Zhukovsky, Shimon (father of Ida
    Maza), 68, 91–92
Žižek, Slavoj, 186 n.10